Integrating Spirituality *and* Religion Into Counseling

A Guide to Competent Practice

D0169611

Edited by

Craig S. Cashwell

and

J. Scott Young

AMERICAN COUNSELING ASSOCIATION
5999 Stevenson Avenue
Alexandria, VA 22304
www.counseling.org

Integrating
Spirituality *and*
Religion
Into
Counseling
A Guide to Competent Practice

10 9 8 7 6 5 4 3 2

American Counseling Association
5999 Stevenson Avenue
Alexandria, VA 22304

Director of Publications
Carolyn C. Baker

Production Manager
Bonny E. Gaston

Copy Editor
Elaine Dunn

Cover and text design by Bonny Gaston.
Cover art is "Dreams," a handmade paper sculpture by Bonny Gaston.

Library of Congress Cataloging-in-Publication Data

Integrating spirituality and religion into counseling: a guide to competent practice/
edited by Craig S. Cashwell, J. Scott Young.
    p. cm.
  ISBN 1-55620-233-4 (alk. paper)
   1. Counseling—Religious aspects.   2. Psychology and religion.   3. Spirituality—Psychology. I. Cashwell, Craig S. II. Young, J. Scott.

  BF637.C6I52 2004
  206′.1—dc22   2004015465

To Tammy Hoyle Cashwell and Sara DeHart Young,
our partners on this journey.

Table of Contents

About the Editors

Craig S. Cashwell, PhD, is a professor in the Department of Counseling and Educational Development at the University of North Carolina at Greensboro. He has worked as a counselor in private practice, community agencies, and college counseling centers. He served as president of the Association for Spiritual, Ethical, and Religious Values in Counseling (ASERVIC) during 2003–2004. He lives in North Carolina with his wife, Tammy, and daughter, Samantha.

J. Scott Young received his PhD in counselor education in 1996 from the University of North Carolina at Greensboro. He is an associate professor in the Department of Counseling, Educational Psychology and Special Education at Mississippi State University. He served as president of ASERVIC during 2002–2003. His research has focused on the interface of counseling practice with religion and spirituality and the training of counselors to address spirituality in counseling. He lives in Mississippi with his wife, Sara, and daughters, Savannah and Sophie.

About the Contributors

Alan Basham, MA, Eastern Washington University

Michele Kielty Briggs, PhD, James Madison University

Craig S. Cashwell, PhD, University of North Carolina at Greensboro

Christopher Faiver, PhD, John Carroll University

Mary A. Fukuyama, PhD, University of Florida

Carman S. Gill, MA, University of North Carolina at Greensboro

W. Bryce Hagedorn, PhD, LMHC, NCC, MAC, Florida International University

Melanie C. Harper, MA, University of North Carolina at Greensboro

R. Elliott Ingersoll, PhD, Cleveland State University

Geri Miller, PhD, Appalachian State University

Judith G. Miranti, PhD, Dean of Humanities, Education, and Counseling, Our Lady of Holy Cross College

Mike O'Connor, PhD, Seattle University

Andrea Dixon Rayle, PhD, Arizona State University

Todd D. Sevig, PhD, University of Michigan

Farhad Siahpoush, J. Hillis Miller Presidential Fellow, PhD candidate, University of Florida

Marsha Wiggins-Frame, PhD, University of Colorado at Denver

J. Scott Young, PhD, Mississippi State University

Acknowledgments

We wish to gratefully acknowledge the inspiration and guidance of many who have influenced this project. We have been blessed with diligent authors who grasped the importance of this project and committed themselves accordingly. Carolyn Baker of the American Counseling Association has been very patient in working with two editors developing their first book. Our respective Department Chairs (DiAnne Borders at The University of North Carolina at Greensboro and Tom Hosie at Mississippi State University) and our colleagues have supported and encouraged this project. Finally, to our parents (John and Joyce Young and Sybil and the late Johnny Cashwell), we give thanks that you showed us your path and allowed us our own.

Foreword

$\mathcal{I}$t is a distinct privilege and opportunity to advance this seminal edited text by two enthusiastic and farsighted professionals whose only goal is to offer trainees and practitioners the competencies, tools, and techniques needed to effectively address the spiritual and religious issues presented by clients. I have had the good fortune to be closely associated with Drs. Cashwell and Young and to observe their intensity and passion when dealing with the topics of spirituality and religion. Their research and publications have significantly contributed to the growing literature on counseling and spirituality, but it is their vision and fortitude to launch this work with competent and skilled contributing authors that the competencies, developed a decade ago, can be operationalized. They have approached this difficult task and produced a text/handbook that will be in demand by counselor educators and practitioners from various mental and allied health professions.

Ten years ago in 1994, a group of practitioners and counselor educators from various specialties and practice settings attended the first Invitational Summit on Spirituality. In the city of Belmont, just miles from the University of North Carolina at Charlotte, under the leadership of Dr. (Sr.) Mary Thomas Burke, they begin the arduous task of attempting to define, describe, and distinguish spirituality and/or religion, a task which seemed to elude and frustrate the participants. After several long days, a draft of competencies was developed that would assist counselors in honoring the various faith and spiritual traditions and practices of their clients. Several years and town meetings later, a final draft was submitted for acceptance by the Association for Spiritual, Ethical, and Religious Values in Counseling (ASERVIC). Now, these very competencies are given definition and substance by providing examples, case studies, techniques, and attitudes in this guide to competent practice.

How proud our association founders would be to see the significant strides that the association has made to advance the integration of spirituality in counseling. From its humble beginnings in 1951 by a group of counselors in New York City to several thousand members in 2004, the purpose of ASERVIC has always been to provide resources, training, and professional development to its members. Today, the organization is composed of members from diverse ethnic, racial, religious, and spiritual backgrounds and has remained committed to the infusion of spiritual, ethical, and religious values in counselor preparation and practice. It has continued to nurture and support its members by sponsoring master works such as this text.

Religion and spirituality continue to be controversial topics because of the difficulty to define terms and to determine best practice in approaching these domains within the context of presenting client issues. Accurately conceptualizing cases is the first step toward providing constructive and effective interventions. This text provides hands-on approaches and techniques that will facilitate client exploration. It will sharpen counselor awareness and the competencies/skills needed to deal with these deeply sensitive and personal client issues. But the text goes beyond competent practice and provides opportunities for counselor educators, trainees, and practitioners to explore their own religious and spiritual journeys so that when they walk this journey with their clients, they too will be the better for it. The editors are to be commended and the contributing authors applauded for their insight, experiences, and shared approaches in this resource and guide to the competent practice of integrating spirituality into counseling.

—*Judith G. Miranti,* Our Lady of Holy Cross College

Chapter 1

Integrating Spirituality and Religion Into Counseling: An Introduction

Craig S. Cashwell and J. Scott Young

May all beings everywhere, with whom we are inseparably interconnected, be fulfilled, awakened, and free. May there be peace in this world and throughout the entire universe, and may we all together complete the spiritual journey.
—Lama Surya Das (1997, p. 3)

$\mathcal{A}$ Native American Shaman journeying to the lowerworld in search of a cure for a tribal illness. A Buddhist monk practicing mindfulness meditation. A Jewish person saying the mourner's Kaddish after the death of a loved one. A member of a Christian church participating in the sacrament of communion. While the basic beliefs of these people may differ, they share the commonality of integrating spirit into their life.

That living a spiritual life is important within American culture is clear. Researchers have found that 96% of people living in the United States believe in God, over 90% pray, 69% are church members, and 43% have attended church, synagogue, or temple within the past 7 days (Princeton Religion Research Center, 2000). Beyond this, however, is the fact that many other people engage in some form of spiritual practice that does not involve participation in an organized religion or that may not include a Higher Power.

Accordingly, it is beyond question that there has been a substantial upsurge in the interest in spirituality among mental health professionals. There has been a proliferation of articles and books on the topic over the past 10 years. A relevant question is *why?* Related to the question of why spirituality has become such a ubiquitous topic in our professional conversation is *how.* How are counselors and other mental health professionals to address in session the most personal of topics with clients in appropriate and ethical ways? Therein lies the purpose of this book: to iterate and operationalize the competencies for integrating spirituality in counseling sessions. Miller (1999) provided a thorough account of the development of the spirituality competencies addressed in this book. One point of interest about these competencies is that they were the result of a grassroots effort of a small group of counseling professionals interested in promoting the appropriate integration of spirituality into the counseling process. Out of the efforts of this small group, a set of nine competencies were developed as an attempt to provide a guiding set of knowledge and skills that counselors should possess to effectively engage clients in the exploration of their spiritual and religious lives as they relate to other psychological concerns.

The nine spirituality competencies as they have been published (Miller, 1999) are as follows:

1. The professional counselor can explain the relationship between religion and spirituality, including similarities and differences.
2. The professional counselor can describe religious and spiritual beliefs and practices in a cultural context.
3. The professional counselor engages in self-exploration of religious and spiritual beliefs in order to increase sensitivity, understanding, and acceptance of diverse belief systems.
4. The professional counselor can describe her or his religious and/or spiritual belief system and explain various models of religious or spiritual development across the life span.
5. The professional counselor can demonstrate sensitivity and acceptance of a variety of religious and/or spiritual expressions in client communication.
6. The professional counselor can identify limits of her or his understanding of a client's religious or spiritual expression and demonstrate appropriate referral skills and generate possible referral sources.
7. The professional counselor can assess the relevance of the religious and/or spiritual domains in the client's therapeutic issues.
8. The professional counselor is sensitive to and receptive of religious and/or spiritual themes in the counseling process as befits the expressed preference of each client.
9. The professional counselor uses a client's religious and/or spiritual beliefs in the pursuit of the client's therapeutic goals as befits the client's expressed preference.

For the purpose of developing these competencies further for implementation, we have chosen to combine Competencies 8 and 9. While we agree with distinguishing between Competency 8 and Competency 9 at a conceptual level, at a practical level the use of a client's religious and/or spiritual beliefs in the pursuit of client goals is predicated on the counselor's sensitivity and receptivity to these themes in the counseling process. Accordingly, we have asked Alan Basham and Mike O'Connor to integrate these two competencies into chapter 8.

While the spirituality competencies have been previously presented in the counseling literature (Miller, 1999), they have not been discussed in adequate detail to inform the practice of counseling. Further, there is empirical evidence

(Young, Cashwell, Wiggins-Frame, & Belaire, 2002) that counseling practitioners and counselor educators support the competencies as important but report that they need more information to be able to implement the competencies.

It also bears note here that we chose the title *Integrating Spirituality and Religion Into Counseling* with intention. Our intention here is to distinguish between spirituality and religion *in* counseling and *spiritual or religious counseling*. Counselors trained and working in a variety of settings, including secular settings, generally are not "spiritual counselors" (i.e., pastoral counselors), yet they should use every approach available that will support a client's progress, including interventions oriented to promote healthy spiritual development. Regardless of the presenting concern a client brings to the counseling process, the person is attempting to make meaning of life in relation to her or his particular clinical issues. Meaning-making is a fundamental aspect of religious and spiritual beliefs. Further, transformative religious or spiritual practice may enable the client to transcend aspects of the ego that make the presenting issues so problematic in their day-to-day life. It is a foundational tenet of this book that drawing from, and working within, the existing spiritual, religious, and existential perspectives of a client enhances the impact of the counseling process.

Spirituality in the counseling process is gaining emphasis within the postmodern framework. A spiritual life is constructed by the client, yet the counselor may facilitate or co-construct this developmental process. Inherent in this co-constructed journey is the imperative that the counselor knows the territory through which the client is journeying. For example, the counselor should understand what spiritual transformation looks like, how psychological issues interface with spiritual issues, and vice versa. The counselor should have sufficient experience with techniques designed to facilitate psychospiritual growth that the client can be guided in their use. In essence, then, counselors can only facilitate this developmental process if they, too, are on a spiritual journey toward the Higher Self. A counselor who focuses only on the translative purpose of spirituality (i.e., spiritual traditions and beliefs) may not be able to help the client on a transformative journey (i.e., through spiritual practices and experiences). Similarly, the counselor interested only in the transformative purpose of spirituality may be less effective with the client who is searching for meaning in life, the translative aspect of spirituality. Although the spirituality competencies are an attempt to codify the appropriate and ethical integration of spirituality into the counseling process, it is imperative to acknowledge the importance of the person of the counselor who hopes to address the spiritual domain. Being able to assist clients in exploring the role of spirituality and religion in their clinical healing requires the counselor to work on her or his own spiritual development. There is a developmental process, a lifelong commitment to growth, inherent for counselors in this work.

Defining Spirituality

It is no small task to define spirituality. One of the challenges in promoting spirituality within the mental health profession has been the diversity of definitions that has emerged. When we strive to define spirituality, we discover not its limits, but our own (Kurtz & Ketcham, 1992). While we believe that spirituality is a universal phenomenon (i.e., all are spiritual beings), we also believe that spirituality is both developmental and highly personal. Various developmental models are discussed fully by Geri Miller in chapter 6. As will be apparent from that chapter, people at various levels of spiritual development will tend to define spirituality from a perspective consistent with their spiritual evolution.

In chapter 2, Marsha Wiggins-Frame provides a number of definitions that have been offered in the counseling literature in an effort to define spirituality. We begin here with the definition offered by Chandler, Holden, and Kolander (1992): Spirituality is "Pertaining to the innate capacity . . . and tendency to . . . transcend one's current locus of centricity, which transcendence involves increased knowledge and love" (p. 169). In other words, spiritual development involves the increased capacity to love others and self. We choose this definition because it captures both the exoteric, or public aspect of spirituality, and the esoteric, or private aspect, of the spiritual life (Bache, 1990).

Beyond this definition, however, it seems important to distinguish between spiritual beliefs, spiritual practices, and spiritual experiences. All too often, the question "Are you a spiritual person?" is answered with information about belief systems. One's cognitive schemas, however, provide only one aspect of the spiritual life, that of *beliefs*. Fowler (1991) talked about belief as the cognitive acceptance of a set of ideas as "true" with varying degrees of provability. To more completely understand someone's spirituality, it is necessary also to consider her or his *spiritual practice* or day-to-day activities that give rise to *spiritual experiences*. It is only through considering the interaction of beliefs, practices, and experiences that one's spirituality can truly come into focus.

There are many people whose belief systems, spiritual practices, and spiritual experiences are logical extensions of one another. For example, Ray describes himself as a Christian who values contemplative practices. He has studied contemplative prayer and *Vipassana* meditation and daily practices one of these two forms of contemplative practice. Over time, he comes into contact with a range of emotions that were previously repressed. Consistent with contemplative practices, he allows these emotions to come forward and find full expression. As a result of releasing these blocks, he begins to have more transpersonal experiences of communion with the Absolute.

For others, however, the interconnection between beliefs, practices, and experiences is not so solid. Examples include the following:

- A person participates in organized religion out of obligation or the sense that "I should go"; because of this sense of obligation (and fear of what may happen if he or she does not attend religious meetings), however, there is virtually no spiritual experience and no disciplined spiritual practice outside of organized religious meetings.
- A person becomes very interested in religion and studies world religions extensively. However, there is no spiritual practice to promote spiritual development and to occasion spiritual experience.

- A person engages in spiritual materialism (Trungpa, 1973) by frequently exchanging one spiritual practice for another, "spiritual window-shopping" for the mountaintop experience. Such a practice, however, is often grounded neither in a set of spiritual beliefs nor in a disciplined and sustained spiritual practice.

In addition to distinguishing between spiritual beliefs, practices, and experiences, it is important to distinguish between the translative and transformative purposes of spirituality (Wilber, 2000). Discussed more fully by Alan Basham and Mike O'Connor in chapter 8 of this book, and by Christopher Faiver and Elliott Ingersoll in chapter 9, we wish only to distinguish between the two here. The translative purpose of spirituality is to help individuals with the meaning-making and purpose-seeking aspects of life. Thus, the translative aspect of spirituality often is connected to the process of how the individual forms her or his spiritual beliefs. On the other hand, the transformative aspect of spirituality involves those practices and experiences that enable a person to develop transpersonally, or beyond the ego. Both translation and transformation are needed for healthy spiritual development, much like a child needs both the word *ball* and the experience of bouncing a ball to fully integrate the concept. Transformative experiences need integration (or translation). Similarly, translative spirituality without transformative spirituality becomes, at some point, inadequate for many people. It is important, then, for counselors who integrate spirituality into the counseling process to consider with great intention both the translative and transformative purposes of spirituality. The essence of integrating spirituality into the counseling process is to honor a client's belief system while drawing on it to facilitate the client's unique experience of the Divine.

Defining Religion

Religion, in contrast to *spirituality*, is easier to define. While spirituality is considered to be universal, ecumenical, internal, affective, spontaneous, and private, *religion* is considered to be denominational, external, cognitive, behavioral, ritualistic, and public (Richards & Bergin, 1997). That is, religion provides one social context within which a set of beliefs, practices, and experiences occur. Religion is, by definition, more institutional and creedal than spirituality. The relationship between the two (religion and spirituality) is an important consideration as it is highly individualized. For some people, participation in organized religion provides a strong social context for their spiritual lives; that is, their spiritual lives are deeply enriched by their religious practices. For others, however, their spiritual beliefs, practices, and experiences may not involve organized religion in any way. Yet a third relationship exists for those persons who participate in organized religious meetings out of a sense of obligation, habit, or fear of consequences for not participating. Rarely do such people have robust spiritual lives. Such people might be considered to be religious but not spiritual (Frame, 2003).

Pitfall of the "Path"

Before we move more fully into the competencies, it is important to consider spiritual development and formation within the context of overall development, with an emphasis on *spiritual bypass* as a potential pitfall of the spiritual journey. Spiritual bypass (Cashwell, Myers, & Shurts, 2004; Welwood, 2000) is a developmental phenomenon whereby people use spiritual beliefs, practices, and experiences to avoid contact with important unfinished psychological business. That is, a person misuses spiritual beliefs, practices, and experiences to avoid emotional and psychological pain. Such people may be said to be practicing an ungrounded spirituality. While many writers encourage the use of spiritual practice as a coping strategy, the spiritual life is not meant to be one of avoiding pain and may, in fact, cause suffering while transformation is taking place (Marion, 2002). Rather, the spiritual life provides strength and support for the journey through the painful aspects of life. Spiritual bypass occurs when people become polarized in thinking that spiritual practice is "higher" or "better" development and overemphasize their spiritual formation. The cost is often that relationships and other aspects of day-to-day life suffer as a result of the bypass (Sovatsky, 1998). Various faith traditions (e.g., the seven major *chakras* discussed in Hinduism and Buddhism, the Christian sacraments, and the Tree of Life described in the Kabbalah of Jewish origin) all emphasize the importance of avoiding spiritual bypass (Prophet, 2000). Spiritual bypass is analogous to a tree with overdeveloped branches and a weak shallow root system that will eventually topple. When spiritual bypass occurs, spiritual practice is not integrated into the practical realm of the psyche, and, as a result, personal development is less sophisticated than the spiritual practice (Welwood, 2000). Such individuals are hyperspiritual but are not willing or able to work on their psychological patterns and behaviors that cause difficulty for them and others. The term *premature transcendence* also appears in the literature (Harris, 1994; Sovatsky, 1998) and appears to be synonymous with spiritual bypass.

A common example of spiritual bypass occurs when a person experiences a substantial loss in her or his life but avoids the painful, yet vital, mourning process by saying, "It was God's will." There is an important distinction here between *surrender* and *avoidance*. Perhaps another example is useful. Consider a client diagnosed with terminal cancer and given weeks to live. The spiritual practice of *surrender* may help the person find peace with the diagnosis and begin dealing with the emotional and instrumental issues that need to be addressed. On the other hand, a person in spiritual bypass may avoid the reality by saying, "God will heal me." It is highly likely that this client will avoid the necessary, albeit painful, "work" of preparing to die. This avoidance behavior likely will cause the person and close friends and family considerable distress. Spiritual bypass may be used to compensate for low self-esteem, anxiety, depression, narcissism, and dependency issues (Welwood, 2000). Further, people engaged in spiritual bypass often act compulsively good; repress undesirable emotions; are spiritually narcissistic, spiritually materialistic, or spiritually obsessed or addicted; demonstrate blind faith in charismatic teachers; abdicate personal responsibility; and may socially isolate.

In sum, then, spiritual bypass represents a developmental detour best avoided. In a historical period in which people are highly interested in living a spiritual life, it is inevitable that counselors will work with many clients who are misusing spirituality to avoid their psychological pain. An oft-used metaphor seems helpful here. It is fine to have your head in the heavens . . . as long as your feet are firmly planted on the earth.

Organization of This Book

The spirituality competencies provide the organizing framework for this book. We have taken some liberties with the competencies, however, that we believe will make this book easier to read. Specifically, as previously mentioned, we have combined Competencies 8 and 9 into one competency that focuses on the counselor's sensitivity and skill in working with religious and/or spiritual themes in the counseling process to facilitate client development and goal attainment. Also, we have reorganized the order of the competencies to more closely follow the counseling process. After Marsha Wiggins-Frame's chapter on the distinction between religion and spirituality (chap. 2), Melanie C. Harper and Carman S. Gill's chapter on assessment follows (chap. 3). Though assessment is ongoing and occurs throughout the counseling process, assessing religious and spiritual beliefs, practices, and experiences at the outset of the counseling process is particularly vital, for it is only through a thorough and comprehensive assessment that developmentally and culturally sensitive interventions can be introduced. From this, we emphasize the person of the counselor by including W. Bryce Hagedorn's chapter on counselor self-awareness and self-exploration next (chap. 4). The three chapters that follow this (chap. 5 by Michele Kielty Briggs and Andrea Dixon Rayle, chap. 6 by Geri Miller, and chap. 7 by Mary A. Fukuyama, Farhad Siahpoush, and Todd D. Sevig) emphasize that spirituality is uniquely expressed, developmental, and culture specific. Following this, in chapter 8 Alan Basham and Mike O'Connor explore the use of spiritual practices to facilitate client growth. Christopher Faiver and Elliott Ingersoll then explore in chapter 9 the importance of working within the boundaries of one's personal limitations and the importance of appropriate referrals when working with spiritual and/or religious issues.

In the end, then, our hope is that this book introduces you to some new ideas and ways of thinking about spirituality within the counseling process. Because it is part of our belief that all living beings are connected, as we write this paragraph we offer up a prayer of gratitude and hope for your work as a counselor. We ask as you read that you do the same for us. We close this chapter with a quote that adorned the walls of Mother Teresa's home, adapted from the work of Kent Keith (2002):

> People are often unreasonable, illogical and self-centered;
> Forgive them anyway.
> If you are kind, people may accuse you of selfish, ulterior motives;
> Be kind anyway.
> If you are successful, you will win some false friends and some true enemies;
> Succeed anyway.

If you are honest and frank, people may cheat you;
Be honest and frank anyway.
What you spend years building, someone will destroy overnight;
Build anyway.
If you find serenity and happiness, they may be jealous;
Be happy anyway.
The good you do today, people will often forget tomorrow;
Do good anyway.
Give the world the best you have, and it may never be enough;
Give the world the best you've got anyway.
You see in the final analysis it is between you and God.
It was never between you and them anyway.

References

Bache, C. M. (1990). *Lifecycles: Reincarnation and the web of life*. New York: Paragon House.

Cashwell, C. S., Myers, J. E., & Shurts, M. (2004). Using the developmental counseling and therapy model to work with a client in spiritual bypass: Some preliminary considerations. *Journal of Counseling & Development, 82*, 403–409.

Das, L. S. (1997). *Awakening the Buddha within: Tibetan wisdom for the modern world*. New York: Broadway.

Fowler, J. (1991). Stages in faith consciousness. *New Directions for Child Development, 52*, 27–45.

Frame, M. W. (2003). *Integrating religion and spirituality into counseling: A comprehensive approach*. Pacific Grove, CA: Brooks/Cole.

Harris, B. (1994). Kundalini and healing in the West. *Journal of Near-Death Studies, 13*, 75–79.

Keith, K. (2002). *Anyway: The paradoxical commandments: Finding personal meaning in a crazy world*. New York: Putnam.

Kurtz, E., & Ketcham, K. (1992). *The spirituality of imperfection: Storytelling and the journey to wholeness*. New York: Bantam.

Marion, J. (2002). *Putting on the mind of Christ*. Hampton Roads, VA: Hampton Roads.

Miller, G. (1999). The development of the spiritual focus in counseling and counselor education. *Journal of Counseling & Development, 77*, 498–501.

Princeton Religion Research Center. (2000). Americans remain very religious, but not necessarily in conventional ways. *Emerging Trends, 22*(1), 2–3.

Prophet, E. C. (2000). *Your seven energy centers*. Corwin Springs, MT: Summit University Press.

Richards, P. S., & Bergin, A. E. (1997). *A spiritual strategy for counseling and psychotherapy*. Washington, DC: American Psychological Association.

Sovatsky, S. (1998). *Words from the soul: Time, East/West spirituality, and psychotherapeutic narrative*. Albany: State University of New York Press.

Trungpa, C. (1973). *Cutting through spiritual materialism*. Boston: Shambhala.

Welwood, J. (2000). *Toward a psychology of awakening: Buddhism, psychotherapy, and the path of personal and spiritual transformation*. Boston: Shambhala.

Wilber, K. (2000, May). A spirituality that transforms. *Tools for Transformation Newsletter.* Retrieved from http://www.trans4mind.com/news/kenwilber.html

Young, J. S., Cashwell, C. S., Wiggins-Frame, M., & Belaire, C. (2002). Spiritual and religious competencies: A national survey of CACREP accredited programs. *Counseling and Values, 47,* 22–33.

Chapter 2

Spirituality and Religion: Similarities and Differences

Marsha Wiggins-Frame

Competency: *The professional counselor can explain the relationship between religion and spirituality, including similarities and differences.*

American culture in the 21st century appears to be ripe for a spiritual revolution. There is a resurgence of interest in issues of transcendence as evidenced by numerous magazine articles, books, television programs, films, and college courses (Richards & Bergin, 1997). Given that we find ourselves in the age of postmodernism, we are aware that absolutes, objective truth, and empirical knowledge continually are being examined and questioned. How we think about what is real and true and meaningful is shaped by the view that people create their own realities based in their subjective experience of the world, the influence of their families of origin, and their culture and values. As a result, counselors of all persuasions must help clients make sense of their worldviews and grapple with how their perspectives shape their thoughts, feelings, and behaviors. Thus, the intersection of religion, spirituality, values, and counseling is a new frontier of growth of our profession. At this historical juncture, we may focus on our clients as whole persons and take seriously their physical, mental, emotional, and *spiritual* dimensions when they present for counseling.

This chapter provides information on the similarities and differences between religion and spirituality. Key terms are defined, and the relationship between religion, spirituality, and mental health are considered. Reasons why counselors often are not prepared to deal with clients' religious and spiritual issues are explored, and the dangers of counselor incompetence are examined. The chapter concludes with case studies, suggested activities, and recommended readings to provide the reader with additional resources for exploration.

Definitions

Capturing in words a concept as ethereal as *spirituality* is difficult at best. Even attempting to do so is contrary to the subject itself. However, in a book whose major focus is the integration of spirituality into counseling, it is important to address this challenge. The Latin word for spirit, *spiritus*, means breath, courage, vigor, or life. This word, taken from the Greek noun *pneuma*, was an attempt to translate the term for spirit in the New Testament into English (Sheldrake, 1992). *Pneuma*, like its Hebrew counterpart, *ruach*, means "wind," "breath," "life," and "spirit" (Delbane & Montgomery, 1981; Roth, 1990). The central image evoked by the word *spirit* is life force. In fact, the first entry in *Webster's Ninth New Collegiate Dictionary* (1987) suggests this theme: "an animating or vital principle held to give life to physical organisms" (p. 1137). The notion of "spirit" is more than mere respiration, however. It goes beyond physical, organic existence. This aspect of spirit is transcendent, that is, concerned with *otherness*. It is what Rudolph Otto (1958) called "the holy." The human search for life's meaning, purpose, and value is the essence of spirituality. As such, it may or may not include a Supreme Being or a Higher Power.

Several authors have offered definitions of spirituality that are useful in understanding the multidimensionality and the innumerable meanings that this notion of spirituality contains. Cervantes and Ramirez (1992) stated that spirituality involved the search for harmony and wholeness in the universe. Tillich (1959) spoke of one's ultimate concern, the meaning-giving dimension of culture, when referring to spirituality. Booth (1992) characterized spirituality as an "inner attitude that emphasizes energy, creative choice, and a powerful force for living" (p. 25). Elkins, Hedstrom, Hughes, Leaf, and Saunders (1988) portrayed the notion of spiritual values that include sensitivity to the tragic aspects of life, a desire to improve the world, altruism, and a balanced view of material values. Chandler, Holden, and Kolander (1992) defined a spiritual experience as "*any* experience of transcendence of one's former frame of reference that results in greater knowledge and love" (p. 170). Hinterkopf (1994) argued that spirituality includes a sensitivity toward transcendence, is perceived in the body, brings new meaning, and is growth-oriented. Holifield (1983) epitomized spirituality as "less a method than an *attitude*, a posture of one's very being that allows seeing not different things but everything differently" (p. 88). Winarsky (1991) noted that spirituality may or may not involve a Supreme Being or god:

> It may be an inner-generated, thoughtful and sometimes skeptical search—
> a process rather than a product—for universal connections, with no *quid
> pro quo* from a higher power sought or intended. People who consider
> themselves to be spiritual may or may not participate in organized religion.
> Some may find solace in readings, discussion groups, and the like. (p. 186)

Participants in the 1995 Summit on Spirituality, comprised of leaders in the American Counseling Association's division called the Association for Spiritual, Ethical, and Religious Values in Counseling (ASERVIC), were confounded by the task of defining spirituality. Instead, they chose to provide a *description* of spirituality:

The animating force in life, represented by such images as breath, wind, vigor, and courage. Spirituality is the infusion and drawing out of spirit in one's life. It is experienced as an active and passive process. Spirituality also is described as a capacity and tendency that is innate and unique to all persons. This spiritual tendency moves the individual towards knowledge, love, meaning, hope, transcendence, connectedness, and compassion. Spirituality includes one's capacity for creativity, growth, and the development of a values system. Spirituality encompasses the religious, spiritual, and transpersonal. ("Summit Results," 1995, p. 30)

From the above discussion, it is obvious that *defining* spirituality is not an easy task. The construct includes a plethora of ideas and understandings. Nonetheless, it is plain to see that *spirituality* includes one's beliefs, awareness, values, subjective experience, sense of purpose and mission, and an attempt to reach toward something greater than oneself. It may or may not include a deity.

Religion, unlike spirituality, is more concrete and easier to define. The concept of religion often encompasses the ideas and characteristics of spirituality, but there are some important differences. A religion refers to a set of beliefs and practices of an organized religious institution (Shafranske & Maloney, 1990). Religion tends to be expressed in ways that are "denominational, external, cognitive, behavioral, ritualistic, and public" (Richards & Bergin, 1997, p. 13). *Religion,* then, is one form of spirituality. The two concepts are not mutually exclusive. Some religious people find that the organization, doctrine, rituals, programs, and community are means through which their spirituality is experienced and developed. Conversely, many people who think of themselves as *spiritual,* rather than *religious,* find that the institutions of religion intrude into their notion of spirituality that is more private and individualistic. Therefore, *religion* and *spirituality* may be related in a variety of ways and played out differently among individuals. For example, a person may seek diligently the meaning of life, may be very committed to his life's mission and purpose, may even engage in spiritual practices such as yoga, and yet not be connected to a religious organization. Thus, one may be spiritual without being religious (Frame, 2003). Another person may be a member of a church, attend worship regularly, serve on the altar guild, but never really absorb the meaning inherent in these practices. She may go through the motions of being religious without being spiritual. Yet another person may be an active member of a mosque, attend worship regularly, read the Koran, and pray five times a day, finding great exhilaration in these activities and personal support through the institutional religion of Islam. Therefore, one may be religious and spiritual simultaneously (Frame, 2003). Given that the terms *spirituality* and *religion* have different meanings and connotations, it is critical that counselors clarify for themselves which of these ideas fits with their own experience. It is also important that they help their clients identify the ways in which spirituality and/or religion make sense for them.

Case Example: LaTrisha

LaTrisha is a 32-year-old African American woman who sought counseling with Amy because she was concerned about her grandmother's, Willie's, diagnosis of cancer. Willie had undergone both chemotherapy and radiation and appeared to be losing her battle with the cancer. LaTrisha knew her grandmother was dying, and this situation put her in a crisis. Not only was she facing the loss of her grandmother, with whom she was very close, but she was also struggling with her religious views about the afterlife. LaTrisha was a member of a "Bible-believing nondemonimational church" whose doctrine included the belief that "only born-again Christians will go to heaven when they die." LaTrisha's grandmother had never been involved in a church and did not have much use for religion of any kind. LaTrisha's distress over her grandmother's condition included both the sadness associated with losing her grandmother to cancer and a fear about her grandmother's eternal destiny.

In this case, both psychological and theological issues are intertwined. LaTrisha is experiencing grief, but that grief is exacerbated because of her religious belief that her grandmother will die "lost and condemned to hell." While spirituality is certainly at play here, it is expressed primarily as a religious issue because LaTrisha's church doctrine and her own religious beliefs have created havoc with her emotions.

LaTrisha's counselor, Amy, could approach her with empathy, acknowledging LaTrisha's sadness and fear about her grandmother's impending death. She could engage LaTrisha in a conversation about her view of God, faith, and the afterlife. By so doing, Amy may be able to see how integrated and solid LaTrisha's beliefs are. It is possible that LaTrisha has simply introjected a doctrine that she has not examined. Giving her an opportunity to think about her beliefs in a safe environment could result in a shift in belief that reduces LaTrisha's pain. For example, she may be able to adjust her views somewhat to move from the notion of absolute certainty about how God will act to a perspective of "not knowing" but trusting that God is benevolent. In addition, Amy might suggest that LaTrisha read some literature about varying viewpoints about the afterlife. One book in particular, *The Will of God* (Weatherhead, 1987), could be particularly useful. Talking with LaTrisha about her response to the ideas expressed in the book could be helpful to LaTrisha in galvanizing her views. Regardless of the outcome of such a conversation, Amy could help LaTrisha plan a talk with her grandmother in which she (LaTrisha) would share her concerns and express her love. She would also have a chance to hear her grandmother's perspectives on life and death and the afterlife. In addition, Amy could enable LaTrisha to celebrate her relationship with her grandmother and to make a memory book of their special times together. Moreover, Amy might encourage LaTrisha to pray for understanding and peace with this troubling situation.

Case Example: Jean

In a similar case, Jean, a 53-year-old White female, is worried about her husband's, Andy's, kidney failure. Andy has been on dialysis for 3 years and is on a waiting list for an organ transplant. Andy has not been able to work since he began dialysis, and Jean reported that their social life is "nonexistent." She has sought counseling to get support for the stress she experiences as a result of her husband's disability. She worries that another kidney will not become available in time to save Andy's life. When Carla, her counselor, asked Jean how she was coping with the uncertainty and fear, Jean said, "I am not a religious person, I mean, I don't believe in organized churches and catechisms, but I believe that there is a reason for everything. I am trying to meditate and discover what I am supposed to learn from this experience." In this case, Jean has made her own distinction between religion and spirituality. She made it clear that she was not "religious." What seems evident, however, is that although she is not connected to a church or other religious institution, Jean is dealing with issues of meaning and purpose. Her comments suggest that she has some awareness of transcendence, but she does not want to attach a religious interpretation to her views. Here is a case of someone who values spirituality but not religion.

Carla, Jean's counselor, could help Jean explore her beliefs about life and death. She might suggest a support group for primary caregivers who are coping with loved ones' terminal illness. Carla might also offer Jean an opportunity to keep a journal about her feelings and her sense of her spiritual understanding of what is transpiring in the intersection of her life and her husband's illness.

Discussion

In both of these cases, it is important for the counselors to be clear about the difference between religion and spirituality. In the case of LaTrisha, the client has clearly stated a religious belief (an afterlife belongs to those who are born-again Christians) and has attached spiritual meaning to it. This is a situation in which spirituality is manifest through religion. In the case of Jean, the client makes an intentional distinction between her notion of religion (doctrinal and institutional) and spirituality (a personal sense of meaning and purpose). If at the outset of counseling, Amy had tried to get LaTrisha to change her notion of the afterlife, or had introduced ideas about reincarnation or some alternative view of immortality, she would have been imposing her values on her client and would not have been able to help LaTrisha explore more fully the meaning and implications of her religious beliefs. In essence, it was essential for Amy to recognize that LaTrisha was immersed in a religious system that, at the time, was determining her worldview and causing her distress. Moreover, it was important for Amy to create a safe, nonjudgmental environment in which LaTrisha could explore her beliefs and be invited to examine a variety of Christian interpretations of God's nature and the afterlife. Even if LaTrisha continued to espouse beliefs that were troubling to her in the face of her grandmother's death, Amy could help LaTrisha express her love for her grandmother and to create a way of remembering her.

Likewise, had Carla attempted to get Jean interested in religion, or had she invited Jean to consider a religious interpretation of her spiritual perspective, Carla would not have been acting in the best interest of her client. Moreover, the failure to distinguish between spirituality and religion could result in unethical behavior that alienates Jean and results in Carla's needs being placed above those of her client. Instead, Carla could accept Jean's own view of spirituality, encourage her to explore this dimension of her experience more fully, and offer support for her stressful situation.

The Relationship Between Spirituality and Religion

A Continuum Between Spirit and Structure

The concepts of religion and spirituality are linked in important ways, and many people, like a pendulum, swing back and forth between the two. Jaroslav Pelikan (1968) used the phrase *spirit versus structure* to describe Martin Luther's role in the Protestant Reformation. Basically, Pelikan argued that Luther believed the Roman Catholic Church had become so rigid that it was stifling God's spirit. Therefore, Luther was led to call for church reform. What Luther uncovered, however, was that the tenuous, gossamer strands of personal spirituality needed the Church's organizational structures for focus. The spirit-versus-structure paradigm suggests that individuals may move between a need for free expression of their spirituality without the bonds of religion and a need for some kind of structure to create meaning and organization for spiritual practice (Frame, 2003).

Case Example: Eric

Eric, a 63-year-old Caucasian man, sought counseling because of a lack of meaning in his life. Eric reported that his wife had died a year ago and his grown daughters had relocated across the country. He felt lost and abandoned. Eric's counselor, Lucy, asked Eric about the sources of support he had in his life. She also inquired about any religious or spiritual connections that might be drawn upon at this time. Eric indicated that he had not been raised with any particular religious or spiritual beliefs. He reported that, as a child, from time to time he would attend a small country church when he visited his grandparents. Although he was interested in spirituality and had wrestled silently with religious questions, he never did officially join a church because he feared being controlled by it. Eric said to Lucy, "I just didn't think I wanted to be in a church that dictated what I could and couldn't do." Eric said he had spent the last 30 years "trying to figure things out" on his own. He revealed that he would like to explore spirituality more intentionally but was not sure how to go about it. Eric said his neighbors, the Carlsons, "attended a church regularly and seemed to get a lot out of it." Lucy suggested Eric might consider talking with his neighbors and inquiring about the nature of their church and why it was meaningful for them. Eric decided to contact several former coworkers and neighbors about their religious or spiritual experiences.

After several weeks and two invitations, Eric decided to attend church with the Carlsons. After 3 months of going to the worship services, Eric joined a Bible study, a grief group, a Sunday School class, and volunteered at a church-sponsored mission project. Soon he was spending almost all of his waking hours engaged in some church activity. In a session with Lucy, Eric confessed that the quest had become a burden. Lucy helped Eric to discover how he had moved from a very unstructured, almost nonexistent sense of spirituality to a very organized religious experience. She was able to help Eric realize that he needed *some* structure and routine to help him integrate his new spiritual awakening, but also some space for personal reflection. This case illustrates the spirit–structure continuum and indicates a way that a competent counselor may address clients' ambivalence about religion and/or spirituality.

The Difficult Relationship Between Counseling, Spirituality, and Religion

Historically, psychology and religion were connected because psychology emerged as the study of the human mind, soul, or spirit. That is, distinctions were not made between *pneuma,* the spiritual aspect of persons, and *psyche,* the soul or mind of the person (Vande Kemp, 1982). During the Enlightenment period in the 18th century, however, the Age of Reason displaced the Age of Faith (Kurtz, 1999). The emergence of modern science beginning in the 1600s and continuing to the present day led to the current split between science and religion. Pioneers in psychology such as Freud, Watson, Thorndike, Skinner, and others aligned themselves with the scientific worldview and, as a result, gained credibility and respectability for their theories.

For the following reasons, however, few counselors trained in the last half of the 20th century have knowledge about the role of religion or spirituality in clinical practice: (a) conflict between scientific worldviews and those of religion and spirituality, (b) religion and spirituality linked with pathology, (c) the notion that religion and spirituality are the domain of spiritual leaders, (d) a lack of training, and (e) their own religious or spiritual issues (Frame, 2003). We discuss each of these below.

The Conflict Between Scientific and Religious/Spiritual Worldviews

Epistemology (or the question of how we know what we know) was one source of conflict. Scientists pointed to the physical world, to the senses, and to empirical evidence. Religious and spiritual spokespersons acknowledged that these ideas were partially correct but transcendence and inspiration also were valid ways of knowing the truth. Thus, science was, in the words of Mahoney (1976),

> grounded in empirical facts that are uninterpreted, indubitable, and fixed in meaning; that theories are derived from these facts by induction or deduction and are retained or rejected solely on the basis of their ability to survive experimental tests; and that science progresses by the gradual accumulation of facts. (p. 130)

Religion, on the other hand, was focused on "the realms of significance, meaning, values, ultimacy, and ethics; these are regarded as making no factual claims on human reality" (Jones, 1996, p. 117). Thus, science and religion were assumed to be incompatible because science was based on fact and religion on faith.

Religion and Spirituality Associated With Pathology

Many psychologists and other mental health practitioners have been supportive of religion and spirituality and have identified themselves as religious or spiritual (Bergin & Jensen, 1990). Historically, however, most have been disparaging of religion or condemned it as an example of pathology. For example, Sigmund Freud was perhaps the most well-known opponent of religion. Besides the idea that religion is the result of wish fulfillment and fantasy, Freud (1927/1961) also declared religion to be an illusion. Freud was convinced that religious indoctrination created fear-induced repression that resulted in a reluctance to exercise critical thinking.

Albert Ellis, founder of rational-emotive behavior therapy (REBT), also criticized religion. He declared that atheism was the only way to optimal human functioning. He wrote, "Religiosity is in many respects equivalent to irrational thinking and emotional disturbance" (Ellis, 1980, p. 637). Thus, many of his followers in the cognitive-behavioral tradition assume that all religious and spiritual beliefs are irrational distortions that clients should give up.

B. F. Skinner (1953), the well-known behaviorist, claimed that religious behavior occurs because it follows reinforced stimuli. Skinner believed that the clergy, liturgy, and behavior codes were reinforcement contingencies, serving not only the individuals involved but the institutional and social order as well (Wulff, 1996).

Humanists emphasized the natural tendency of people to become self-actualized if surrounded by a positive, supportive environment. Those with a scientific and rational bent generally rejected the notion of a Supreme Being (Goud, 1990). Their emphasis was on the human being as the crown of creation.

Religion and Spirituality as Domains of Spiritual Leaders

The emergence of faith in professionals is a trend that began in the 1920s (Kurtz, 1999). The idea of expertness belonging to "professionals" resulted in each discipline drawing boundaries that separated it from other disciplines. While clergy and other spiritual leaders have ecclesiastical authority and expertise and may be well prepared to deal with religious and spiritual issues, many are not equipped to address psychological ones (Domino, 1990). Therefore, to relegate counseling clients with religious or spiritual issues solely to religious leaders is to abdicate our responsibility to provide psychological services, even if they must be offered within the clients' religious or spiritual worldviews.

Counselors' Lack of Training

One reason that counselors have neglected or opposed integrating religion and spirituality in their practice has to do with competence. Virtually all of the ethical codes governing the practice of psychotherapy speak against practicing in areas in which one is not trained or competent (American Association for Marriage and Family Therapy, 2001; American Counseling Association, 1995; American Psychological Association, 2003; National Association of Social Workers, 1996; National Organization for Human Service Education, 1995). Up until recently, mental health professionals had not been trained in working with clients' religious or spiritual issues (Collins, Hurst, & Jacobson, 1987; Genia, 1994; Jensen & Bergin, 1988; Shafranske & Maloney, 1990). Indeed, Kelly (1994) found that of 341 accredited and nonaccredited counselor education programs, only 25% reported that religion and spirituality were addressed in the curriculum. Pate and High (1995) surveyed 60 programs accredited by the

Council for Accreditation of Counseling and Related Education Programs (CACREP), and 60% reported that some attention was given to these issues in the social and cultural foundations courses. In a subsequent study, Kelly (1997) studied 48 programs that were accredited solely by CACREP and found that just over half reported that religion and spirituality were presented in some aspect of their counselor education curriculum. More recently, Young, Cashwell, Frame, and Belaire (2002) surveyed liaisons in 94 CACREP-accredited programs and found only 46% perceived themselves as prepared or very prepared to integrate material related to spirituality and religion into teaching and supervision. Further, only 28% viewed their colleagues as similarly able to address these issues in counselor preparation.

Counselors' Unresolved Religious and Spiritual Issues

Many counselors have neglected or opposed the inclusion of religion and spirituality because of unresolved personal issues. Those who do venture into an area such as incorporating clients' religious and spiritual concerns in their work may experience countertransference to the degree that it interferes with their effectiveness or, worse, harms the client (Genia, 2000; Kochems, 1993).

One example of such interference is in the case of Charles, a counselor who, raised in a strict, fundamentalist Christian sect, spent years trying to find a more open, accepting Christian denomination. When working with clients who had a similar religious upbringing, Charles was eager to liberate them from what he believed was oppressive religion. As a result, he had a tendency to push his clients too quickly to move beyond their rigid views (Genia, 2000).

Also, counselors who have experienced significant trauma, such as being involved in school shootings or the tragedy of September 11th, may have their own faith tested. They may wonder how God or any loving Supreme Being could permit such atrocities. When clients raise similar concerns in the wake of the death of loved ones or other tragic events, counselors may be unable to manage the strong emotions these topics trigger in them (Frame, 2003). They may also feel powerless to assist their clients in dealing with situations in which "bad things happen to good people" (Kushner, 1981). Such unresolved issues complicate the counseling process.

Another challenge emerges when counselors must work with clients who hold personal views opposed to their own. For example, Nancy, a lesbian counselor, was extremely sensitive to clients who were outspoken against homosexuality and who condemned it based on biblical authority. Because she herself was taught that homosexuality was "an abomination," her internalized homophobia created a serious conflict and countertransference with some clients. Although most of the time Nancy was able to make peace with her sexual orientation, in issues of faith and religion, she often succumbed to self-denigration. As a result of these types of situations of unresolved issues, counselors may avoid dealing with religion and spirituality in clinical settings.

A Rationale for Including Religion and Spirituality in Counseling

There are many reasons that religion and spirituality are appropriate dimensions of counseling. First, the majority of Americans report they believe in a

Higher Power, and many are actively involved in churches, synagogues, mosques, and other religious institutions (Hoge, 1996). This implies that most clients will have some kind of religious or spiritual background that may shape their attitudes, feelings, beliefs, and behavior. Also, there is some overlap in the values and goals between counseling and religion or spirituality. For example, both psychotherapy and religion offer ways of managing life's challenges and transforming the mind and emotions (Bianchi, 1989).

It is interesting to note the etymological connections between the Latin root words for salvation and health. *Salvare* in Latin means "to save." *Salvus* means "safe" and is related to the Latin word *salus* meaning healthy or whole. Thus, the religious word *salvation* is etymologically related to the psychologically oriented words *health, wholeness,* and *well-being.* There is a linguistic history that binds together the spiritual notion of what it means to be whole with the psychological assumption about wellness. The unity of the disciplines, then, is visible from the perspective of language (Frame, 2003).

In addition to both the practical and etymological intersections between spirituality and counseling, there is empirical evidence that suggests that religion and spirituality contribute positively to mental health and, thus, the religious and spiritual aspects of clients' lives may be supplementary tools in the therapeutic process. Bergin (1983) reviewed 24 research studies and found that when religion was correlated with measures of mental health, 23% of the studies revealed a negative relationship, 30% found no relationship, and 47% found a positive relationship. Bergin concluded, "Thus, 77% of the obtained results are contrary to the negative effect of religion theory" (p. 176). Gartner, Larson, and Allen (1991) reviewed 12 studies and found fewer suicidal impulses and more negative attitudes toward suicide in religious participants. Eleven of the 12 studies reviewed revealed a negative relationship between religious commitment and drug use. In addition, those who reported a high level of religious involvement were less likely to abuse alcohol. While religious attitudes were moderately associated with lower criminal and juvenile behavior, high religious participation *consistently* was associated with lower criminal and juvenile delinquency.

Another reason that religion and spirituality are appropriate for the counseling endeavor has to do with the postmodern movement in the latter part of the 20th century. It has been a bridge over the gulf between science and religion, and has opened up new opportunities for expanding a holistic approach to psychotherapy. The postmodern perspective involves a paradigm shift regarding how we think about the world. In this worldview, "there are no metaphysical absolutes; no fundamental and abstract truths, laws, or principles that will determine what the world is like and what happens in it" (Slife & Williams, 1995, p. 54). Instead, there are multiple perspectives and varieties of ways of perceiving. Thus, individuals do not discover reality but rather invent it (Watzlawick, Weakland, & Fisch, 1974). Postmodern thinkers emphasize the context in which human beings find themselves. They claim that meaning and truth are not objective "givens" but that they emerge in light of human relationships, language, culture, and personal meanings. What this shift in perspective means for counselors is that clients' religious or spiritual beliefs are considered human constructions of reality. It does not matter if those constructions include God or not (Zinnbauer & Pargament, 2000) or if they are congruent with the counselor's constructions (Neimeyer, 1995). Thus, counselors enter the subjective reality of their clients and work within their perspectives, using a common language involving shared metaphors and symbols (Bilu, Witztum, & Van der Hart, 1990). Such an approach enables counselors to avoid theological arguments with clients and may reduce the likelihood of their imposing their values on their clients. That philosophical trend, coupled with a renewed interest in religion evident in the popular culture (Richards & Bergin, 1997), makes the time ripe for committing ourselves to integrating spirituality/religion and counseling.

The Dangers of Being Incompetent

The process of becoming a competent counselor not only requires acquiring technical skills but also involves a commitment toward becoming a professional and a person (Whitaker & Keith, 1981). Because counselors bring with them their life experiences, worldviews, values, and personal relationships into the counseling process (Aponte & Winter, 1987), it is imperative to address *person-of-the-therapist* issues (Aponte & Winter, 1987) when working with clients' religious and spiritual concerns. Such issues are what Guerin and Hubbard (1987) referred to as *clinical triggers*. This phrase means that clients may arrive with issues that are similar to the counselor's issues. When both sets of issues collide in the therapeutic process, counselors are more vulnerable to being pulled into their clients' system (Kramer, 1985).

There is a wide range of experiences that may shape counselors' responses to clients' religious and spiritual issues, including countertransference reactions. For example, counselors who were raised in families in which religion was eschewed may feel they are betraying their families of origin if they address their clients' religious issues (Frame, 2003). They may be vulnerable to being drawn into conflicts with dogmatic clients that may result in forging clients' rigid beliefs rather than opening for them new viewpoints. Or, on the other hand, counselors with or without a religious or spiritual upbringing may be unaware of how significantly spirituality may influence their clients and thus not attend to it in ways that would be helpful to their clients (Benningfield, 1998).

Other counselors may have had significant transpersonal experiences of higher consciousness, unity with others and the universe, and a poignant sense of self-transcendence. Despite the positive impact these encounters may have had, some counselors may not have an appropriate spiritual frame for integrating transpersonal experiences into their daily living. They may feel at once excited and fearful about what has occurred for them personally. When counselors find themselves in this situation, their countertransference reaction may cause them to overidentify with clients who present similar circumstances (Frame, 2003). Or counselors' transpersonal revelations may be too intense and unexamined that they cause counselors to refrain from entering that area with their clients.

Benningfield (1998) raised other person-of-the-therapist issues. He suggested that some counselors might not set appropriate limits with their clients.

For example, Audrey became overly invested in providing a positive spiritual experience for her client, Rodney. Consequently, she focused on religion and spirituality to the neglect of important psychological issues. As a result, she failed to balance supportive interventions with confrontational ones. By such omissions, counselors may inadvertently prevent their clients from dealing with serious psychological distress.

An example of positive countertransference may be found in Ben, who, being religiously and spiritually committed himself, neglected to ask probing questions of his client, Sam, regarding Sam's religious beliefs and practices. Because Ben valued religion and spirituality, he was afraid that he might make assumptions about Sam's beliefs and overidentify with Sam's problems. Ben was worried that if he asked deeper questions of Sam, he may have to address these very issues himself. As a result, Ben was reluctant to deal with spirituality in the same way with Sam as he did with other concerns that arose in counseling.

The previous scenarios are illustrations of how person-of-the-therapist issues (Aponte & Winter, 1987) may emerge in the context of working with clients' religious and spiritual concerns. These examples show possible counselor incompetence as a result of counselors' personal issues that may interfere with their counseling effectiveness.

Case Studies

Kristen

Kristen is counseling Renee, who requested assistance handling her husband's, Brian's, resistance to start attending church with her. Renee, an Episcopal, always enjoyed church and the social aspects of it. She reported that she and Brian are planning to have children soon. It is important to Renee to have her children baptized and for all of them to attend church as a family. However, Renee also indicated to Kristen that she was afraid she might lose Brian if she put too much pressure on him about church. Kristen, a devout Catholic, understood and shared the belief that children should be baptized and attend church. In counseling, Kristen focused on gender issues and advised Renee to be assertive regarding her opinion about religion, regardless of what Brian thought. While Renee appreciated the support from Kristen, she remained torn between her religious beliefs and her husband, who staunchly opposed them.

Questions for Discussion or Reflection

1. How well do you think Kristen handled Renee's issues concerning religion? Why?
2. What do you think are some of Kristen's personal issues?
3. Do you think that Kristen's experience with religion influenced the way she worked with Renee? Why or why not?
4. What would you recommend that Kristen do in subsequent sessions with Renee?
5. If you were Renee, how might you be feeling about Kristen's work with you?

6. With a partner, role-play this case, paying particular attention to Renee's concerns about her husband's opposition to religion.

Caroline

Caroline, a counselor in a community mental health center, is counseling Jason, a 32-year-old single father regarding his alcoholism and use of illegal drugs. Jason's young children, Amanda and Travis, have been removed from his home by Social Services and placed in foster care. As part of his treatment, Jason has been attending Alcoholics Anonymous and practicing the 12-step program in an effort to gain sobriety and have his children returned. Jason has been captivated by the notion of a Higher Power and is spending enormous amounts of time exploring various religions and spiritual perspectives. Whenever he has the urge to drink or use drugs, he watches a Pentecostal TV program, reads Jehovah's Witnesses devotional literature, or goes to a prayer meeting. Sometimes Jason moves between religions, attending Buddhist temples or Muslim mosques. While his efforts are sincere, Jason seems unable to focus on any one religion or to commit himself to integrating his belief in a Higher Power into the rest of his life. Caroline, a practicing Buddhist, is frustrated with Jason, especially because his tendency to attach himself to any religion is contrary to her Buddhist beliefs of detachment. Moreover, Caroline believes that Jason is simply substituting one addiction for another. Caroline suggested that Jason stop focusing on the Higher Power aspect of his treatment and begin to take seriously his substance abuse problem.

Questions for Discussion or Reflection

1. In what ways do you think Caroline's work with Jason was helpful or not helpful?
2. What person-of-the-therapist issues do you think Caroline needs to consider?
3. How would you respond to Jason if he were your client?
4. How effective do you think Jason's spiritual path is?
5. With a partner, role-play this case, paying particular attention to Jason's spiritual needs.

Suggested Activities

The following types of activities will be developed more fully in chapter 4; however, those presented here are related specifically to the tasks and goals described in this chapter on similarities and differences between religion and spirituality.

Write a Spiritual Autobiography

What are your earliest memories of religion and/or spirituality in your home or family life? Describe your experiences with religion and spirituality through childhood, adolescence, young adulthood, and beyond. Write about episodes when your religious or spiritual beliefs and values were challenged or changed. Reflect on where you are with religion and spirituality at this time in your life.

Where are you with this aspect of your life now? What would you like to do regarding religion and spirituality in the future?

Keep a Journal

Keep a journal in which you can reflect on challenging life questions to which religion and spirituality provide responses. Remember that your clients will be grappling with these same issues. It can be very helpful for you to think and write about where you stand on these matters. Use the questions below to structure your thinking and writing (Frame, 2003, p. 32).

1. What is your view of human nature? Are people good, evil, neutral?
2. What about free will? Do people have the ability to make their own choices or are their thoughts, feelings, and actions determined by some other force such as instincts, reinforcements, God?
3. "Why do bad things happen to good people?" Who is responsible for evil? Is there an evil spirit that struggles against a good spirit? Is there a God who is powerless to contain evil? Do bad things happen because people make poor choices? Do bad things happen to good people because the "good people" aren't really as good as they think they are? Do bad things happen randomly?
4. What happens to people after they die? What do you believe about an afterlife? Describe it.
5. Do you believe in a Higher Power? What are the qualities of the Supreme Being if you believe in one? Why do you believe in a Higher Power or God? If you do not believe in a Higher Power or God, what are the reasons for your disbelief?
6. What is your understanding of spirituality? How have you experienced it in your life?
7. Which of the "person-of-the-therapist" issues (or others not mentioned) seem to fit best for you? Where do you think you are most vulnerable to countertransference when clients raise religious or spiritual issues? What experiences have you had that lead you to believe that you are particularly vulnerable to "clinical triggers"?
8. Which types of clients or client problems involving religion or spirituality would be the most challenging for you? Why? Which ones would be the most exiting? Why?

Interview a Practicing Counselor

Select someone who is currently working in the mental health field providing direct service counseling to clients. Interview that counselor regarding issues raised in this chapter. Consider using some of the questions below to guide your interview (Frame, 2003, pp. 32–33):

1. How do you understand the differences between religion and spirituality?
2. How would you describe your own spiritual path if you have one?
3. What is your opinion about working with clients' religious or spiritual issues in counseling? How comfortable do you feel doing so?

4. How does your theoretical orientation to counseling contribute to your approach to working with clients' religious or spiritual issues?
5. If you do address religion and/or spirituality in your work with clients, what is your reason for doing so?
6. Which types of clients or client problems involving religion or spirituality would be the most challenging for you? Why? Which ones would be the most engaging? Why?

Expose Yourself to New Religious or Spiritual Experiences

Attend one religious or spiritual activity/event that is different from your background or religious/spiritual tradition. Cross-cultural events/activities are strongly encouraged. Team up with other friends or colleagues, and after your experience discuss the following questions:

1. Why did you choose to do this activity?
2. What did you learn about yourself and your own spirituality from engaging in this activity?
3. What implications for counseling did you learn from this experience?

Recommended Reading

Anderson, W. T. (1990). *Reality isn't what it used to be.* San Francisco: Harper & Row.
> This readable book is a helpful treatise on postmodern thought and its implications for contemporary life. It includes a very enlightening chapter regarding a postmodern perspective of counseling.

Kushner, H. S. (1981). *When bad things happen to good people.* New York: Schocken Books.
> Written by a rabbi, this book reveals the author's personal struggles with the question of how a loving God can permit tragedy to occur. Kushner addresses, in a very straightforward way, the difficult questions that most people ask when struggling with the problem of evil.

Shafranske, E. P. (1996). *Religion and the clinical practice of psychology.* Washington, DC: American Psychological Association.
> This edited book is a well-done volume containing several chapters related to integrating spirituality into existing theoretical perspectives. It provides a solid basis for practitioners who are beginning to make these connections.

Web Sites of Interest

The following Web sites may provide additional information or resources for exploring the relationships between religion, spirituality, and counseling:

http://www.accta.net/2001Handouts/armstrong.html
> This Web site provides a list of recommendations for training in using spirituality or religion in counseling.

http://www.apa.org
  This Web site lists the American Psychological Association (APA) ethics code (www.apa.org/ethics) and provides a link to APA's Division 36: Psychology of Religion.

http://www.aservic.org
  This Web site lists the Association for Spiritual, Ethical, and Religious Values in Counseling (ASERVIC, a division of the American Counseling Association) competencies related to counseling and spirituality.

http://www.csuohio.edu/oaservic/bib.htm
  This Web site lists an annotated bibliography of materials on spirituality and counseling. Additions to the list may be made by Web site visitors.

Summary

The purpose of this chapter has been to explicate the first competency and focus on the similarities and differences between religion and spirituality. Further, the historical and current relationship between religion, spirituality, and mental health have been explored. The case studies and suggested activities provide the reader with a context for examining the remaining chapters.

References

American Association for Marriage and Family Therapy. (2001). *AAMFT code of ethics.* Washington, DC: Author.

American Counseling Association. (1995). *Code of ethics and standards of practice.* Alexandria, VA: Author.

American Psychological Association. (2003). *Ethical principles of psychologists and code of conduct.* Washington, DC: Author.

Aponte, H. J., & Winter, J. E. (1987). The person and practice of the therapist: Treatment and training. *Journal of Psychotherapy and the Family, 3,* 85–111.

Benningfield, M. F. (1998). Addressing spiritual/religious issues in therapy: Potential problems and complications. In D. S. Becvar (Ed.), *The family, spirituality and social work* (pp. 25–42). New York: Haworth Press.

Bergin, A. E. (1983). Religiosity and mental health: A critical reevaluation and meta-analysis. *Professional Psychology: Research and Practice, 14,* 170–184.

Bergin, A. E., & Jensen, J. P. (1990). Religiosity of psychotherapists: A national survey. *Psychotherapy, 27,* 3–7.

Bianchi, E. C. (1989). Psychotherapy as religion: Pros and cons. *Pastoral Psychology, 38,* 67–81.

Bilu, Y., Witztum, E., & Van der Hart, O. (1990). Paradise regained: "Miraculous healing" in an Israeli psychiatric clinic. *Culture, Medicine, and Psychiatry, 14,* 105–127.

Booth, L. (1992). The stages of religious addiction. *Creation Spirituality, 8*(4), 22–25.

Cervantes, J. M., & Ramirez, O. (1992). Spirituality and family dynamics in psychotherapy with Latino children. In L. A. Vargas & J. D. Koss-Chioino (Eds.), *Working with culture: Psychotherapeutic interventions with ethnic minority children and adolescents* (pp. 103–128). San Francisco: Jossey-Bass.

Chandler, C. K., Holden, J. M., & Kolander, C. A. (1992). Counseling for spiritual wellness: Theory and practice. *Journal of Counseling & Development, 71,* 168–175.

Collins, J. R., Hurst, J. C., & Jacobson, J. K. (1987). The blind spot extended: Spirituality. *Journal of College Student Personnel, 28,* 274–276.

Delbane, R., & Montgomery, H. (1981). *The breath of life: Discovering your breath prayer.* San Francisco: Harper & Row.

Domino, G. (1990). Clergy's knowledge of psychopathology. *Journal of Psychology and Theology, 18,* 32–39.

Elkins, D. N., Hedstrom, L. J., Hughes, L. L., Leaf, J. A., & Saunders, C. (1988). Toward a humanistic-phenomenological spirituality. *Journal of Humanistic Psychology, 28,* 5–18.

Ellis, A. (1980). Psychotherapy and atheistic values: A response to A. E. Bergin's "Psychotherapy and Religious Values." *Journal of Consulting and Clinical Psychology, 48,* 635–639.

Frame, M. W. (2003). *Integrating religion and spirituality into counseling: A comprehensive approach.* Pacific Grove, CA: Brooks/Cole.

Freud, S. (1961). The future of an illusion. In J. Strachey (Ed. & Trans.), *The standard edition of the complete psychological words of Sigmund Freud* (Vol. 21, pp. 1–56). London: Hogarth Press and the Institute of Psychoanalysis. (Original work published 1927)

Gartner, J., Larson, D. B., & Allen, G. D. (1991). Religious commitment and mental health: A review of empirical literature. *Journal of Psychology and Theology, 19,* 6–25.

Genia, V. (1994). Secular psychotherapists and religious clients: Professional considerations and recommendations. *Journal of Counseling & Development, 72,* 395–398.

Genia, V. (2000). Religious issues in secularly based psychotherapy. *Counseling and Values, 44,* 213–220.

Goud, N. (1990). Spiritual and ethical beliefs of humanists in the counseling profession. *Journal of Counseling & Development, 68,* 571–574.

Guerin, P. J., & Hubbard, I. M. (1987). Impact of therapists' personal family system on clinical work. *Journal of Psychotherapy and the Family, 3,* 47–60.

Hinterkopf, E. (1994). Integrating spiritual experiences in counseling. *Counseling and Values, 38,* 165–175.

Hoge, D. R. (1996). Religion in America: The demographics of belief and affiliation. In E. P. Shafranske (Ed.), *Religion and the clinical practice of psychology* (pp. 21–41). Washington, DC: American Psychological Association.

Holifield, E. B. (1983). *A history of pastoral care in America.* Nashville, TN: Abingdon Press.

Jensen, J. P., & Bergin, A. E. (1988). Mental health values of professional therapists: A national interdisciplinary survey. *Professional Psychology: Research and Practice, 19,* 290–297.

Jones, S. L. (1996). A constructive relationship for religion with the science and profession of psychology: Perhaps the boldest model yet. In E. P. Shafranske (Ed.), *Religion and the clinical practice of psychology* (pp. 113–147). Washington, DC: American Psychological Association.

Kelly, E. W., Jr. (1994). The role of religion and spirituality in counselor education: A national survey. *Counselor Education and Supervision, 33,* 227–237.

Kelly, E. W., Jr. (1997). Religion and spirituality in variously accredited counselor training programs: A comment on Pate and High. *Counseling and Values, 42,* 7–11.

Kochems, T. (1993). Countertransference and transference aspects of religious material in psychotherapy. In M. L. Randour (Ed.), *Exploring sacred landscapes: Religious and spiritual experiences in psychotherapy* (pp. 34–54). New York: Columbia University Press.

Kramer, J. R. (1985). *Family interfaces: Transgenerational patterns.* New York: Bruner/Mazel.

Kurtz, E. (1999). The historical perspective. In W. R. Miller (Ed.), *Integrating spirituality into treatment* (pp. 19–46). Washington, DC: American Psychological Association.

Kushner, H. S. (1981). *When bad things happen to good people.* New York: Schocken Books.

Mahoney, M. (1976). *Scientist as subject.* Cambridge, MA: Ballinger.

National Association of Social Workers. (1996). *Code of ethics.* Washington, DC: Author.

National Organization for Human Service Education. (1995). *Ethical standards of the National Organization for Human Service Education.* Austin, TX: Author.

Neimeyer, R. A. (1995). An appraisal of constructivist psychotherapies. In M. J. Mahoney (Ed.), *Cognitive and constructive psychotherapies* (pp. 163–194). New York: Springer.

Otto, R. (1958). *The idea of the holy.* New York: Oxford University Press.

Pate, R. H., & High, H. J. (1995). The importance of client religious beliefs and practices in the education of counselors in CACREP-accredited programs. *Counseling and Values, 40,* 2–5.

Pelikan, J. (1968). *Spirit versus structure.* New York: Harper & Row.

Richards, P. S., & Bergin, A. E. (1997). *A spiritual strategy for counseling and psychotherapy.* Washington, DC: American Psychological Association.

Roth, N. (1990). *The breath of God: An approach to prayer.* Cambridge, MA: Cowley.

Shafranske, E. P., & Maloney, H. N. (1990). Clinical psychologists' religious and spiritual orientations and their practice of psychotherapy. *Psychotherapy, 27,* 72–78.

Sheldrake, P. (1992). *Spirituality and history: Questions of interpretation and method.* New York: Crossroad.

Skinner, B. F. (1953). *Science and human behavior.* New York: Macmillan.

Slife, B. D., & Williams, R. N. (1995). *What's behind research: Discovering hidden assumptions in the behavioral sciences.* Thousand Oaks, CA: Sage.

Summit results in information of spirituality competencies. (1995, December). *Counseling Today,* p. 30.

Tillich, P. (1959). *Theology of culture.* New York: Oxford University Press.

Vande Kemp, H. (1982). The tension between psychology and theology: I. The etymological roots. *Journal of Psychology and Theology, 10,* 105–112.

Watzlawick, P., Weakland, J., & Fisch, R. (1974). *Change: Principles of problem formation and problem resolution.* New York: Norton.

Weatherhead, L. D. (1987). *The will of god.* Nashville, TN: Abingdon.

Webster's ninth new collegiate dictionary. (1987). Springfield, MA: Merriam-Webster.

Whitaker, C. A., & Keith, D. V. (1981). Symbolic-experiential family therapy. In A. S. Gurman & D. P. Kniskern (Eds.), *Handbook of family therapy* (pp. 187–225). New York: Bruner/Mazel.

Winarsky, M. (1991). *AIDS-related psychotherapy.* New York: Pergamon Press.

Wulff, D. M. (1996). *The psychology of religion: An overview.* In E. P. Shafranske (Ed.), *Religion and the clinical practice of psychology* (pp. 43–70). Washington, DC: American Psychological Association.

Young, J. S., Cashwell, C., Frame, M. W., & Belaire, C. (2002). Spiritual and religious competencies: A national survey of CACREP-accredited programs. *Counseling and Values, 47,* 22–33.

Zinnbauer, B. J., & Pargament, K. I. (2000). Working with the sacred: Four approaches to religious and spiritual issues in counseling. *Journal of Counseling & Development, 78,* 162–171.

Chapter 3

Assessing the Client's Spiritual Domain

Melanie C. Harper and Carman S. Gill

Competency: *The professional counselor can assess the relevance of the religious and/or spiritual domains in the client's therapeutic issues.*

This chapter provides information related to the appropriate and ethical integration of spiritual assessment into the counseling process. Reasons for spiritual assessment are explored, challenges counselors face in assessing spirituality are discussed, and specific assessment techniques are described. The chapter concludes with activities that can be used to practice applying spiritual assessment concepts and skills and resources for further exploration of spiritual assessment.

Explanation of Spiritual Assessment Competency

The Association for Spiritual, Ethical, and Religious Values in Counseling (ASERVIC) identifies spiritual assessment skills as a requirement for the counselor to appropriately and ethically integrate religion and spirituality into the counseling process (Miller, 1999; Summit on Spirituality, 1996). The relating competency is: "The professional counselor can assess the relevance of the religious and/or spiritual domains in the client's therapeutic issues" (Association for Spiritual, Ethical, and Religious Values in Counseling, n.d., ¶ 7). The following sections examine the intended meaning of this competency.

Assessment

Assessment in counseling is a process that begins as soon as a client enters the counseling setting (Frame, 2003). As a result, it is imperative for counselors to know what assessment is, the purpose for using assessments, and how assessment relates to other spirituality competencies. *Oxford English Dictionary Online* (Simpson & Weiner, 1989) defines *assessment* as the action or an instance of assessing, and *assessing* is defined as "to determine the importance, size, or value of." This definition implies not only the action of determination but also determination of amount of value or importance. Locke, Myers, and Herr (2001) defined assessment as involving how the counselor facilitates awareness of the clients' belief systems that are "relevant to the resolution of issues that the clients bring to counseling" (p. 608). For the purpose of this chapter, assessment is defined as the act of determining the amount of value or importance an individual assigns to a specific construct, such as spirituality. Counselors must be aware not only of the actions they are taking when assessing a client but also that they are determining the portion of value or amount of importance that the client assigns to spirituality. Because of this responsibility, counselors should understand the purpose for assessing client spirituality.

Counselors need to be conscious of their purpose or rationale for assessing client spirituality. Spirituality can be assessed to understand the client's worldview and context, to encourage client self-exploration (Kelly, 1995; Locke et al., 2001), to assist in diagnosis, to investigate religion and spirituality as client resources, to uncover religious and spiritual problems, and to determine what interventions may be appropriate (Frame, 2003). Identifying the purpose for assessing spirituality can provide guidance for counselors who are working in this area and clearly relates to these competencies.

Relevance

Oxford English Dictionary Online (Simpson & Weiner, 1989) describes *relevant* as "bearing upon, connected with, pertinent to, the matter in hand." Thus, the spiritual domain is relevant to therapeutic issues if there is a connection between the spiritual domain and the therapeutic issues or if the spiritual domain has or can have some bearing on or pertinence to the therapeutic issues. Relevance can be obvious at the beginning of counseling, uncovered through exploration, or established during the course of counseling, as in the case of the client who learns to draw from strengths in the spiritual domain to cope more effectively with her or his presenting problem.

Spiritual Domain

The spiritual domain has been referred to as involving meaning, hope, and love or relatedness (Newshan, 1998). For others, the spiritual domain is equivalent to specific religious practices or traditions. The spiritual domain may refer to a private experience of connection or unity or a sense of peace or belonging. The spiritual domain appears to encompass the complete area of human meaning-making, sense of connectedness, and belief in or understanding of the Divine. The spiritual domain may overlap or directly affect the physical or mental domains of functioning.

Therapeutic Issues

When defining a client's presenting problem, the counselor considers all components of the problem, events that contribute to the problem, the duration of the problem, and the client's coping skills, resources, and strengths (Hackney & Cormier, 1996). By working with any of these areas of the problem, the counselor can perform therapeutic work, or work that results in positive change, prevention of further problems, or life enhancement. Thus, each area of the problem definition contains therapeutic issues, or targets for exploration, change, or further strengthening of or utilization of skills and resources.

In relating therapeutic issues to the spiritual domain, the counselor can identify how such elements of the spiritual domain as the client's conscience, beliefs, values, spiritual experiences, meaning, responsibility, and practices contribute to the ways the client experiences the problem and to ways the client might cope with the problem. The problem might be viewed as wholly in the realm of the spiritual domain, such as a conflict between beliefs and tragic realities (e.g., the belief that God takes care of innocent people and the reality that the client's 4-year-old daughter was killed in a drive-by shooting). Alternatively, dissonance between elements of the spiritual domain and pressures from outside that domain might contribute to the client problem, or elements within the spiritual domain might be utilized as resources, skills, or strengths for coping with problems that appear to be wholly outside the spiritual domain. Once a relationship between the spiritual domain and the problem is made, the associated elements from the spiritual domain are considered therapeutic issues.

Importance of Spiritual Assessment to Competent Counseling

The counselor and client simultaneously perform assessment. While the counselor performs a professional assessment of the client, client's systems, and the issues that motivated the client to seek or accept counseling, the client informally assesses the counselor. The client might contemplate: "How much can I safely say to this person?" "What does this person want to know?" and "How will this person judge me?" In group and family counseling, assessment extends further to each client assessing the other clients' behaviors. The clients might wonder: "Who are these people?" "How do I compare with them?" and "What aspects of me might they accept and reject?" The choices the counselor makes during the initial assessment phase of counseling can influence the client's level of safety with disclosure and the counselor's level of accuracy and completeness of client conceptualization. The following sections describe factors that have influenced counselors' decisions related to assessment of the client's spiritual domain. Historical considerations are presented along with considerations of how the spiritual domain can relate to therapeutic issues. Concerns related to avoidance of nonmaleficience also are explored.

Historical Separation of Counseling From Spiritual Assessment

Much of the history of spirituality and religion in counseling can be traced back to Freud and Jung (Kelly, 1995). The traditional Freudian view of religion as an immature method of coping influenced much of the early psychoanalytic therapy and literature. This belief contributed to the historical separation of counseling from spiritual assessment (Genia, 1995). With the onset of existential therapies and Carl Jung, counselor belief toward spirituality and religion began to broaden. Carl Jung's belief in the intrinsic value of meaning and purpose to life, inseparable from spirituality, gave room for informal assessment of the spiritual domain.

Because assessment in counseling begins in the initial session (Frame, 2003), the counselor's theoretical orientation has an impact on how client spirituality is assessed (Kelly, 1995). Counselors who worked from a Jungian theoretical stance and other theoretical backgrounds that acknowledge the importance of spirituality began informally assessing the client's spiritual domain as part of treating the whole individual. Counselors soon began to integrate assessment of the spiritual domain into counseling assessment. As the integration of spirituality and informal spirituality assessments developed, so did the need for more formalized assessments.

One of the first uses of a formal spirituality instrument came in the early 1950s and resulted directly from concerns about the links between religion and prejudice (Hill & Pargament, 2003). Allport (1950) described the difference between religiously mature and immature individuals to this end. Additionally, Allport and Ross (1967) used assessment measures to determine whether extrinsically oriented individuals, those who identified religion as peripheral to their values (Sherman, 2001), would display more prejudice than would intrinsically oriented religious individuals, those who identified religion as an inherent value (Sherman, 2001). From this point until the introduction of wellness, use of spirituality assessment in counseling diminished.

Formal spirituality assessments seem to have been reintroduced through holistic models as subsets of a larger factor. Dunn (1961) introduced a model for holistic wellness in the medical field. Dunn's model included spirituality as part of holistic wellness. Hettler (n.d.) introduced a six-dimension model of holistic wellness, which included spirituality as a portion of holistic wellness. Additionally, he developed the Lifestyle Assessment Questionnaire based on this model and included spirituality as a subscale with 14 questions specific to spirituality (National Wellness Institute, 1983). Travis (1981) introduced a holistic model of wellness and an assessment, the Wellness Inventory, which evaluated spirituality as part of the wellness factor. In addition, Moos and Moos (1981) published the Family Environment Scale that included spirituality as a Moral/Religion subscale score. This trend introduced formal spirituality assessments as a part of holistic counseling, and the separation of counseling from spiritual assessment further decreased.

Other types of spirituality assessments were introduced in the early 1980s as spirituality and religion became widely recognized as an important part of holistic treatment. Research regarding the impact of spirituality in clients' lives followed, and models of spiritual development and integration evolved. However, concerns about the integration of spirituality and counseling still lingered (Bergin, 1983; Larson, Pattison, Blazer, Omran, & Kaplan, 1986).

Locke et al. (2001) identified four reasons why counselors might be hesitant to address, and we would add *assess*, the spiritual domain. First, fear of imposing personal values is often a reason for avoiding spirituality and spirituality assessments. Counselors may fear that even initial informal assessment questions could be leading for the client and introduce a value that will be leading for the client. This fear is prevalent throughout counseling and psychology literature (Kelly, 1995; Tjeltveit, 1986) and can be traced back to the historical separation of counseling and spirituality (Locke et al., 2001). Confounding this issue is the belief that if the spiritual domain is avoided, the counselor may be overlooking important interventions or problems. A second reason for counselors to avoid assessing the spiritual domain is the counselor's own negative experiences with organized religion or spiritual abuse (Locke et al., 2001). Lack of knowledge about addressing, assessing, or intervening in the spiritual domain is a third reason that counselors often do not work in this area. Finally, the lack of integration of spirituality into theoretical models or the lack of facilitative models may contribute to the counselor's avoidance of spirituality assessments.

Recent literature focuses on the difficulties facing spirituality assessment. Counselors and theorists have noted the challenges associated with defining spirituality, especially as a concept separate from other aspects of the individual. Hill and Pargament (2003) identified changes in spiritual assessment from the conceptualization of spiritual as external to spiritual as internal. They stated that as assessments, both formal and informal, grow in depth and sophistication, these assessments give a more thorough picture of the client's spiritual domain and religious belief system.

Finally, theorists and counselors call for further development of spiritual assessment. Suggestions include more cultural sensitivity in assessments. Large portions of the current spirituality assessments use Judeo-Christian references that are no longer applicable to all clients in our increasingly diverse population (Hill & Pargament, 2003). Assessments that focus on the client's spiritual change and development over time are needed as well. Advancement in the area of spirituality assessment is sure to be a focus in the future of counseling.

Relationship Between Spirituality and Therapeutic Issues

Clients bring into counseling therapeutic issues that arise from problems within the spiritual domain, between the spiritual domain and other personal domains (such as work and leisure), and between the spiritual domain and various systems (such as the family and the community). Within the framework of group counseling, additional therapeutic issues, such as guilt and shame that may be related to the spiritual domain, can arise. In many instances, clients also bring into counseling resources from their spiritual domains that can be utilized as part of counseling interventions. The following sections explore these ways in which the spiritual domain can relate to a client's therapeutic issues.

Spiritual Domain as a Contributor to Therapeutic Issues

What happens when one's belief system is in conflict with one's behavior or view of one's self? Where does one turn when tragic events in this world clash with one's view of a just or benevolent God who is in control of each person's destiny? Are shame and guilt strictly spiritual issues or also therapeutic issues? Can a person delve into the spiritual domain too deeply or in psychologically dangerous ways? How does an individual develop purpose and meaning or, at the end of life, recognize that one's life has been lived well? From these questions, a counselor can begin to explore how the spiritual domain might contribute to some clients' therapeutic issues. Conflicts involving the spiritual domain and difficulties resulting from spiritual beliefs, practices, and experiences can contribute to the development of therapeutic issues.

Conflicts involving the spiritual domain (within the spiritual domain and between the spiritual domain and other personal domains) can manifest in numerous forms. Heyse-Moore (1996) explained that people who are dying reveal their spiritual pain through their physical symptoms, emotional distress, mental outlook and expression, and spiritual stance. The relationship between physical, emotional, and mental symptoms and spiritual distress can be difficult to assess. Counselors can explore these symptoms by looking for symbolic associations to spiritual difficulties. For example, anger can indicate a spiritual struggle, and anxiety can represent fear of the unknown. Spiritual pain might appear in the form of a dark night of the soul (O'Connor, 2002), as described by St. John of the Cross (1578/1959), or a cloud of unknowing, as described by an English mystic (see Wolters, 1961). The *dark night of the soul* refers to loss of satisfaction with spiritual practices, and the *cloud of unknowing* describes the inability of one to connect with God through the intellect. Although Heyse-Moore's work focused on spiritual pain in people who are dying, spiritual pain might manifest in similar ways for people who are not facing death. Regardless of whether a client is facing mortality, empathic exploration into the client's spiritual domain is necessary for the counselor to determine whether symptoms are related to spiritual pain.

Although the spiritual domain can contribute resources for effectively coping with life's challenges (as described in the next section), spiritual practices and beliefs also can impede a person's recognition and resolution of emotional and relational difficulties (Cashwell & Rayle, 2005). A *spiritual bypass* occurs when an individual assigns exclusive or excessive responsibility to the spiritual domain for an issue that transcends the spiritual domain. This bypass allows the person to avoid action, responsibility, or immediate emotional distress. As an example of a spiritual bypass, consider Brenda, who, when faced with relationship problems, increases her involvement in prayer, spiritual reading, and public worship in place of directly working on the relationship with her partner. Instead of alleviating the relationship problems, Brenda's increase in spiritual activities reduces time available for the relationship and further strains the relationship. Brenda views her actions as positive. Her increased spiritual activities reduce her personal responsibility for her relationship difficulties by placing responsibility for the relationship in the hands of a Higher Power and reduce her emotional distress because of faith that the relationship is in better hands than her own. In this case, the counselor assesses Brenda's spiritual bypass as a contributing factor to the couple's relationship difficulties. The counselor does not invalidate Brenda's efforts or her spiritual views. Instead, the counselor helps Brenda to determine how she can assume more personal responsibility for the relationship and increase her efforts to work on the relationship with her partner while retaining a satisfying level of involvement in spiritual activities. Brenda's case exemplifies a spiritual bypass in which personal responsibility is abdicated and in which spiritual obsession overshadows the needs of the family relationship. Spiritual bypass also can manifest as compulsive goodness, repression of undesirable emotions (hiding normal emotions that are thought to be bad), spiritual narcissism (feeling superior because the person possesses a perceived more highly developed spiritual domain), spiritual materialism (seeking a peak spiritual experience by experimenting with a variety of practices from different paths instead of sustaining disciplined practice from one spiritual path), blind faith in spiritual teachers, and social isolation (detaching from the world to avoid unfinished psychological business). Assessing for these types of spiritual bypasses can help the counselor identify ways that the spiritual domain might contribute to the development or escalation of therapeutic issues.

Spiritual Domain as a Contributor of Resources for Therapeutic Interventions

The use of assessment in counseling often is linked to treatment planning and therapeutic interventions. As earlier noted, determining effective treatment planning and intervention is one of the purposes for using spirituality assessments (Kelly, 1995; Stanard, Sandhu, & Painter, 2000). Clinicians often point to assessment of the client's religious beliefs and doctrinal understanding as a guideline for working with clients in the spiritual domain (Richards & Potts, 1995). When appropriate assessment is used, the therapist may find that clients have many resources available to them. In addition, the therapist is more likely to use appropriate treatment planning and intervention techniques.

Wellness-based models have traditionally acknowledged spirituality as a component of holistic treatment. Myers, Sweeney, and Witmer (2000) emphasized the importance of spirituality by placing it in the center of their Wheel of Wellness. From this strength-based, holistic perspective, the counselor has a duty to assess the spiritual domain and determine if interventions are needed. If the counselor determines that intervention is needed, a variety of resources for therapeutic interventions are available for clinicians and clients.

The spiritual beliefs and values of clients can be a resource for strength-based approaches such as wellness. Understanding these beliefs and values is crucial for effective intervention, and assessment can play a strong role in this understanding. Beliefs, such as a responsibility to a Higher Power, can be rationale for clients to become more self-actualized and can be the client's motivation for building on personal strengths. In addition, values, such as forgiveness and altruism, will help the client function more fully in the social realm.

Specific spiritual interventions can be used more effectively when assessment methods are utilized. Studies have shown that therapists use prayer as a resource when counseling (Ball & Goodyear, 1991; Payne, Bergin, & Loftus, 1992). According to Richards and Potts (1995), therapist silent prayer is used frequently among therapists who identify themselves as traditionally Christian and as Mormon. Clients can also be encouraged to use prayer as a coping resource. Meditation is a resource of the spiritual domain that is essentially different from prayer (Kelly, 1995). This resource has the added benefit of proven stress reduction (Kelly, 1995). The spiritual domain may be a client's primary resource for social support. A thorough assessment and understanding of the spiritual domain before, during, and after using these interventions will provide the counselor with valuable information. This information will assist the therapist in making decisions about how to proceed with treatment.

Therapists who use spiritual interventions often integrate these interventions into mainstream approaches. As stated earlier, wellness-based approaches integrate resources from the spiritual domain. Also, counselors have used spiritual resources when working from cognitive-behavioral (Propst, Ostrom, Watkins, Dean, & Mashburn, 1992), psychodynamic, and existential therapies (Payne et al., 1992). However, research on positive or negative outcomes from specific spiritual interventions has only recently begun being conducted (Richards & Potts, 1995).

Spiritual Domain as a Part of the Client's Systems

How does a client's spiritual domain interact with a system's spiritual domain? Each of the client's systems (e.g., family, work, school, community) has its own spiritual domain. For example, the client's family of origin has a spiritual history, a set of values and beliefs, and possibly a set of spiritual-based customs and practices. Although the family spiritual domain overlaps the client's spiritual domain, the two domains might not be equivalent. Take for example the case of Ann. Ann grew up in a multigenerational Roman Catholic family. The family attended mass every weekend and on holy days, and Ann learned from her parents a sense of right and wrong that was based heavily on the church's teachings. During college, Ann developed close friendships with a few classmates whose families did not attend church as regularly and whose views were somewhat in conflict with the Catholic Church's teachings and the teachings of Ann's family. Ann modified some of her views and spiritual practices. She began attending mass less regularly, took a part-time job at a restaurant on Saturdays and Sundays, and started contemplating moving in with her boyfriend. Ann's spiritual domain continued to intersect and match her family's spiritual domain in some areas, but in other important areas Ann's spiritual domain grew in conflict with the spiritual domain of her family system.

The family is not the only system in which a client lives and derives meaning (Becvar & Becvar, 2000). In Ann's case, we know that Ann is part of a friendship system, a school system, a work system, and a community system. Even though her friends influenced some of the changes in Ann's spiritual domain and provide her with a place of belonging, Ann has integrated only pieces of her friends' spiritual domains into her own spiritual domain. Thus, the friendship system contains a spiritual domain that is characterized by varied spiritual histories, values, beliefs, and practices. We know very little about the other systems in which Ann participates. If Ann's college were a Catholic university, Ann might experience some dissonance between her evolving spiritual domain and the traditions and values of the school. Similarly, Ann might find resistance or support from her work and her community as her spiritual domain changes.

Striving for Nonmaleficence While Assessing Spirituality

Kitchener (1984) identified five considerations for ethical behavior when working with clients, but of particular concern when assessing spirituality is the area of nonmaleficence. When assessing the spiritual domain, counselors need to avoid harm to the client. Avoiding harm involves (a) steering clear of assumptions about the client's spiritual and religious belief systems, (b) using language appropriate for the client's view of spirituality, and (c) providing respectful focus on spirituality topics. For example, considerable harm could be done if the counselor begins using language oriented toward a specific religious belief system without knowledge about the client's actual religious beliefs. A client with Buddhist beliefs may be reluctant to disclose spiritual information to a counselor who has used Judeo-Christian language when referring to spiritual matters.

Avoiding Assumptions

While the Judeo-Christian faith is still the leading belief system in the United States, the last decade has seen increased diversity. Assumptions about a person's belief systems based on the individual's physical characteristics or geographic location or based on the counselor's religious belief system may result in verbal or nonverbal expression that damages the counselor–client relationship. Choosing an assessment method based on assumptions about a client can be equally as damaging. Imagine, for example, a person who identifies with Judaism being asked to complete an assessment that has questions about Jesus.

The Language of Spiritual Exploration

The value of language cannot be understated when striving for nonmaleficence in spirituality assessment. Because assessment begins when the client enters, a counselor working within Kitchener's (1984) ethical guidelines will attend to the client's verbal representation of spirituality. By using the client's own language in initial, informal assessment procedures, the counselor gains a better understanding of the client's spiritual domain without damaging the trust relationship that is just forming.

Often, the language of the client is broad. The client may refer to a denomination when asked about spirituality. The problem lies in the fact that people from the same denomination often have very different values and beliefs. For example, clients identifying themselves as Baptist may have very different views on issues such as divorce, birth control, and abortion. These different views stem from differing belief systems. In this instance, the counselor needs to gather more information to understand the client's spiritual domain rather than making assumptions based on a denominational category.

Focus as a Vehicle for Validation of Client Values

In addition to promoting nonmaleficence, focusing on the spiritual domain can validate the client's values. Clients may begin to feel that the counselor is genuinely attempting to understand their values and beliefs. Unconditional positive regard demonstrated by the counselor during the initial assessment process will set the tone for the therapeutic process.

Choosing Between Qualitative and Quantitative Methods of Assessment

Assessment methods are categorized as either qualitative or quantitative. Counselors can choose between qualitative and quantitative methods or can incorporate techniques and instruments from each of these methods when performing a spiritual assessment.

Qualitative and quantitative methods of assessment each have advantages and drawbacks. Qualitative assessment methods allow for flexible exploration of the client's spiritual domain, and quantitative methods provide structured and focused exploration. Figure 3.1 summarizes the advantages and disadvantages of qualitative and quantitative assessment methods, and the following sections provide more detailed information about these methods, their differences, and some common techniques and instruments that counselors use in spiritual assessment.

Qualitative Assessment Methods

Qualitative assessment methods provide the counselor with techniques for gaining an understanding of the client's unique spiritual domain. Although the elements of the spiritual domain might be similar to the elements found in other clients' spiritual domains, the counselor relies on qualitative assessment to discover how a specific client integrates spirituality with the other domains in life, interprets personal spiritual experiences and beliefs, and constructs an overall worldview and a localized self-view. The following sections describe uses of qualitative assessment techniques, limitations of these techniques, and some of the more common techniques used in qualitative assessment.

Uses of Qualitative Assessment Techniques
Qualitative assessment techniques are designed for exploration in a flexible manner. The counselor can use the client's language and can follow the client's

Quantitative Benefits	*Qualitative Benefits*
• Quantifiable results	• Flexible terminology
• Comparable results	• Flexible exploration
• Preset coverage of themes	• Focus on strengths
• Time efficient	• Assessment can be an intervention
Quantitative Limitations	*Qualitative Limitations*
• Focus limited by instrument	• Focus limited by assessor and client
• Predetermined terminology	• Not quantifiable
• Search for deficits	• Limited comparability
	• Time intensive

Figure 3.1
Comparison of advantages and disadvantages of qualitative and quantitative assessment methods.

pace, direction, and emphasis. The focus of exploration can be on identifying ways the spiritual domain provides strength to the client. For the counselor who is unfamiliar with elements of a client's spiritual domain (e.g., the client's religion or a specific spiritual practice), qualitative assessment can serve to educate the counselor. For the counselor who is familiar with all aspects of the client's spiritual domain, qualitative assessment can serve to verify or dispel assumptions the counselor might make about the client's spiritual domain. Because of its exploratory nature, qualitative assessment also can function as an intervention through which the client gains self-knowledge.

Limitations of Qualitative Assessment Techniques
The exploratory characteristics of qualitative assessment make this form of assessment time-intensive. Unlike quantitative assessment, qualitative assessment does not have a clear ending point or firm boundaries. Exploration continues for as long as the counselor feels the process is needed for accurate assessment or is beneficial to the client's development of self-knowledge. Without a specific map to follow, the counselor and client can explore a limited area of the client's spiritual domain. The counselor inadvertently can disregard important areas of the client's spiritual domain because the client does not mention those areas and the counselor fails to consider those areas. For example, the counselor can focus exploration on elements in a couple's current spiritual domain and miss exploring the evolution of this spiritual domain, or the counselor can ask about specific spiritual practices and miss learning about other spiritual practices.

The process of qualitative assessment unfolds uniquely for each client. Only areas that the counselor deems important are explored. As such, the counselor cannot consistently and accurately compare the results across assessments with various clients. No numerical scores are generated, so assessment results are not quantifiable. This lack of comparability and quantification can make qualitative assessment results difficult to interpret, summarize, and use as justification for treatment.

Qualitative Assessment Techniques
Traditional qualitative assessment techniques can be adapted for use with spiritual assessment. The following sections provide information about using behavioral observations, histories and interviews, sentence completion exercises, autobiographies, genograms, and ecomaps to assess therapeutic issues related to the client's spiritual domain.

Behavioral observations. Behavioral observation occurs when someone (possibly the counselor or in the case of self-observation, the client) watches a person or a group and records information about specific behaviors that are present or absent (Cohen & Swerdlik, 1999). The observer records instances of the behaviors and such related information as behavior intensity, preceding situations, and consequences of the behaviors. In self-observation, the client also can record accompanying thoughts and emotions. So how can watching and recording behaviors be used in assessing the spiritual domain of a client and the relationship between spirituality and the client's therapeutic issues?

First, consider a basic form of observation, the assessment of a client's appearance. Some people display their spiritual beliefs and personal values through their dress, hairstyle, grooming, makeup, and jewelry. Wedding and engagement rings, cross and star pendants, bindis, Masonic rings, novelty T-shirts, uncut or shaved hair, flag pins, colored ribbons, tattoos, and an imaginatively endless assortment of other ways people choose to present themselves can imply personal or spiritual beliefs and values. Through observation of the client's appearance, the counselor can obtain clues about the client's beliefs and values. The counselor then can use these clues to begin a discussion with the client about the client's spiritual domain.

Behavioral observation goes beyond simple observation of appearance. A counselor might note spiritual-related behaviors, such as invocations of a higher power. Invocations of a higher power can take the form of statements (e.g., "God willing and the creek don't rise") and gestures (e.g., the sign of the cross, folded hands with uplifted gaze, or the touch of a spiritual symbol that the client wears or carries). A counselor also might choose to direct a client in spiritual self-observation as a way to explore the client's connection to and use of the spiritual domain. Consider Charles, who comes to counseling to gain a sense of balance in his life. He talks sadly about not being a very spiritual person. He says that he works too much, takes walks on a nature trail near his work at lunch, and crams in time with his wife and son during the late evenings and on the occasional free weekends. As Charles talks, you recognize that his lunchtime walks have a spiritual quality. During his time in nature, Charles says he experiences "wholeness." Charles also states that he offers his work as service to fellow humanity, so he generally does not feel guilty working so much. As he talks, Charles realizes that since childhood he has viewed church involvement as the only legitimate spiritual activity, and lacking involvement in a church has caused him to view himself as not very spiritual. The counselor and Charles discuss Charles's view of spirituality and elements of his spiritual domain. The counselor then directs Charles to observe activities and behaviors that Charles thinks might involve his spiritual domain. Through this self-observation and exploration with the counselor, Charles gains understanding of how he has found ways to integrate spirituality in his life. Charles reports that the action of self-observation also encourages him to find additional ways of connecting his everyday activities with his spiritual domain. Assessment of Charles's spiritual domain through self-observation informs both the counselor and the client and provides the client with an effective initial intervention.

Spiritual histories and interviews. Spiritual histories and interviews involve questions that prompt clients to describe their spiritual development (Hodge, 2001). The goals often include gaining understanding of the environment in which the client's spiritual development has taken place, the progression of the client's spiritual development, the client's current spiritual domain, and the extent to which the client connects with a spiritual tradition or faith community. Public spiritual-related experiences (e.g., baptisms, bar mitzvahs, weddings, and divorces) are explored along with more private spiritual experiences (e.g., transcendent experiences, spiritual awakenings, and spiritual challenges and disillusionments).

The process of taking a spiritual history usually involves open-ended exploratory questions (e.g., "How did you come to believe in your religion or spiritual tradition?") but can include questions on intake forms (such as "Religion or spiritual tradition?"). The counselor remains empathic during the exploration and directs the dialogue so that specific themes are explored along with chronological influences, experiences, and spiritual domain changes. For example, the counselor might ask questions customized for the client but similar to the following questions: "What do you value in life?" "What gives you a sense of purpose?" "How do you stay connected with your religion or spiritual path?" "How has marriage (or becoming a parent, worker, or caregiver) affected your religious or spiritual practices?" "What experiences have strengthened, diminished, or shaped your beliefs?" and "How have your spiritual beliefs changed throughout your life?"

Horovitz-Darby (1994) cautioned that, depending on the client's personality and mental health status, the counselor might need to refrain from examining some aspects of the client's spiritual domain to protect the client from possible intensification or aggravation of psychosis. Thus, exploration of a client's spiritual domain should be conducted intentionally and with awareness of possible complications presented by the client's psychological status. Although the counselor selects the spiritual themes that are to be explored, several authors have proposed varied frameworks for spiritual histories (e.g., Dombeck & Karl, 1987; Richards & Bergin, 1997). Richards and Bergin (1997) suggested covering the following themes during the spiritual interview: the client's worldview, connection with any religious affiliation or spiritual tradition, level of orthodoxy (i.e., adherence to religious or spiritual traditions, beliefs, and practices), knowledge of religious or spiritual doctrine, approach to integrating spirituality into developing solutions to problems, perception of the client's relationship to God and the universe, perception of God, congruence of values and lifestyle, and spiritual maturity and health (as indicated by level of intrinsic vs. extrinsic spiritual motivation). Through exploration of these themes, the counselor can gain a broad view of the client's spiritual domain. The counselor then can determine whether further assessment of the spiritual domain is required.

Sentence completion. Sentence completion tests contain sentence stems, which clients are asked to complete. The stems usually are very general and allow for a wide range of responses. Although sentence completion tests have high face validity, they are vulnerable to faking (Cohen & Swerdlik, 1999). Clients who want to appear more spiritual can anticipate what the counselor would consider a positive spiritual answer. For other clients, spiritual-based sentence completion tests might spur deep consideration in the client as well as provide the counselor with insight into the client's spiritual domain. This section describes two sentence completion tests that prompt for information about client spirituality: the Oshodi Sentence Completion Index (OSCI; Oshodi, 1999) and the Spiritual Quest Form (SQF; Niño, 1997).

The Oshodi Sentence Completion Index (OSCI; Oshodi, 1999) is a 20-stem test designed to assess need for achievement in people of African descent (Oshodi, 1999). Six sentence stems are identified as prompts for attitudes toward spirituality. These stems are "I depend," "My skin color," "Reality to me," "In this world," "With my human spirit," and "When good or bad things happen to me, I attribute them to" (p. 218). Although Oshodi classified responses to other sentence stems in his test as indicating attitudes toward aspiration, obstacles, risk taking, persistence, and communality, many of these other stems could elicit information about the client's spiritual domain. For example, the following stems could return information about values and spiritual-based coping resources: "I emulate or imitate," "I would like to be seen as," "When I feel weak," "During misfortune," and "School, work, and pleasure are" (p. 218). In describing the interpretation of client responses to these sentence stems, Oshodi gave examples of enhancing responses and stumbling responses. Some enhancing responses are "When I feel weak, I pray to be strong" (p. 222) and "With my human spirit, I will overcome any difficult task that comes my way" (p. 228). Some stumbling responses are "When I feel weak, I worry" (p. 222) and "With my human spirit, I am limited" (p. 228). The OSCI stems provide counselors with a structure to assess the spiritual domain with African and African American clients in a manner that respects African influences on spirituality.

The Spiritual Quest Form (SQF; Niño, 1997) is a 10-stem test designed to explore attitudes of the client related to the client's movement toward spirituality. The SQF contains the following stems:

> I see myself now ...
> I think the spiritual ...
> The people I have met ...
> Thinking about my past ...
> When I feel fragmented ...
> My relation to God ...
> The world around me ...
> A meaningful life ...
> The best I have ever done ...
> What I really would like to do ... (p. 207)

Niño (1997) emphasized that the counselor must administer the SQF in an empathic environment to obtain satisfactory exploration. Exploration should go beyond the completion of the sentences. The counselor should assist the client in identifying values and meanings, in evaluating answers from new perspectives, and in identifying ways the client can expand behaviors that enrich the client's spiritual domain.

Stems from the OSCI and the SQF can be used to explore client spirituality at the beginning of assessment and throughout treatment. By using the same stems at different points in treatment, the counselor can identify changes in the client's spiritual domain. Substantial changes in answers could reflect actual changed beliefs, attitudes, and behaviors or could reflect a difference in the client's desire to fake a particular level of spirituality. As Niño (1997) noted, spiritual assessment using sentence stems can be a base for exploration, but further inquiry regarding the client's answers to the stems results in more useful and therapeutic assessment.

Spiritual autobiographies. A spiritual autobiography is a written form of a spiritual history. The advantages of the autobiography format is that the client can choose to devote more time to reflection on past experiences and consideration of how those experiences have influenced spiritual development and how spiritual development has extended out to influence other areas of life. One type of spiritual autobiography is the Exceptional Human Experience (EHE) autobiography (Palmer, 1999). In the EHE autobiography, the client describes, explores, and possibly integrates mystical, psychic, death-related, and other EHE experiences. In addition to learning about the client's EHEs, the counselor can use the EHE autobiography to learn about the client's willingness to disclose spiritual information, the qualities of experiences that provide meaning to the client and that facilitate transformation in the client's life, and other aspects of the client's spirituality. Through joint exploration of a client's spiritual autobiography, the counselor also can assist the client in gaining deeper understanding and more meaningful interpretation of past experiences.

Spiritual genograms. Counselors use genograms for a variety of purposes, including for the assessment of the spiritual domain in a family system (Frame, 2000; Hodge, 2001). Genograms provide the counselor and the client with a pictorial representation of the client's family. Through the genogram, patterns in the family emerge, and the counselor gains a clearer understanding of confusing relationships. For the counselor who thinks a systemic view of a client's spiritual domain would be beneficial, genogram development during assessment should be considered. The basic genogram can be developed at the onset of assessment, and information can be added as the client provides more information during the course of counseling.

A standard genogram (e.g., Figure 3.2) contains a description of the two generations preceding the client, the client's generation, and any following generations (McGoldrick & Gerson, 1985). The counselor and client can choose

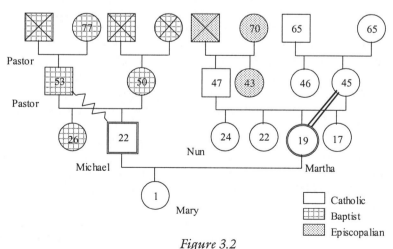

Figure 3.2
Spiritual genogram of a couple with a 1-year-old daughter and varied religious backgrounds.

a different depth for the genogram based on such factors as the client's knowledge of family history and the relevance of family members to the client's spiritual domain and to current clinical issues. For example, a genogram for a client who is having difficulty relating to children or grandchildren might work with the counselor to create a spiritual genogram that extends back only to the client's parents and continues on down to the client's grandchildren and great-grandchildren. The counselor and client then can explore the genogram for changing values, beliefs, and practices that might relate to the client's relationship difficulties.

Genograms can be as simple or complex as needed to assess the family system. Typically, men are depicted using squares, women are depicted using circles, and an "X" through a square or circle indicates the individual has died (McGoldrick & Gerson, 1985). A double circle or square represents the client. A solid horizontal line indicates a marriage, slashes in the horizontal line indicate a divorce, and a dashed horizontal line indicates a union that is not a marriage. Vertical lines lead to subsequent generations of family members. Multiple lines connecting family members represent exceptionally close relationships, jagged lines indicate strained relationships, and broken lines indicate a split in the relationship. A genogram can contain ages, dates, careers, achievements, physical and mental disorders, notations about alcohol and drug use, and other snippets of family history. A spiritual genogram focuses primarily on the spiritual domain of the family but can contain any other information the counselor and client think is important to the client's assessment and treatment.

Figure 3.2 illustrates a simple spiritual genogram for a couple that reports conflicts related to child-rearing decisions. Michael grew up in a small Baptist family. His father and grandfather both were pastors. Instead of following in his father's footsteps, Michael married Martha, a Catholic, and converted to Catholicism. Martha came from a larger family. Similar to Michael, Martha's father converted from the Episcopal faith to Catholicism when he married Martha's mother. Martha's eldest sister is a nun. Although the only aspects of the spiritual domain identified in this genogram are religious affiliation and religious careers, the counselor can use this genogram as a base to probe further into beliefs and values that might underlie conflicts between Michael and Martha and stress from either of their families of origin. As assessment and therapy continue, the counselor might add spiritual beliefs, values, and significant spiritual and religious events to this genogram. If the counselor were to decide to delve deeper into family patterns, the counselor could add information about the families of Martha's aunts. The counselor also could combine this assessment tool with other assessment tools, such as the spiritual ecomap.

Spiritual ecomaps. Instead of describing a multigenerational view of a family, the spiritual ecomap graphically describes the spiritual domain of the immediate family (Hodge, 2000). The counselor and client can co-create a spiritual ecomap of the family while taking a spiritual history.

Although taking a spiritual history without creating an ecomap might provide the counselor with an equivalent level of information, creation of the ecomap results in a document that can be used throughout the counseling process to identify any changes in the spiritual domain. These changes can include improved relationships or strengthened connections to rituals or practices. Use of an ecomap provides structure for the counselor to obtain ongoing knowledge about the family's spiritual domain in a way that respects the family's spiritual tradition.

Creation of an ecomap begins with the counselor creating a genogram-style representation of the immediate family in the middle of a page (Hodge, 2000). The counselor draws a circle around the family. Outside the family circle, the counselor draws additional circles representing components (or systems) of the family's spiritual domain. Solid lines connect systems with the family members who relate most to those systems and to the family circle if the entire family unit is affected by the system. Heavier lines indicate stronger relationships than lighter lines. Similar to the genogram, jagged lines indicate strained relationships and broken lines indicate severed or disconnected relationships. Hodge suggested that counselors include each of the following systems that are relevant to the family's spiritual domain: rituals and practices, God/transcendence, faith communities, spiritual leaders, parents' spiritual traditions, and transpersonal beings (e.g., saints, angels, significant others who have died, and good or evil spirits). Any other identified spiritual systems also should be included in the ecomap. The counselor explores each of the spiritual systems through open-ended questions that invite descriptions of meaning to the family and intensity of relationships. Descriptive notes are added to the ecomap as needed to clarify meaning and relationships.

Figure 3.3 illustrates an ecomap for the family described in Figure 3.2. This ecomap shows that Michael has conflicted relationships with his parents' religious tradition (Baptist denomination) and with his current parish priest. The

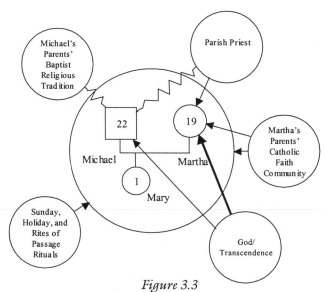

Figure 3.3

Spiritual ecomap of a couple with a 1-year-old daughter and varied religious backgrounds.

Catholic faith community of Martha's parents also is the family's faith community. Martha enjoys a close personal relationship with this faith community, whereas Michael's relationship with this faith community is at the family level rather than at a personal level. Martha's connection with or belief in God is stronger than the connection Michael experiences. The ecomap also indicates that the family has adopted some spiritual rituals that they celebrate together on Sundays and holidays and as rites of passage (such as baptism).

Quantitative Assessment Methods

Quantitative assessment methods differ from qualitative methods in that they tend to have more focused functions, have different limitations than qualitative methods, measure more specific constructs, and often have psychometric properties to report. In this section, we report the basic uses and limitations of quantitative instruments. Additionally, several instruments are listed, basic information regarding these instruments is given, psychometric properties are addressed where applicable, and a brief discussion of each is presented.

Uses of Quantitative Assessment Instruments

Formal spiritual assessment inventories can be used to understand specific aspects of the client's spiritual domain. Because formal assessment inventories tend to be more closed-ended than informal assessments, the counselors should be aware of the specific constructs the instrument they choose to administer measures. For example, if the counselor and client want to learn more about spiritual experience and personal relationship, the Index of Core Spiritual Experiences (INSPIRIT; Kass, Friedman, Leserman, Zuttermeister, & Benson, 1991) may be an appropriate choice. Holistic inventories, such as the Wellness Evaluation of Lifestyle (WEL; Hattie, Myers, & Sweeney, 2004), give a more global picture of the client's functioning. In these assessments, spirituality may be a portion or subset of what is measured. This provides information about additional areas of the client's life.

Formal spirituality assessments can be useful for diagnosis. Kelly (1995) stated that this type of assessment question asks whether religious faith contributes to the problem, to what extent, and how does religious faith contribute to the client's presenting problem. For example, clients who struggle with sexual orientation issues may also struggle with guilt and shame if their primary care system believes that homosexuality is a sin. Formal assessments may assist both the counselor and client in identifying the underlying issues.

Limitations of Quantitative Assessment Instruments

All formal assessments involve certain limitations. These assessments are subject to the conditions under which they are taken. If the client is having a bad day or difficulty reading the assessment, the results may be skewed. In addition, if the assessment does not hit on the specific client issue, valuable data can be overlooked. The language of the assessment may be confusing for some test-takers who could misread a question and be misrepresented as a result.

Many of these limitations can be minimized through proper presentation of the results. Results of formal inventories should never be presented as the "correct" answers or as a perfectly accurate representation of the client. The client should be asked to make the ultimate determination about whether or not the results accurately reflect his or her personal beliefs. The counselor has a duty to explain how and what has been measured, and the results should be presented in a nonjudgmental way. The client should understand how the scores are represented and should not be left to figure out the meaning of the scores without assistance from the counselor.

Quantitative Assessment Instruments

A variety of quantitative assessment instruments are available to counselors who are working in the spiritual domain. The instruments we have selected for the purposes of this chapter can be categorized into three areas: those that measure values, those that measure beliefs, and those that measure experiences. This may assist counselors in determining which assessment is most appropriate.

Assessing values. Spirituality instruments that assess the spiritual values of an individual often report definitions of spirituality different from traditional definitions. We have chosen to report the Spirituality Scale (SS; Jagers & Smith, 1996) as a values assessment instrument because of the unique definition of spirituality, the focus on differing cultures, and the representation of diverse values. Further, the Human Spirituality Scale (HSS; Wheat, 1991) defines spirituality through personal valuing or experiencing and, as a result, is included in this section along with the SS.

The Spirituality Scale (SS; Jagers & Smith, 1996) was developed by Jagers, Boykin, and Smith to evaluate spirituality from an Afro cultural perspective (Stanard et al., 2000). In this assessment, spirituality is conceptualized as a fundamental organizing factor in African culture. Spirituality not only organizes but also permeates life and transcends physical death, embracing a connection with ancestors (Jagers & Smith, 1996). The instrument currently includes 20 items based on this definition of spirituality. The questions are answered on a 6-point Likert scale.

Reliability for this instrument includes coefficient alphas of .84 and .87 and test–retest reliability of .88, both of which indicate good internal consistency. Personal agency, spiritual well-being, and religious motivation were used as constructs for establishing construct validity (Stanard et al., 2000). In addition, statistical differences were found between the responses of African Americans and European Americans. The data indicate that the instrument measures a definition of spirituality consistent with that of African Americans (Jagers & Smith, 1996).

The SS is short, easy to score, and easy to administer. In addition, it seems to be a more appropriate measure of spirituality for those who identify with African American culture (Stanard et al., 2000). The language includes some Judeo-Christian references such as a prayer, and the counselor should be aware of the client's basic belief system before administering this instrument. When used appropriately, this instrument could yield useful data for insight into the spiritual domain of African American clients.

The Human Spirituality Scale (HSS; Wheat, 1991) was developed through factor analysis in response to the lack of a generally accepted operational definition of spirituality. Wheat (1991) defined spirituality as "(a) a larger context or structure in which to view one's life, (b) an awareness of and connection to life itself and other living things, and (c) a reverent compassion for the welfare of others" (p. 3230). The 20-item instrument uses a 5-point Likert-type scale to measure three dimensions of spirituality based on Wheat's definition of spirituality (Frame, 2003).

Evidence of reliability has been reported as a Cronbach's alpha coefficient of .89 that was obtained through item analysis (Wheat, 1991). Each item had a reported item discrimination index of >.30. Three studies demonstrated construct validity. This scale approaches spirituality as a psychological construct that can be defined and measured for research purposes. The instrument demonstrates potential for the measurement of spirituality that does not necessarily have a theistic basis (Frame, 2003). However, the instrument has been criticized for lacking a theoretical framework explaining the dimensional interrelationships and for lacking adequate reference to a spiritual reality (Niederman, 1999). Little information exists regarding use of this instrument in a clinical setting.

Assessing beliefs. Some quantitative spiritual assessment instruments are designed to focus primarily on the client's belief system. Use of these instruments can be helpful especially when the client is struggling in the area of spiritual beliefs or the counselor has had difficulty recognizing the client's belief system. Counselors can use the Spirituality Assessment Scale (SAS; Howden, 1992), the Spiritual Health Inventory (SHI; Veach & Chappel, 1992), and the Spiritual Well-Being Scale (SWBS; Ellison, 1983) to measure the client's spiritual beliefs. The SHI and SWBS also may be used to measure spiritual experiences, but these instruments are discussed in this section because each contains more questions pertaining to beliefs than to experiences.

The Spirituality Assessment Scale (SAS; Howden, 1992) is a 28-item Likert-type scale that measures four attributes of spirituality. These attributes or subscales include unifying interconnectedness, purpose and meaning in life, innerness, and transcendence. The attributes are affected by age, gender, marital status, and income. Items are rated from 1 (*strongly disagree*) to 6 (*strongly agree*), and all statements are positively worded.

Evidence of reliability for this instrument has been reported by a Cronbach's alpha coefficient of .92 (Howden, 1992). The alpha coefficient for unifying interconnectedness was .91, the coefficient for purpose and meaning in life was reported as .91, the coefficient for innerness was .79, and the coefficient for transcendence was the lowest at .71. Howden (1992) reported evidence of content, factorial, and criterion validity. Stanard et al. (2000) reported high face validity for this instrument.

The SAS is well conceptualized, model and factor-analysis based, and avoids religious language (Stanard et al., 2000). The four scales reflect a more in-depth approach to evaluating spirituality, and information gained will be useful for the counselor in understanding the spiritual orientation of the client and for treatment planning/intervention purposes. The assessment would be applicable to Eastern religions as well.

The Spiritual Health Inventory (SHI; Veach & Chappel, 1992) is an 18-item self-report instrument that measures four factors of spirituality: personal experience, spiritual well-being, sense of harmony, and personal helplessness.

Answers can range from *strongly disagree* to *strongly agree*. The assessment is based on the belief that spirituality includes contributions from the biological, psychological, social, and spiritual dimensions. The SHI highlights the spiritual aspects of these dimensions and is meant to be used along with other assessments of these dimensions (Stanard et al., 2000; Veach & Chappel, 1992).

Reliability for this instrument is reported as "high" for the first three scales; however, the coefficients are not given (Veach & Chappel, 1992). The personal helplessness scale reports only moderate internal consistency, and authors have stated that additional items are needed for clarification (Stanard et al., 2000). Several studies have suggested evidence of some construct validity, but further studies are needed.

The SHI has the advantage of brevity (Kelly, 1995) and has been used frequently for research purposes (Stanard et al., 2000). In addition, the information provided for counseling may be helpful in understanding the client's spiritual awareness more fully. The counselor should note that Judeo-Christian language is incorporated and this instrument may not be appropriate for all clients. Additional items to strengthen subscales have been recommended (Stanard et al., 2000).

The Spiritual Well-Being Scale (SWBS; Ellison, 1983) is a 20-item scale with available answers ranging from *strongly agree* to *strongly disagree*. The instrument is based on Ellison's conceptualization of spiritual well-being as the expression of both spiritual health and spiritual maturity, yet separate from these two underlying concepts (Kelly, 1995). Ellison believed spiritual well-being to be a continuous, dynamic reflection of one's spiritual health and maturity (Stanard et al., 2000), and the subscales reflect a two-part belief that spiritual well-being results from religious well-being and existential well-being (Frame, 2003). The religious well-being subscale attempts to measure the client's relationship with God or concept of God, whereas the existential well-being scale addresses sense of life satisfaction and purpose apart from religion (Frame, 2003; Stanard et al., 2000). These scales are combined into one overall spiritual well-being factor (Stanard et al., 2000).

Evidence of reliability for this instrument has been reported as test–retest reliability with correlation coefficients of .93 for the overall scale and .96 and .86 for the religious well-being and the existential well-being subscales, respectively (Stanard et al, 2000). The coefficient alphas include .96 for the religious well-being subscale, .78 for the existential well-being subscale, and .89 for the overall scale (Stanard et al., 2000). The SWBS and its religious well-being and existential well-being subscales were negatively correlated with the University of California, Los Angeles Loneliness Scale and positively correlated with the Purpose in Life Test, Intrinsic Religious Orientation, and self-esteem to establish concurrent validity (Frame, 2003; Stanard et al., 2000). Unfortunately, the SWBS lacks norms (Frame, 2003), and with religious samples, the SWBS may have a ceiling effect or be unable to measure clinically significant scores above the mean (Frame, 2003; Ledbetter, Smith, Vosler-Hunter, & Fischer, 1991).

The SWBS has been well researched, despite the possible ceiling effect and lack of norms (Frame, 2003). Additionally, the SWBS can provide useful initial information for the counselor in a clinical setting (Kelly, 1995). The acceptance of the concept of God as inherent to spiritual well-being, however, can limit the instrument's usefulness for diverse populations (Stanard et al., 2000).

Assessing spiritual experiences. Counselors and clients who wish to gain a better understanding of the client's spiritual experiences may find the assessments listed in this section useful. Each instrument—the Index of Core Spiritual Experiences (INSPIRIT; Kass et al., 1991), the Wellness Evaluation of Lifestyle (WEL; Hattie et al., 2004), and the Phenomenology of Consciousness Inventory (PCI; Pekala, Steinberg, & Kumar, 1986)—focuses on a person's unique spiritual experiences. In addition, the WEL is a holistic scale that includes additional information about other dimensions of the client.

The Index of Core Spiritual Experiences (INSPIRIT; Kass et al., 1991) evaluates two factors: a specific spiritual event and a personal relationship with a powerful spiritual force. This instrument originally had 11 items, but after factor analysis, several items were dropped, leaving 7 current items. The items are worded as questions with the 7th and final question including 13 parts scored on a 4-point Likert scale. Item 7 also includes an open-ended question for additional, unlisted spiritual experiences (Kass et al., 1991).

Reliability for this instrument includes a Cronbach's alpha reliability coefficient score of .90. To establish concurrent validity, the INSPIRIT was compared with the Intrinsic scale of the Religious Orientation Inventory with a correlation of .69 ($p < .0001$). In addition, the INSPIRIT discriminated between different populations on the degree of core spiritual experiences in both analysis of covariance and multiple regression analysis (Stanard et al., 2000).

Sources have cited the INSPIRIT as both a promising instrument and a quick, helpful tool for counselors (Kelly, 1995; Stanard et al., 2000). This instrument does use language consistent with a Judeo-Christian faith and may be most appropriate for clients who identify with that faith system. Counselors may find that when used appropriately, the information gained in a short amount of time can be useful for holistic understanding of the client, treatment planning, case conceptualization, and selection of intervention.

The Wellness Evaluation of Lifestyle (WEL; Hattie et al., 2004) is based on the model of holistic wellness proposed by Myers et al. (2000). This instrument is a 114-item inventory with a 5-point Likert scale that measures 19 dimensions of wellness. The corresponding model places spirituality at the center of a Wheel of Wellness, and spirituality is a subscale of this assessment. The subscale reports spiritual wellness on a scale of 1 to 10 in addition to other holistic data for the test-taker.

The WEL has been extensively tested with male and female participants, ethnically diverse populations, various age groups, and people of differing education levels. Test–retest reliability exceeded .68 for all scales, with most above .80. The essence (spirituality) scale has reported evidence of reliability by Cronbach's alpha of .76 (Hattie et al., 2004). In addition, validity for the essence (spirituality) scale has been established through correlations with other spirituality assessments.

The WEL is a longer, more global assessment with spirituality examined along with the whole person. This evaluation offers the advantage of providing a breadth of data about the client within a solid wellness perspective. The assessment may take about 45 minutes to administer, however, and scoring may be difficult.

Pekala et al. (1986) developed the Phenomenology of Consciousness Inventory (PCI) to measure dimensions of phenomenological experience. The assessment has 53 items and 12 subscales as follows: positive affect, negative affect, altered experience, visual imagery, attention, self-awareness, altered awareness, internal dialogue, rationality, volitional control, memory, and arousal. Answers are given on a 7-point response scale.

Pekala et al. (1986) reported an internal consistency or alpha for each scale ranging from .65 to .90. There is some evidence of criterion validity. This assessment offers global language that will incorporate various religious beliefs and a variety of faith values. However, the construct this assessment is designed to measure focuses on experience of phenomenon. This may not result in the data a counselor needs to assist in treatment.

Applications

Questions for Reflection and Discussion

Many intake forms contain a blank for "Religion."

1. By itself, what does identification of a religion tell you about the client's spiritual domain?
2. What does this blank on the intake form tell the client about the counselor, counseling agency, or institution?
3. What are the advantages and disadvantages of assigning spiritual assessments as homework?
4. What client characteristics might influence your decision to perform spiritual assessments in the office as opposed to assigning spiritual assessments as homework?
5. How does the spiritual domain relate to diagnosis and intervention selection?
6. What influence does the client's level of awareness related to spiritual concerns have on the counselor's approach to assessment, diagnosis, and treatment planning?
7. How can you use spiritual assessment to validate the client's culture and to strengthen the client?
8. How might spiritual assessment cause harm to the client?
9. When working with a family, how can you demonstrate respect for opposing or conflicting spiritual values and beliefs?

Directed Journaling

1. What difficulties do you anticipate encountering in your attempt to assess your clients' spiritual domains? How will you minimize those difficulties?

2. Which spiritual assessment methods do you feel will be more useful to you and your clients? What makes these methods more comfortable for you? What makes other methods less comfortable for you?
3. What is your level of knowledge and understanding of spiritual beliefs, experiences, and practices, and how might this influence your ability to accurately assess the spiritual domains of your clients?
4. What views do you hold that might encourage you to value some beliefs, experiences, and practices more than others?

Case Study

Physical description: Jerry is a 43-year-old Caucasian male. He reports that he has not had any significant health problems anytime during his life.

Problem description: Client reports an increasing lack of desire to interact with people, including family members and long-standing friends. He states that over the past 6 months he has gradually stopped attending religious activities, Rotary Club meetings, and his daughter's high school basketball games. He states that he has no interest in sex, has lost his sense of humor, and no longer has energy enough to play basketball with his daughter. He states that although he is tired and lacks energy all the time, he has difficulty sleeping and spends most of the day and night staring at the television or sitting on the back porch watching the weather. He states that he feels worthless, unacceptable, and like a failure. He says that he can no longer bring himself to face more rejection, so he has stopped making any real effort to search for a job. Jerry states that he thinks his family would be better off with him dead but that he knows suicide is wrong, so he continues to exist.

Psychosocial description: Jerry reports that he has been married since 1982 and has a 20-year-old son and a 16-year-old daughter. He describes his relationship with his wife as increasingly more distant. He states that his wife works as a nurse, his daughter attends public high school, and his son recently dropped out of a private college. Jerry reports that he was laid off from a managerial job in the textile industry almost 1 year ago and has been unable to obtain work. He states that he is a single child and that both of his parents are in good health and living in a retirement community in Florida. He says that although his relationship with his parents has been close in the past, he has recently pulled away from them and avoids their calls. Jerry reports that he has insurance through his wife's work and that her salary is enough to pay the mortgage and basic expenses. He states that the family has had to economize and drop financial assistance to their son to pay for the necessities. Jerry identifies his religion as Baptist.

Process of assessment: After reviewing information Jerry reported, the counselor determines that Jerry is experiencing symptoms consistent with major depressive disorder. After establishing an empathic environment, the counselor administers the SQF sentence stems. Exploration of the stems indicated to the counselor and Jerry that he had lost a sense of meaning and purpose in life. What Jerry identified as a personal relationship with God seemed to deteriorate. Jerry states that this occurred about the time he lost his job. When questioned closely, Jerry states that he often feels guilty about the angry statements he made concerning God's cruelty in not protecting him against unemployment. He feels that he has always done the right thing and now he is being punished unfairly.

Case conceptualization: The counselor hypothesizes that Jerry's depression may be a developmental result of conflict in his spiritual and religious belief system. Jerry's admission of his guilt and anger toward God is a strong indicator of problems in the spiritual domain. The counselor believes Jerry's awareness of this problem is basic and somewhat limited. The treatment plan includes use of the WEL so that the counselor can verify the hypothesis and Jerry can holistically understand how he is suffering spiritually.

Questions for Reflection

1. What additional information would be helpful to your assessment of Jerry?
2. How would your assessment process differ from the process described in this study?
3. How would your assessment conclusions differ from those identified in this study?
4. What benefits do you think the assessment process provides to Jerry and his counselor?

Scenarios for Discussion

For each of the following scenarios, discuss how you would assess the client's spiritual domain and determine whether the spiritual domain is relevant to the therapeutic issues. How would your assessment decisions influence your relationship with the client and the client's relationship with spirituality?

Doug's Move

Doug is a 41-year-old man who has entered counseling because of the onset of panic attacks 4 months ago. Doug reports that he relocated from his and his wife's small hometown to a large city because of a new job at about the time the panic attacks began. Doug seems ecstatic about the job and says he has wanted this job for years. He says that he prayed about the job and the move and then accepted the job after sensing that this was the right direction for him. Doug says that although his wife expressed reservations about the job and the move, he had expected that she would follow him and adapt to the new environment. Instead, Doug reports that his wife returned to their hometown shortly after they moved and filed for divorce. Doug says that his wife revealed that she was unhappy in the 20-year marriage and unwilling to adapt to the new city. The couple had two children, both of whom are in high school and who moved back to their hometown with their mother. Doug expresses distress as he states that he did not want a divorce, thinks that divorce is a sin, does not want to lose his children, and thought that the new job and move were in keeping with God's direction for his life. Doug describes his family as against divorce for religious reasons and indicates that no one in his family has ever divorced. Doug says that his parents and siblings have not spoken to him since the separation, except to encourage him to "get right with God" and resume his marriage. Doug says that he has begun questioning his religious beliefs and wonders if his panic attacks are related to all the changes in his life.

Andrea and Phil's Premarital Challenges

Andrea and Phil are in their 20s and planning to wed in 6 months. They have begun premarital counseling at the request of their parents, who have expressed concerns about their differing religious beliefs. Andrea identifies herself as Mexican American and says that she has been raised in the Catholic Church and has lived a sheltered life in her parents' home. Andrea describes having a curfew even as she is approaching marriage. Prior to meeting Phil, she said that her parents' expectations had been for her to become a nun. Phil says that he was raised as a Southern Baptist, currently does not identify with any particular religion, but has thought about joining the Catholic Church because Andrea is so invested in that religious path. Phil describes himself as "spiritually free" and hesitates to restrict his spiritual freedom. Phil says that his parents are concerned because they do not recognize Catholics as Christians and do not want Phil to attend the Catholic Church. Andrea and Phil report that they have not discussed such issues as birth control, alcohol use, discipline of children, marital expectations and roles, and previous relationships.

Rebecca's Stomachaches

Rebecca is an 8-year-old girl of slightly above-average intelligence referred to you, the school counselor, by her teacher. The teacher stated that the class had been discussing Pilgrims and Indians when Rebecca said that her stomach hurt her and her conscience hurt her too. From talking with the teacher, you learned that Rebecca's parents are devout Jehovah's Witnesses and that Rebecca has not participated in any holiday-related activities until this year, when she began voluntarily participating in some of the Thanksgiving activities. The teacher stated that she felt Rebecca wants to participate in holiday discussions and activities and appears hurt when she is left out of these activities. Rebecca's teacher also stated that Rebecca has complained of numerous stomachaches and headaches since school started 3 months ago.

Suggested Activities

Create your own spiritual genogram or a genogram for someone you know. As you add notations related to the spiritual domain, consider how these beliefs, values, attitudes, and experiences might have affected the individual's mental health, the mental health of other family members, relationships with other family members, and relationships outside the family.

Select sentence stems from the OSCI and SQF, and administer those stems to a friend. Explore your partner's responses to the stems, discuss possible interpretations of the responses, and discuss any further methods of assessment you would consider to gain a more complete understanding of your partner's spiritual domain.

Administer the SAS (Howden, 1992) or another quantitative spiritual assessment to a classmate or a friend. Score your partner's responses, and share the results with your partner. Discuss possible interpretations of the results and any further methods of assessment you would consider to gain a more complete understanding of your partner's spiritual domain. Note that you can obtain a copy of the SAS from http://www.gbmhealing.org/downloads/spirituality_assessment.pdf.

Summary List of Assessment Instruments

The following list provides summary information for the assessment instruments described in this chapter.

- The Index of Core Spiritual Experiences (INSPIRIT; Kass, Friedman, Leserman, Zuttermeister, & Benson, 1991) is a seven-item instrument designed to measure spiritual events and personal relationship with a powerful spiritual force.
- The Oshodi Sentence Completion Index (OSCI; Oshodi, 1999) is a 20-stem instrument designed to assess need for achievement in people of African descent. The OSCI contains some stems that can be used for exploration of the spiritual domain.
- The Phenomenology of Consciousness Inventory (PCI; Pekala, Steinberg, & Kumar, 1986) contains 12 subscales that are designed to measure dimensions of phenomenological experience. This assessment offers global language that incorporates a variety of religious beliefs and faith values.
- The Spirituality Assessment Scale (SAS; Howden, 1992) is designed to measure unifying interconnectedness, purpose and meaning in life, innerness, and transcendence. This instrument contains general, non-religious language and might be applicable to diverse populations.
- The Spiritual Health Inventory (SHI; Veach & Chappel, 1992) is designed to measure four factors of spirituality: personal experience, spiritual well-being, sense of harmony, and personal helplessness. This instrument is based on the belief that spirituality includes contributions from the biological, psychological, social, and spiritual dimensions.
- The Spiritual Quest Form (SQF; Niño, 1997) is a 10-stem instrument designed to explore attitudes of the client related to the client's movement toward spirituality.
- The Spirituality Scale (SS; Jagers & Smith, 1996) is designed to evaluate spirituality from an Afro cultural perspective, which conceptualizes spirituality as a fundamental organizing factor.
- The Wellness Evaluation of Lifestyle (WEL; Hattie, Myers, & Sweeney, 2004) is designed to measure 19 dimensions of wellness and is based on the model of holistic wellness proposed by Myers, Sweeney, and Witmer (2000). The corresponding model places spirituality at the center of a Wheel of Wellness. Spirituality is one of the subscales reported for this instrument.

Recommended Reading

The following resources contain further information about spiritual assessment and were selected because the topics they address could not be discussed adequately in the context of this chapter. The first resource covers spiritual assessment through art therapy, an assessment method that was not described in this chapter because we felt that an adequate introduction to the method would require more information and examples than could be supplied in this chapter. The second and third resources provide information about a broader assortment of instruments that assess elements of the spiritual domain than this chapter could cover. It is our hope that readers will explore these valuable resources to learn more about ways of assessing clients' spiritual domains.

Horovitz-Darby, E. G. (1994). *Spiritual art therapy: An alternate path.* Springfield, IL: Charles C Thomas.

> In this book, Horovitz-Darby describes a process for assessing spiritual beliefs, history, and development through a combination of interviews with a client and directed artistic creation by the client. Guidelines are given for assessing the resultant artwork. Horovitz-Darby provides numerous examples that contain information from interviews, pictures of drawings and sculptures, information about the process of assessment and case conceptualization, and questions for contemplation and discussion.

MacDonald, D. A., Friedman, H. L., & Kuentzel, J. G. (1999). A survey of measures of spiritual and transpersonal constructs: Part One. Research update. *Journal of Transpersonal Psychology, 31,* 137–154.

> This article was written as a companion piece to the next annotated article. Additional measures of spiritual constructs are introduced, psychometric properties are reviewed, and advocated uses are presented. The authors encourage increased use of spirituality assessments in research and counseling.

MacDonald, D. A., LeClair, L., Holland, C. J., Alter, A., & Friedman, H. L. (1995). A survey of measures of transpersonal constructs. *Journal of Transpersonal Psychology, 27,* 171–235.

> In this article, the authors present a review of the literature regarding transpersonally oriented survey measures. The authors give details about the conceptualization of the instruments, give detailed descriptions of each instrument, and provide psychometrics of each measure. In addition, a list and references for measures not discussed are provided.

Web Sites of Interest

http://www.aac.ncat.edu/

> This is the Web site of the Association for Assessment in Counseling and Education (AACE, a division of the American Counseling Association).

http://www.apa.org/science/jctpweb.html

> This is the Web site of the American Psychological Association's Joint Committee on Testing Practices.

http://www.aservic.org

> This Web site lists the Association for Spiritual, Ethical, and Religious Values in Counseling (ASERVIC, a division of the American Counseling Association) competencies related to counseling and spirituality.

http://www.fetzer.org/pdf/total-fetzer-book.pdf

Fetzer Institute, National Institute on Aging, & National Institutes of Health. (1999). Multidimensional measurement of religiousness/spirituality for use in health research. In *A report of the Fetzer Institute/National Institute on Aging Working Group.* Kalamazoo, MI: Fetzer Institute. Retrieved September 20, 2004.
    This Web site contains information about the Multidimensional Measure of Religiousness/Spirituality, an extensive instrument that measures fundamental dimensions of spirituality and religiousness as related to mental and physical health.

http://as800.chcr.brown.edu/pcoc/spirit.htm

Puchalski, C. (n.d.). *Toolkit of instruments to measure end-of-life care: Spirituality.* Providence, RI: Center for Gerontology and Health Care Research, Brown Medical School. Retrieved September 20, 2004.
    This Web site contains information about assessment instruments that can be used to measure quality of life, attitudes toward life and death, religiousness, and overall spirituality with clients who are facing the end life.

Summary

The purpose of this chapter has been to emphasize the importance of competent assessment of the spiritual domain among clients. After a consideration of why counseling and assessment of the spiritual domain have been historically separated, a primary point of emphasis for the chapter was a consideration of the pros and cons of qualitative and quantitative approaches to assessing client spirituality. Finally, specific assessment strategies and instruments were discussed, and case studies were provided to facilitate further exploration of these topics. The competent and thorough assessment of the spiritual domain of a client provides the necessary background to inform the case conceptualization and treatment planning discussed throughout the remainder of this book.

References

Allport, G. W. (1950). *The individual and his religion: A psychological interpretation.* New York: Macmillian.

Allport, G. W., & Ross, J. M. (1967). Personal religious orientation and prejudice. *Journal of Personality and Social Psychology, 5,* 432–443.

Association for Spiritual, Ethical, and Religious Values in Counseling. (n.d.). *Competencies for integrating spirituality into counseling.* Retrieved November, 2003, from http://www.aservic.org/new_page_1.htm#Competencies%20for%20Integrating%20Spirituality%20into%20Counseling

Ball, R. A., & Goodyear, R. K. (1991). Self-reported professional practices of Christian psychologists. *Journal of Psychology and Christianity, 10,* 144–153.

Becvar, D. S., & Becvar, R. J. (2000). *Family therapy: A systemic integration* (4th ed.). Boston: Allyn & Bacon.

Bergin, A. E. (1983). Religiosity and mental health: A critical reevaluation and meta-analysis. *Professional Psychology: Research and Practice, 14,* 170–184.

Cashwell, C. S., & Rayle, A. D. (2005). Spiritual bypass. In D. S. Sandhu (Ed.), *Spirituality as a fifth force in counseling and psychology: Implications for practice, training, and research.* Alexandria, VA: American Counseling Association.

Cohen, R. J., & Swerdlik, M. E. (1999). *Psychological testing and assessment: An introduction to tests and measurements.* Mountain View, CA: Mayfield.

Dombeck, M., & Karl, J. (1987). Spiritual issues in mental health care. *Journal of Religion and Health, 26,* 1–15.

Dunn, H. L. (1961). *High-level wellness.* Arlington, VA: R. W. Beatty.

Ellison, C. W. (1983). Spiritual well-being: Conceptualization and measurement. *Journal of Psychology and Theology, 11,* 330–340.

Frame, M. W. (2000). Spiritual genogram in family therapy. *Journal of Marital and Family Therapy, 26,* 211–240.

Frame, M. W. (2003). *Integrating religion and spirituality into counseling: A comprehensive approach.* Pacific Grove, CA: Brooks/Cole.

Genia, V. (1995). *Counseling and psychotherapy of religious clients: A developmental approach.* Westport, CT: Praeger.

Hackney, H. L., & Cormier, L. S. (1996). *The professional counselor: A process guide to helping* (3rd ed.). Boston: Allyn & Bacon.

Hattie, J. A., Myers, J. E., & Sweeney, T. J. (2004). A factor structure of wellness: Theory, assessment, analysis, and practice. *Journal of Counseling & Development, 82,* 357–364.

Hettler, B. (n.d.). *Balance the six dimensions of your life.* Retrieved November 21, 2003, from http://www.hettler.com

Heyse-Moore, L. H. (1996). On spiritual pain in the dying. *Mortality, 1,* 297–315.

Hill, P. C., & Pargament, K. L. (2003). Advances in the conceptualization and measurement of religion and spirituality: Implications for physical and mental health research. *American Psychologist, 58,* 64–74.

Hodge, D. R. (2000). Spiritual ecomaps: A new diagrammatic tool for assessing marital and family spirituality. *Journal of Marital and Family Therapy, 26,* 217–228.

Hodge, D. R. (2001). Spiritual genograms: A generational approach to assessing spirituality. *Families in Society: The Journal of Contemporary Human Services, 82,* 35–48.

Horovitz-Darby, E. G. (1994). *Spiritual art therapy: An alternate path.* Springfield, IL: Charles C Thomas.

Howden, J. W. (1992). Development and psychometric characteristics of the Spirituality Assessment Scale. *Dissertation Abstracts International, 54*(01), 166B. (UMI No. AAG 9312917)

Jagers, R. J., & Smith, P. (1996). Further examination of the Spirituality Scale. *Journal of Black Psychology, 23,* 429–442.

Kass, J., Friedman, R., Leserman, J., Zuttermeister, P., & Benson, H. (1991). Health outcomes and a new measure of spiritual experience. *Journal for the Scientific Study of Religion, 30,* 203–211.

Kelly, E. W. (1995). *Spirituality and religion in counseling and psychotherapy: Diversity in theory and practice.* Alexandria, VA: American Counseling Association.

Kitchener, K. S. (1984). Intuition, critical evaluation, and ethical principles: The foundation for ethical decisions in counseling psychology. *Counseling Psychology, 12,* 43–55.

Larson, D. B., Pattison, E. M., Blazer, D. G., Omran, A. R., & Kaplan, B. H. (1986). Systemic analysis of research on religious variables in four major psychiatric journals, 1978–1982. *American Journal of Psychiatry, 143,* 329–334.

Ledbetter, M. F., Smith, L. A., Vosler-Hunter, W. L., & Fischer, J. D. (1991). An evaluation of the research and clinical usefulness of the Spiritual Well-Being Scale. *Journal of Psychology and Theology, 19,* 49–55.

Locke, D. C., Myers, J. E., & Herr, E. L. (2001). *The handbook of counseling.* Thousand Oaks, CA: Sage.

McGoldrick, M., & Gerson, R. (1985). *Genograms in family assessment.* New York: Norton.

Miller, G. (1999). The development of the spiritual focus in counseling and counselor education. *Journal of Counseling & Development, 77,* 498–501.

Moos, R. H., & Moos, B. S. (1981). *Manual for the Family Environment Scale.* Palo Alto, CA: Consulting Psychologist Press.

Myers, J. E., Sweeney, T. J., & Witmer, J. M. (2000). The wheel of wellness counseling for wellness: A holistic model for treatment planning. *Journal of Counseling & Development, 78,* 251–266.

National Wellness Institute. (1983). *Lifestyle Assessment Questionnaire* (2nd ed.). Stevens Point: University of Wisconsin, Stevens Point Institute for Lifestyle Improvement.

Newshan, G. (1998). Transcending the physical: Spiritual aspects of pain in patients with HIV and/or cancer. *Journal of Advanced Nursing, 28,* 1236–1242.

Niederman, R. (1999). *The conceptualization of a model of spirituality.* Retrieved November 21, 2003, from http://www.geocities.com/randynied/ch2.html

Niño, A. G. (1997). Assessment of spiritual quests in clinical practice. *International Journal of Psychotherapy, 2,* 192–212.

O'Connor, M. (2002). Spiritual dark night and psychological depression: Some comparisons and considerations. *Counseling and Values, 46,* 137–148.

Oshodi, R. E. (1999). The construction of an Africentric sentence completion test to assess the need for achievement. *Journal of Black Studies, 30,* 216–231.

Palmer, G. T. (1999). Disclosure and assimilation of exceptional human experiences: Meaningful, transformative, and spiritual aspects. *Dissertation Abstracts International, 60*(05), 2358B.

Payne, I. R., Bergin, A. E., & Loftus, P. E. (1992). A review of attempts to integrate spiritual and standard psychotherapy techniques. *Journal of Psychotherapy Integration, 2,* 171–192.

Pekala, R. J., Steinberg, J., & Kumar, V. K. (1986). Measurement of phenomenological experience: Phenomenology of Consciousness Inventory. *Perceptual and Motor Skills, 63,* 983–989.

Propst, L. R., Ostrom, R., Watkins, P., Dean, T., & Mashburn, D. (1992). Comparative efficacy of religious and non-religious cognitive-behavioral therapy for the treatment of clinical depression in religious individuals. *Journal of Consulting and Clinical Psychology, 60,* 94–103.

Richards, P. S., & Bergin, A. E. (1997). *A spiritual strategy for counseling and psychotherapy.* Washington, DC: American Psychological Association.

Richards, P. S., & Potts, R. W. (1995). Using spiritual interventions in psychotherapy: Practices, successes, failures, and ethical concerns of Mormon psychotherapists. *Professional Psychology: Research and Practice, 26,* 163–170.

Sherman, R. M. (2001). Religious orientation and identity formation: A study of adolescent girls. *Dissertation Abstracts International: The Physical Sciences and Engineering, 61,* 6168.

Simpson, J. A., & Weiner, E. S. C. (Eds.). (1989). *Oxford English dictionary online.* New York: Oxford University Press. Retrieved July 29, 2003, from http://dictionary.oed.com

Stanard, R. P., Sandhu, D. S., & Painter, L. C. (2000). Assessment of spirituality in counseling. *Journal of Counseling & Development, 78,* 204–211.

St. John of the Cross. (1959). *Dark night of the soul* (3rd ed.). (E. A. Peers, Trans.). Garden City, NY: Image. (Original work published 1578)

Summit on Spirituality. (1996, October 4). *Spirituality competencies.* Retrieved July 31, 2003, from http://www.aservic.org

Tjeltveit, A. C. (1986). The ethics of value conversion in psychotherapy: Appropriate and inappropriate therapist influence on client values. *Clinical Psychological Review, 6,* 515–537.

Travis, J. W. (1981). *The Wellness Inventory.* Mill Valley, CA: Wellness Associates.

Veach, T. L., & Chappel, J. N. (1992). Measuring spiritual health: A preliminary study. *Substance Abuse, 13,* 139–147.

Wheat, L. W. (1991). Development of a scale for the measurement of human spirituality (measurement scale). *Dissertation Abstracts International, 52*(09), 3230A.

Wolters, C. (Trans.). (1961). *The cloud of unknowing and other works.* New York: Penguin. (Original work published n.d.)

Chapter 4

Counselor Self-Awareness and Self-Exploration of Religious and Spiritual Beliefs: Know Thyself

W. Bryce Hagedorn

Competency: *The professional counselor engages in self-exploration of religious and spiritual beliefs in order to increase sensitivity, understanding, and acceptance of diverse belief systems.*

Look well into thyself; there is a source of strength which will always spring up if thou wilt always look there.
—Marcus Aurelius

Throughout history, great thinkers (e.g., Aristotle, Socrates, Confucius, and Nietzsche) have written of self-awareness as the key to understanding ourselves, others, and the world in which we live. Socrates' "know thyself" represented the importance of self-knowledge as the means to a productive and satisfying life. The third spiritual competency, the focus of this chapter, speaks to this ongoing need for self-awareness: The competent counselor engages in self-exploration of religious and spiritual beliefs in order to increase sensitivity, understanding, and acceptance of diverse belief systems. Before exploring this competency in depth, let us begin with a look at the larger picture.

Why are spiritual competencies necessary? Are counselors-in-training not taught from day one to be accepting and tolerant of those clients who are different from them? I remember learning in Counseling 101 the necessity of such core conditions as unconditional positive regard, genuineness, congruence, empathy, and warmth (which included respect for others; Murphy & Dillon, 2002). Whereas this may be true in terms of learning the need for multicultural awareness when working with clients (i.e., race, gender, ethnicity, and sexual orientation), the need for tolerance and the need for acceptance are not uniformly taught as they apply to clients' religion and spirituality. Much of this discord results from the traditional rift between religion/spirituality and the counseling process, a phenomenon that I will explore further.

The focus for this chapter can best be encapsulated by the following statement: Clients desire "therapists who will honor their seeking for something sacred and who can respect their whole being in its psychological and spiritual fullness—rather than belittling or minimizing their spiritual seeking, as much of traditional psychotherapy has historically done" (Cortright, 1997, pp. 13–14). Young, Cashwell, Wiggins-Frame, and Belaire (2002) noted that although current counselor preparation programs are making strides toward providing curricular experiences directed at religion and spirituality, there is a lack of consensus for how this information is disseminated. Additionally, it is difficult to measure the assimilated knowledge as it pertains to clinical practice. Therefore, one of the purposes for developing spiritual competencies in the first place, as well as the more immediate purpose of this chapter, is to challenge practicing clinicians to assess their own beliefs and knowledge as these pertain to their spiritual selves. It is hoped that an increase in self-awareness will result in improved client service.

This particular competency serves as the bridge between counselors' *conceptual* and *experiential* understanding of religion and/or spirituality. Whereas the first two competencies stressed the importance of learning significant concepts of religion and spirituality (e.g., key definitions, similarities and differences, and the importance of the cultural context), the focus of the third competency is more on the counselor's personal experience and exploration of religion and/or spirituality. As will be demonstrated in this chapter, individual exploration is preeminent to the other competencies; without self-awareness, practicing counselors likely will fail in empathically bonding with clients. Upon completing this chapter, readers should recognize the importance of actively exploring their own systems of belief. Similarly, readers are encouraged to actively engage in this exploration process before moving on to describe their own religious and/or spiritual belief systems, before demonstrating sensitivity and acceptance of other belief systems, and even before identifying limits of understanding (competencies explored in later chapters).

This chapter begins with a discussion of the traditional separation between religion/spirituality and the practice of counseling, which is important for understanding why a need for spiritual competencies exists in the first place. Next, the significance of addressing religion and spirituality within the therapeutic setting is explored. The fundamental concepts found in Competency 3 follow, to include the need for clinician self-awareness (both in general and as it relates to religion and spirituality) and the need for increased sensitivity and acceptance of client belief systems. Following this are some additional resources (e.g., seminal works by authors advocating the importance of religion and spirituality to the practice of counseling, as well as a list of related Web sites for relevant professional associations/organizations) for those seeking to increase self-knowledge and self-awareness related to religion and spirituality. Finally, for those interested in increasing their awareness of held religious and/or spiritual beliefs, experiential exercises are provided to facilitate this self-exploration process.

The Rift Between Religion/Spirituality and the Practice of Counseling

Traditionally, the study and practice of counseling and psychology made a clear distinction between spirituality and psychotherapy. This assumption was originally articulated by Freud, who believed that "psychotherapy is a technical procedure, like surgery, that does not involve the values or life-style of the treatment agent" (Bergin, 1991, p. 396). The separation of the counselor's values (religious and otherwise) from the therapeutic process was based on the theory of countertransference, the belief that counselors would unconsciously impose their values and beliefs onto clients. Many theorists, most notably Albert Ellis and a young Carl Rogers, followed suit, calling for the separation of religious and spiritual values by advocating that the counselor act as a blank slate (Grimm, 1994). In fact, counselors were originally trained to isolate all personal values from the therapeutic process (McLennan, Rochow, & Arthur, 2001; Sacks, 1985).

Other justifications have perpetuated the separation of religious and spiritual values from therapy. One is based on the notion that many mental health problems were once thought to have origins in extreme religiosity (Bergin, 1991). For example, psychological disorders like anxiety and depression were once believed to be directly related to the shame and guilt experienced by individuals who engaged in acts that were believed to be evil or sinful. Another, more current view maintaining the separation is rooted in the Western philosophy of individualism, autonomy, and personal freedom (Fukuyama & Sevig, 1997). Religious and spiritual clients often exhibit submissiveness to a higher authority and may appear dependent on God or a higher power as the source of answers to their problems. Some counselors have viewed these clients' dependence as a way to avoid personal responsibility. As avoiding responsibility is common with different types of clients, a thorough assessment and exploration of religious and spiritual beliefs would prove invaluable to determine how much dependence is adaptive and how much is avoidant.

Whereas many in the counseling field continue to demonstrate strong advocacy for the separation of religion and psychotherapy, religious institutions have also called for this same severance. Many religious leaders have viewed psychotherapy as a secular competitor and influence over people's minds (Grimm, 1994), believing that human philosophy is in opposition to many of the tenets of the major religions. Many religious clients hold similar beliefs, tending to avoid secular counselors who they believe will negate the values that they hold to be true (McLennan et al., 2001; Worthington, Kurusu, McCullough, & Sandage, 1996). Whereas bias, fear, and strong beliefs continue, much work has been accomplished in integrating religion and spirituality with the counseling process. It is to this progress that I now turn.

The Importance of Religion and Spirituality to the Therapeutic Process

There has been increased attention given to the importance of addressing religious and spiritual issues within the counseling arena. One reason for this resurgence of interest can be attributed to the general public's attention to religious and spiritual matters. This is due in part to the influx of New Age spirituality, rekindled practices of conservative Christians, as well as the influence of the religious traditions of new immigrants seeking outlets for their belief systems (Worthington et al., 1996). As a result, more clients are seeking assistance from professional counselors who identify themselves as religiously or spiritually competent. Similarly, because of the impact of managed care on the amount of attainable counseling services, more clients are seeking assistance from clergy, who often do not charge for their services.

There are several reasons for counselors to be adept at discussing religious and spiritual matters, most notably the impact that these dimensions have on clients' presenting issues. For example, McLennan et al. (2001) noted the importance of spirituality for some clients when considering such issues as intimate relationships, career choice, and the experience of birth and death. Similarly, spirituality may be embedded in a host of other concerns brought to the counselor, including family issues (e.g., sexuality, child rearing, deciding on the family's religion), recovery from addictive substances or behaviors (e.g., alcoholism, eating disorders, sexual addiction), or survival of past abuse (i.e., emotional, physical, psychological, and sexual). As a consequence of these increased interests, researchers and authors have sought to quantify the connection between mental health and spirituality, leading to an increase in empirical research efforts.

An example of research that demonstrated the positive links between mental health and spirituality were the landmark studies by Bergin throughout the 1980s and 1990s. These studies helped to dispel many of the aforementioned reasons for justifying the separation of religious values and psychotherapy. In answer to the assumption that mental illness resulted from client religiosity, Bergin (1991) performed a meta-analysis across 24 studies that measured variables for both mental illness and religiosity. This seminal study concluded that no correlation existed between religion and mental illness. Regarding the goal of remaining value neutral, Bergin also concluded that this goal did not work "because (a) it often amounts to taking a value position in that silence may be viewed as consent for certain actions, and (b) one subtly communicates one's inclinations at critical points essentially involuntarily" (p. 397). Other researchers such as Chappelle (2000), Karasu (1999), and McLennan et al. (2001) made similar conclusions: Religion and spirituality are an essential piece of the individual psyche that warrants attention by trained clinicians.

In response to the resurgence of interest in religion and spirituality, as well as the foundation laid by empirical research, helping professions are honoring this heightened awareness. Young et al. (2002) provided several examples of how this has occurred, including (a) the inclusion of religion as an important component of human diversity in the code of ethics of both the American Counseling Association and the American Psychological Association; (b) the addition of spiritually related problems to the 1994 edition of the *Diagnostic and Statistical Manual of Mental Disorders* (American Psychiatric Association, 1994); and (c) the introduction by the Council for Accreditation of Counseling and Related Educational Programs (CACREP) for the inclusion of discussions of values, as they relate to religion and spirituality, as a core element of counselor education programs.

In summary, the competent counselor, intent on working with spiritual matters, will need to learn to balance his or her formal science-based education with matters that are more intangible. This balancing process necessarily begins with an awareness of one's own religious and spiritual beliefs and how these affect work with clients. The need for self-awareness therefore warrants close examination.

Counselor Self-Awareness

The process of self-exploration and self-awareness is crucial for the ethical practice of counseling (Bishop, 1992; Fukuyama & Sevig, 1997). Sensitivity to how personal feelings, attitudes, and biases affect work with clients (e.g., countertransference issues) is tantamount to assisting hurting individuals (Bergin, 1991). Ideally, the development and nurturance of accurate introspection begins long before counselors see their first client. Several researchers have demonstrated the efficacy of actively fostering such skills in students through experiential exercises and even personal therapy (Meier, Back, & Morrison, 2001; Merwin, 2002; Richardson & Molinaro, 1996), whereas others have noted the need for the advance of curricular changes to meet this need (Williams, Judge, Hill, & Hoffman, 1997). Before noting the specific impact of self-awareness as it pertains to religious and spiritual beliefs, I discuss the influence of self-awareness on the counseling process in general.

Can clinicians truly assist clients through the self-exploration process if they themselves (the clinicians) are not committed to the continual exploration of their own feelings, motives, and experiences? Most clinicians and educators would say no. In fact, in exploring the key components for optimized psychological health, Kinnier (1997) noted the need for clinicians to pursue self-knowledge and self-awareness. Through regular self-exploration and introspection, clinicians are encouraged to recognize their internal motivations, awareness of countertransference, and true feelings as these pertain to the therapeutic setting. Kinnier concluded that, "Of all the goals of psychotherapy and counseling, the goal of self-knowledge is probably the most central and universal" (p. 52).

Self-awareness and self-knowledge are key components to just about every theory of counseling and psychotherapy. Freudian psychoanalysis calls for clinicians to closely monitor countertransference reactions—how they unconsciously relate to client behavior (Prochaska & Norcross, 1999). Similarly, Jungian psychology notes the importance of the clinician's perseverance to explore his or her own psychological and physical needs before engaging clients in the therapeutic setting (Schwartz, 2003). Without a clear awareness of their own issues, clinicians can hinder the therapeutic process. Other theories call for the clinician to be authentic and congruent (e.g., Adlerian, existential, person-centered, gestalt, reality, and rational-emotive theories), two characteristics that require a strong awareness of one's own internal motivations, biases, strengths, and weaknesses. Even when using specific techniques, independent of particular theories, it is important to be aware of one's reactions. For example, when using EMDR (eye movement desensitization and reprocessing) to treat clients with posttraumatic stress disorder, it is imperative that clinicians recognize negative reactions to client behaviors to accurately assess the impact of information gained through this technique (Dworkin, 2002). Regardless of the theory or technique, awareness is a key component of the healing process, for both the clinician and the client (Walsh, 1999).

Additional needs for professional self-awareness and self-knowledge include maintaining personal wellness and monitoring the differences between clinician and client cultural systems. Coster and Schwebel (1997) noted that clinicians considered self-awareness/self-monitoring to be one of the most important aspects of professional wellness, especially when confronted with professional and personal stressors. The authors asserted that "the process of self-awareness and self-monitoring serves the essential purpose of maintaining our bearings and avoiding self-deception" (p. 11) as well as to recognize the need for personal therapy. Clinicians also must maintain certain levels of self-awareness when working with chronically (physically or mentally) ill clients. Without understanding the impact of one's own emotions in working with suffering individuals, clinicians not only stand the risk of inadequate client care but also chance personal and professional distress, disengagement, burnout, and poor judgment (Meier et al., 2001).

One final general need for clinician self-awareness and exploration involves areas in which there are notable differences between counselor and client, particularly with cultural diversity. Given that culture can be defined as "the customary beliefs, social norms, and material traits of a racial, religious, or social group [which result in a] set of shared attitudes, values, goals, and practices" (*Merriam-Webster Online*, 2003), religious and spiritual beliefs definitely fall within a cultural context. Whereas this topic is covered more thoroughly in chapter 3, the point needs to be made here as well: Without self-awareness, it is unlikely that counselors will develop the necessary empathy, attitudes, and insights to work with clients different from them (Richardson & Molinaro, 1996), likely resulting in substandard and incompetent care for culturally (i.e., religiously/ spiritually) diverse clientele (Wilson & Weis, 1995). Karasu (1999) summarized the necessity for self-awareness well by asserting that the competent clinician will pursue personal growth, a broad education that goes beyond psychotherapy per se, and a life philosophy:

> It is for the therapist—as it is for everyone else—the issue of being and becoming, insofar as the therapist can help a patient grow only as much as he, himself, has grown. That is why what really matters is not schools of therapy, but the psychotherapists themselves. (p. 154)

Self-Exploration and Self-Awareness in Religion and Spirituality

Just as insight into one's psychodynamic issues is critical to ethically and therapeutically sound professional counseling, so is awareness of one's religious/

spiritual issues. "Who am I? Where did I come from? Where am I going? What does life mean? What is worth living for?" (Helminiak, 2001, p. 163) are questions for which clinicians should have their own answers or be in the process of answering, especially as these are questions common to working with clients. Other topics commonly addressed during the therapeutic process include forgiveness, transcendence, understanding the purpose of tragedy, sin, faith, the afterlife, morality, sacredness, leading a religious/spiritual life, altruism and high ideals, understanding one's relationship with God or a higher power, and the value of material possessions (Weinstein, Parker, & Archer, 2002). If clinicians do not recognize the role that the aforementioned issues play in their own lives, can they effectively explore these same issues with clients?

Leaders in the helping field assert that before counselors seek to assist clients with spiritual concerns, they must both acknowledge and be comfortable with their own spiritual and religious beliefs, values, and spiritual journey (Capuzzi & Gross, 2003; Fukuyama & Sevig, 1997; Sacks, 1985; Tuck, Pullen, & Wallace, 2001). Hickson, Housley, and Wages (2000) noted that although counselors are becoming more aware of the importance of an understanding of their own spirituality as it pertains to working with clients seeking spiritual answers, more work remains.

To answer the question posed earlier—"Can clinicians take clients where they themselves have not gone?"—let us investigate (a) some current opportunities for developing self-awareness, (b) the impact of clinician value systems on clinical work, (c) a brief synopsis of the components involved with spiritual self-awareness, and (d) the benefit of engaging in continual self-exploration as this applies to religious and spiritual beliefs and values.

Opportunities for Developing Self-Awareness

Whereas clinician preparation programs stress the importance for self-awareness as a component of professional development, many do not put the same emphasis on religious/spiritual self-awareness. Opportunities for exploring religious/spiritual awareness would likely transpire during coursework related to spirituality, but given that programs either do not offer such courses (Williams et al., 1997) or lack a systematic way to prepare future clinicians to assess and treat those seeking spiritually related answers (Constantine, 1999; Fukuyama & Sevig, 1997; McLennan et al., 2001), where are beginning-level counselors to obtain this valuable experience?

Similarly, experienced mental health professionals often lack the necessary training for working with spiritual and religious experiences therapeutically (Fukuyama & Sevig, 1997; Genia, 2000; Hickson et al., 2000; Zinnbauer & Pargament, 2000). Psychotherapeutic settings traditionally offer little in the way of opportunities for the discussion of religious and spiritual issues among professional colleagues (Genia, 2000). Without actively seeking opportunities to foster religious/spiritual self-awareness, many clinicians have found themselves unprepared to incorporate their clients' religious/spiritual experiences into the therapeutic process (Weinstein et al., 2002).

Recently, in response to the lack of self-awareness opportunities, many have called for the systematic addition of a spiritual component to clinician preparation programs (Chappelle, 2000; Hickson et al., 2000; Hinterkopf, 1994; Kelly,

1994; Young et al., 2002). This addition would encourage the active exploration of clinicians' spiritual awareness, as well as teach the necessary skills to work with clients for whom spirituality is important. Although progress has been made, much work remains in assisting clinicians with developing self-awareness as it pertains to their own religious and spiritual belief systems.

The Impact of Clinician Value Systems

Another vital area for clinician self-exploration involves personal value systems. McLennan et al. (2001) called for counselors to explore the impact of their attitudes and beliefs about religion and spirituality on both the formation of their values and their overall professional practice. Values (including religious and spiritual) held by counselors are an integral part of the therapeutic process and there exists a high likelihood that counselors' values will be imposed on clients.

Understanding one's own value system also increases sensitivity to the value systems of others. Without self-awareness, ignoring others' value systems is unfortunately a possible consequence. For example, one common occurrence among clinicians is their reluctance to refer clients to local religious leaders. Worthington et al. (1996) listed three possible reasons for this situation. First, it may be due to counselors' lack of awareness of the importance of religious/spiritual values in their clients' lives (or in the counseling process itself). Second, counselors may doubt the professional competency of clergy. Finally, it may simply be due to the lack of contact with a variety of religious leaders. Without a good referral base (as highlighted in chap. 7, this volume), the responsibility of assisting clients with exploring spiritual values is left to counselors. Counselor self-awareness of his or her religious/spiritual values is therefore even more crucial to learn the importance of spirituality, to learn one's own limits, and to learn to whom to refer.

Values also play a crucial role in counselors' conceptualization of mental health and their choice in theoretical orientations (McLennan et al., 2001). Left unexplored, counselor beliefs and attitudes can negatively impact the conditions necessary for a therapeutic alliance. Worse yet, without understanding one's own feelings about spirituality, the counselor can invalidate the client's spiritual experiences (Hinterkopf, 1994), resulting both in harm to the counseling relationship and the likelihood of premature termination.

The importance of understanding one's values, biases, and competencies cannot be overstated. With this understanding, counselors increase their effectiveness in assessing and treating religious/spiritual clients, referring religious/spiritual clients when necessary, and recognizing clients who fall within the scope of their professional competence (Worthington et al., 1996). Similarly, overtly religious counselors must be able to make the same observations and distinctions when working with nonreligious clients.

Other authors assert that the therapeutic relationship can promote the candid exploration of spiritual values only so far as counselors are committed to their own spiritual growth. For example, when clients use religious terminology with which counselors are unfamiliar, the likelihood of counselor discomfort exists. Hinterkopf (1994) suggested that counselors, committed to self-examination, seek a thorough processing of such uncomfortable feelings (with appropriate supervision) so as to maintain high levels of competent client care. Vaughan and Wittine (1994) stated that whereas most competent counselors can offer emotional support for the searching client, it is those committed counselors who have personal experience with spiritual values who can offer the most valuable encouragement for clients seeking the same.

When working with spiritual values, counselors need more than an education in counseling skills and techniques, more than devouring religious/spiritual literature, and more than supervision/consultation with religious and spiritual leaders to assist in the exploration of that which is crucial and yet intangible. Those counselors who have made significant movement toward awareness of their own values, who are in touch with deeper spheres of being, and who are familiar with the spiritual world are those who can successfully facilitate this discovery process with clients (Vaughan & Wittine, 1994).

Components of Spiritual Self-Awareness

At this point, the careful reader may be asking, "What does *spiritual self-awareness* actually encompass?" McLennan et al. (2001) asserted that spiritual self-awareness entails four integrated processes. First, one should reflect on the development of one's value system across the life span. This would include the transition from accepted childhood beliefs (often held as a result of parental religious/spiritual practices), through the rejection of such beliefs that often takes place during adolescence, to the integration of beliefs occurring in adulthood. The second process involves the self-exploration of personally held biases, fears, doubts, and prejudices. Such domains can be explored through involvement in spiritual experiences as well as through existential inquiry with colleagues, clergy, or spiritual mentors. Exploring how one assimilates religion/spirituality with the counseling process (as a whole) is the third component of self-awareness. Exploring the connections between mind, body, and spirit would facilitate this process. Finally, the fourth component of religious/spiritual self-awareness requires an ongoing assessment of one's comfort level in exploring religious/spiritual matters with clients, particularly with clients of faiths different from one's own.

Additional paths to self-exploration and awareness were offered by Chappelle (2000). These include (a) gathering religious/spiritual information from clients themselves, (b) learning about specific religious or spiritual beliefs through the study of religious texts and other materials, and (c) exposing oneself to experiences with specific groups of religious or spiritual clients, which would necessitate appropriate supervision from those familiar with such belief systems. The reader is reminded that each of the suggestions offered by McLennan et al. (2001) and Chappelle (2000) are *processes* rather than *events*. Ideally, self-awareness will be an ongoing and developmental practice for the competent counselor.

The Benefits of Continual Self-Exploration

Similar to other events that bring new perspectives and meaning, continual self-awareness and exploration is necessary for the counselor intent both on maturing spiritually and meeting the needs of future clients. Counselors who take the time to continually explore their religious and spiritual beliefs are more likely to

> (a) fully understand and empathize with their religious clients, (b) contextualize their interventions so that they are in harmony with the client's religious belief system, (c) competently use religious and spiritual resources in the client's life, and (d) recognize cultural blind spots that cause them to unknowingly show disrespect or a lack of sensitivity to their client's religious values. (Richards & Potts, 1995, p. 169)

To this list of reasons for continued counselor self-exploration, Bishop (1992) added (a) the need for counselors to be aware of their biases to circumvent them when necessary and (b) the need for counselors to perform periodic values clarification to assist with the identification of client issues or values with which the counselor cannot effectively work.

In avoiding such introspective work, counselors may unwittingly ignore or invalidate their clients' spiritual experiences. Similarly, counselors may try to impose their belief system onto clients. For example, Richards and Potts (1995) noted one case in which a counselor unwittingly referred to Jesus during a religious discussion with a Jewish client. If a client believes that the counselor has not taken the time to understand her or his belief system, the client may terminate therapy without alerting the counselor to the blunder. Without continual self-evaluation, introspection, supervision, and awareness, even those counselors who make significant efforts at connecting with religious and spiritual clients may lose the ability to do so. Having explored the nature of and need for self-awareness, let us now turn to a brief discussion of why self-awareness is important to the development of sensitivity.

The Need for Increased Sensitivity

As the wording of Competency 3 suggests, the purpose of increasing one's self-awareness of religious and spiritual beliefs is to enhance one's sensitivity, understanding, and acceptance of diverse belief systems. This is directly related to (a) addressing some of the biases that continue despite increased educational and training initiatives and (b) viewing religion and spirituality as an aspect of the "whole" client. If a counselor can both rise above bias *and* see the importance of a holistic approach, he or she is well on the way to meeting the essence of Competency 3.

Addressing Clinician Bias

Ambivalence, confusion, and even hostility concerning client spiritual and religious values are all too common (Bergin, 1991; Grimm, 1994). It was not long ago that Bergin (1991) called for the counseling profession to adopt a more tolerant view of client belief systems:

> It is important to recognize that many clients are not treated within a congenial values framework because so many counselors do not understand or sympathize with the cultural content of their clients' religious world views but instead deny their importance and coerce clients into alien values and conceptual frameworks. (p. 399)

In response to the insensitivity exhibited by many counseling professionals, Ingersoll (1994) suggested three provisions for counselors interested in understanding the impact of religion and/or spirituality on their clients' lives: (a) actively acknowledge and affirm the importance of spirituality in the lives of clients, (b) join with clients by integrating their terminology and imagery into the therapy process, and (c) with clients' approval, willingly consult with spiritual leaders belonging to the clients' belief system.

Utilizing a Holistic Approach

In addition to addressing bias and insensitivity, another reason for increased sensitivity involves acknowledging spirituality as an aspect of a holistic/wellness approach to working with clients (Fukuyama & Sevig, 1997). Many authors and theorists have advocated for a wellness approach as being the best way to conceptualize clients (e.g., Chandler & Holden, 1992; Myers, Sweeney, & Witmer, 2000). These same authors assert that a "well" person is one who is balanced evenly among six major life dimensions: intellectual, emotional, physical, social, occupational, and spiritual. Others have asserted that to be optimally well, one must continually seek spiritually based meaning and purpose (Ardell, 1996). Still others advocate that for counselors themselves to be well, spirituality is a must (Coster & Schwebel, 1997).

To ignore the importance that religion and spirituality play in the overall development of clients' lives is to invalidate a crucial part of individual identity (McLennan et al., 2001). To demonstrate the importance of spirituality to the overall human existence, Myers et al. (2000) placed a strong sense of spirituality at the core of human wellness, the hub around which other life dimensions successfully emanate. Chandler and Holden (1992) went further and suggested that spiritual health not be viewed as distinct from the other wellness dimensions. Instead, they promoted the idea of spirituality as a component within each of the other five dimensions. The conclusion drawn from these theorists is that the competent counselor, intent on increasing sensitivity, will consider all aspects of the client's persona to include a careful examination of the religious and spiritual dimension.

Applications

To assist in the self-exploration of religious and spiritual beliefs, the following exercises are offered. The first series of questions are more cognitive in nature and focus on past experiences (and their impact on current self-awareness). Following these questions are some mini meditations (particularly the practice of mindfulness) that can assist with increasing your awareness of spiritual and religious matters. Finally, an experiential exercise is included that focuses attention and centers on the readers' body awareness. As this chapter has demonstrated, self-awareness is fundamental for the counselor intent on working with clients seeking religious and spiritual answers. As many client questions have answers grounded in religious and spiritual belief systems, every clinician can benefit from these exploration exercises.

According to Bishop (1992), readers who partake in these exercises should come to a new understanding of how their value systems relate to religion and spirituality. Readers who find these exercises too invasive, or who find themselves feeling resentful or apathetic toward their spiritual selves, should at the very least refer clients with spiritual issues, and at best seek additional opportunities for personal growth in these areas.

Application 1: Questions for Self-Exploration

One way to assist in the personal exploration of spirituality and religion is through questions that address one's specific spiritual journey. The following list of questions was adapted from work by Fukuyama and Sevig (1997), Bishop (1992), and Vaughan and Wittine (1994).

These questions can be used in a variety of ways (e.g., contemplative meditation, journaling, dyad sharing, and classroom discussion). Not all questions need to be answered at one time, and considerable time can be spent exploring each one individually.

1. What were the specific religious/spiritual beliefs and values of my parents (or those of my family of origin)? [The reader may choose to construct a family tree to track the development of religious/spiritual beliefs and values.]
2. What religious/spiritual beliefs and values was I taught as a child? Who influenced these beliefs and values outside of my immediate family?
3. Were these values and beliefs common to my peers or were they unique to my experience?
4. How have my religious/spiritual beliefs and values changed as I have moved through developmental life stages (i.e., adolescence, young adulthood, midlife, and old age)? How has the *practice* of these beliefs and values changed?
5. Did I assimilate those values and beliefs different than my own into my current beliefs and values?
6. What factors caused me to accept or reject the religious/spiritual values of my family or peer group?
7. Where and when were some of the turning points along the development of my religious/spiritual beliefs and values?
8. Where am I now on my religious/spiritual journey?
9. Am I active in organized religion? Why or why not?
10. Do I see a distinction between religion and spirituality? Why or why not?
11. How does religion help or restrict my spirituality?
12. What meaning does this period of my life have in the context of my life as a whole?
13. What are my current struggles/challenges as they relate to my religious/spiritual beliefs and values? What is the likely outcome and will I grow as a result?

Application 2: Expressions of Self-Exploration

Another way to approach self-exploration is to use creativity and the arts to express your spiritual history. For example, you might draw and color a picture that symbolizes your spiritual journey. You might choose to create a collage from pictures selected from popular magazines. You may even write a poem, use interpretive dance, or create a music collage, picking pieces of music to represent the different periods of your spiritual development. Whatever the method chosen, you are encouraged to share your journey with others in a safe and supportive environment.

Application 3: Mindfulness Exercise for Increased Self-Awareness

Increasing one's self-awareness is, at best, an ongoing process. By investigating our motives, discovering how our beliefs and values shape our interactions with others, and being purposeful in bringing the unconscious into awareness, we not only grow emotionally and spiritually but also become better conduits of change for clients. But as the self-awareness process involves training, the practice of mediation offers an excellent way to "guide" our mind, body, and soul toward increased awareness. Walsh (1999) said it succinctly:

> Without awareness training, we are strangers to ourselves. We remain prisoners of our subliminal psychological dynamics: moved by unconscious motives and directed by unrecognized thoughts and beliefs. Meditative mental microscopy allows us to become aware of, and therefore free from, the unconscious dynamics that otherwise rule our lives and reduce us to semiconscious automatons. (p. 180)

One particularly practical way to facilitate the self-awareness training process is through the practice of mindfulness. Walsh (1999) and others (Ott, Longobucco-Hynes, & Hynes, 2002; Teasdale, Segal, & Williams, 1995; Vacarr, 2001) have advocated for the practice of mindfulness as a necessary adjunct to increased self-awareness with a variety of populations and clinical issues. Mindfulness can briefly be defined as focusing one's attention on the present moment. A more thorough definition is offered by Tacón, McComb, Caldera, and Randolph (2003): "Mindfulness encourages detached, non-judging observation or witnessing of thoughts, perceptions, sensations, and emotions, which provides a means of self-monitoring and regulating one's arousal with detached awareness" (p. 27). The following exercises have been adapted from those offered by Walsh (1999) and can be found in greater depth in his work *Essential Spirituality*.

Exercise 1: Eating Mindfully

This exercise involves your focused attention to what you are eating. Begin by treating yourself to one of your favorite meals, and find a way to enjoy this meal in a quiet and solitary environment. Sit down in front of your meal and use some rudimentary relaxation techniques (e.g., diaphragmatic breathing, guided imagery) to rid yourself of the thoughts and cares carried in from the day.

Upon reaching a relaxed state of mind, become aware of the meal in front of you: How does the food look (how many colors are there, are there different textures, different shapes) and smell (is there an underlying sweet scent, a salty smell, are the scents strong or subtle)?

Take your first bite of food and then place your eating utensil down on the table. Become aware of each sensation as it occurs: What tastes can you detect (are there dominant flavors and more subtle ones?), do the flavors change as you chew, what is the texture of the food against your tongue and teeth, what is the temperature of the food and does it change the longer you chew?

Be aware of your tendency to want to chew quickly and swallow to get to the next bite of food; resist the temptation to do so as this is your *special* meal. When you do decide to swallow, be aware of all the feelings involved in this act, to include your natural inclination to want to pick up your fork for another bite. When you do pick up your next morsel, go through a similar process as outlined above—note how your sensations and expectations change with each bite.

Eat the meal as carefully, consciously, and enjoyably as you can. There may be times during the meal that your mind wanders and you find that you have forgotten to pay attention to what is happening in front of you. Observe this occurrence and then return to eating mindfully. Upon completing the meal, take time to explore your feelings—are you satisfied, are you still hungry, are you too full?

Meditative eating is a valuable exercise to do regularly, so you may want to find a regular time during your week to schedule such a meal. The overall goal is to increase your awareness of the eating experience, an experience that many either rush through or consider to be an inconvenience to a hectic schedule.

Exercise 2: Mindful Music

Too often we find ourselves oblivious to the benefits of music; it is usually something that is simply "on" as we proceed through a busy day. This exercise invites you to take the time to experience all that music has to offer (i.e., evoking pleasant memories or facilitating spiritual connectedness, worship, healing, etc.).

Proceed through a relaxation exercise as suggested above. Find a favorite piece of music, preferably something comforting and easygoing, and find a quiet and solitary environment where you can sit or lay down to enjoy this experience. Begin the music and be mindful of all aspects of the piece: How does the music begin, what instruments are involved, are their voices, how do the instruments/voices blend into one another, does the rhythm change throughout the song, what emotions or thoughts are evoked by the music?

You may find your mind wandering during this exercise, or you may even drift into a peaceful sleep. If this happens, observe it for what it is, and then return to listening mindfully. The goal of this exercise is to train your mind to be sensitive to everything that is happening in the moment that the music is playing. Increased concentration and sensitivity can prepare you for other areas of your life.

Exercise 3: Momentary Beauty

This exercise involves your taking a moment, maybe three or more moments throughout a day, to focus attention on your current surroundings. Look around you, even now as you are reading this, and find the beauty in something near you. Look at how the sun shines through the mini-blinds, watch a particle of dust as it dances in the air, or observe a child playing with her toys.

Whatever you choose, direct your full attention to all the sensations that you experience about the moment—if it is the child, note the different colors, the sounds, the movements, and the interactions between these. Also observe your own feelings about what you are experiencing, but attach no judgment to these feelings, simply observe. Appreciate the beauty of the moment, how it is connected with all other moments, and seek a sense of thankfulness for your presence in this moment. Then bring all these feelings with you as you continue throughout your day.

Application 4: Focusing on Self-Awareness

Another exercise known as the *experiential focusing method* was developed by Eugene Gendlin, an existential-phenomenological psychologist and philosopher at the University of Chicago (Hinterkopf, 1994). This technique was based on the notion that stuck individuals do not attend to their internal, bodily consciousness when considering the issues for which they seek assistance. Gendlin (1978) believed that clients who were taught to focus on these bodily reactions could more easily reach a successful solution to their problems.

Whereas this technique was originally developed as a method to help counselors process their clients' spiritual experiences, it is just as effective for assisting counselors through the same process. Given the focus of this chapter, this technique might be utilized for those who find themselves stuck or unclear about the impact of past religious and/or spiritual experiences. By attending to these experiences in a new way and allowing them to unfold in a safe and structured format, new meanings can be discovered and assigned to these old experiences, resulting in psychospiritual growth (Hinterkopf, 1994).

As noted by Hinterkopf (1994), the purposes of this six-step integration method are threefold. First, many individuals have had negative religious experiences during their youth that make the discovery of their current spiritual belief system difficult. This method can be an effective way to process these events in such a way that they are able to integrate the positive aspects of these early experiences. Second, using the focusing method can assist with developing and solidifying current spiritual experiences and beliefs. Finally, focusing can help individuals experience new connections with their spirituality.

The experiential focusing method can be used individually or with groups as a way to work through a spiritual block or impasse. Either way, a guide can lead others through the six steps (outlined below). Whereas formal training in focusing can be obtained for use with groups, the individual can effectively follow the six-step sequence on his or her own. Following the exercise, participants can process their experiences through discussion, journaling, or some other artistic expression.

Before starting the exercise, it is important that individuals prepare themselves by becoming both physically and emotionally at peace. One way to do so would be through diaphragmatic breathing. By focusing on expanding the abdomen rather than the chest, take 10 deep breaths, breathing in through the nose and out through the mouth. Slowly count to four with each inhalation and note how cool the air feels on the nostrils. After holding the breath for a count of four, exhale, again counting to four, noting how warm the air feels on the lips. One may also imagine each inhalation as bringing peace and tranquility into the body and each exhalation as expelling any negative energy or concerns.

The following sequence of steps was closely adapted from the original work of Gendlin (1978), the subsequent work by Hinterkopf (1994, pp. 165–175), and through personal communication (E. Hinterkopf, personal communication, July 27, 2003). Each step is followed by questions and suggestions to facilitate the work suggested by that particular step.

Step 1: Clearing a Space
Take an internal examination of your current problems or issues (as they relate to religion/spirituality). Check to see how you somatically experience each issue (noting how your body reacts; e.g., does your breathing increase or decrease, do your palms begin to sweat, etc.). As you identify and explore each issue, imagine yourself placing each problem outside yourself: Take time to examine it more closely without having to attach any physical sensations. After you have briefly explored each issue, choose one to focus on, probably the issue that is felt most strongly.

> How are you?
> Don't answer, let whatever comes, come:
> Don't go into anything.
> Just greet each thing that comes. (Gendlin, 1978, p. 177)

Step 2: Getting a Felt Sense
Whatever issue is chosen from Step 1, attend to all of the feelings associated with this issue. This attending is what Gendlin (1978) called the *felt sense* of the issue. This felt sense has multiple aspects, including the emotions, somatic impressions, and associated meanings of each. Also observe and attend to related images, movements, sounds, and smells. At first, this felt sense can be quite ambiguous. One example of how a felt sense is experienced is how you may have experienced déjà vu, the feeling when you believe that you have experienced a present situation in the past but cannot quite put your finger on the events or people involved. As you explore the felt sense, don't try to describe it to yourself with words, don't try to figure it out, just *experience* it all.

> Pick a problem
> Which feels the worst right now:
> Don't go into it: What does it feel like to have the problem there?
> "Feel all of that"—of the whole thing. (Gendlin, 1978, p. 177)

Step 3: Finding a Handle
Throughout the focusing process, you are asking yourself a series of open-ended questions, while at the same time striving not to answer these questions with words. Rather, you are learning to allow the answers to come to you in their own way without your having to impose your "preferred way of answering" on them. In this stage, you ask yourself some more open-ended questions: "What

is the crux of this problem? What is the worst of it? What is the main thing in it that makes me feel bad?" (Gendlin, 1978, p. 58). Again, do not seek to answer these questions, just ask them, and then *wait*. As you begin to experience some of the answers, see if a word can describe what you are sensing. Some examples of words might be "empty," "scratchy," "bumpy," "shrinking," or "expanding."

> Stay with that feeling
> What is the main thing in it?
> Wait, let words or images come out of this feeling. (Gendlin, 1978, p. 177)

Step 4: Resonating

Take time to decide if the words you chose to describe the felt sense are the most accurate as you experience the felt sense in the here and now. Don't force this association process, simply allow it to happen. Allow the time for words and images to ebb and flow, allowing yourself the latitude to change descriptors or find additional words to describe the felt sense. Don't rush this process. Most people fail in making a connection during the focusing technique because they are in too much of a hurry to explain a feeling rather than allowing the feeling to produce its own words and images.

> Go back and forth between words (images) and the feeling
> Try to get them to match—if the feeling changes, follow it
> Check it. Ask your body "Is that right?"
> When you get a perfect match, the words (images) being just right for this feeling, let yourself feel that for a minute. (Gendlin, 1978, pp. 177–178)

Step 5: Asking

Ask the felt sense some open-ended questions. Rather than asking closed-ended questions, which usually result in rhetorical answers, open-ended questions can bring about new meanings. Ask questions like, "Do these words accurately describe this feeling?" "What is the worst thing about this for me?" and "What does this whole thing need from me?" Again, don't make the mistake of answering for the felt sense, wait for an answer. An answer (and new meanings) may emerge in a minute or less. If you feel stuck or an answer doesn't emerge, don't worry about it, just wait it out.

When new meanings emerge from this process, the actual feeling itself changes. This event is called a *felt shift*. This felt shift is a physiological change that brings a feeling of liberation, with an accompanying increase in life energy. These feelings are similar to when you remember the past situation that was causing your déjà vu. When this felt shift occurs, you should experience it as a genuine event rather than mere intellectualization, and if you do, it indicates that psychospiritual growth has occurred.

When stuck, ask questions:

> What is the worst of this feeling?
> What's really so bad about this?
> What does it need?
> What should happen?
> Don't answer: wait for the feeling to stir and give you an answer. (Gendlin, 1978, p. 178)

Step 6: Receiving

Receiving involves taking time to assimilate the new answers that came as a result of the felt shift. Affirm the felt shift by taking the time to notice how it occurred, as well as the answers that came with it. Vocalize this felt shift with someone with whom you feel comfortable.

Again, do not fret if you do not experience a felt shift. This, like other meditative practices, takes *practice*. During an individual or group focusing session, Steps 2 through 5 can be cycled through until a felt shift occurs. Eventually, with additional practice, you will not need six distinct stages—each step will blend into an overlying process of focusing.

> What would it feel like if it was all O.K.?
> Let the body answer:
> What is in the way of that?
> Could I come back to it later? (Gendlin, 1978, p. 178)

Concluding Comments

As part of the focusing method, you need to recognize the importance of maintaining a number of attitudes while attending to your feelings. For example, a receptive attitude would involve *allowing* both feelings and symbols to emerge rather than *forcing* them to surface. Additional attitudes include being friendly, kind, patient, and accepting with yourself. Similarly, during the focusing process, learn to keep some "professional distance" from your problems. Experience the problem in its full nature (the point of which is to get the felt sense), while at the same time examining it from far enough away to recognize that your life is much greater than the issue. Develop an *observer self* where you learn how closely you can get to a problem without becoming overwhelmed by it. (I would like to thank Elfie Hinterkopf for her significant contribution to this exercise.)

Recommended Reading

Bergin, A. E. (1991). Values and religious issues in psychotherapy and mental health. *American Psychologist, 46,* 394–403.
  This article discusses the historical separation between religion and psychology.

Helminiak, D. A. (2001). Treating spiritual issues in secular psychotherapy. *Counseling and Values, 45,* 163–189.
  This article is an exploration of spirituality as independent from, yet connected to, personal religious practices.

Karasu, T. B. (1999). Spiritual psychotherapy. *American Journal of Psychotherapy, 53,* 143–162.
  In this article, Karasu describes the art of becoming a spiritual therapist.

Web Sites of Interest

http://www.emdrportal.com/clinical_applications_notes/DworkinQ_ver5.htm
  Dworkin, M. (2002). *The Clinician Self-Awareness Questionnaire in EMDR—Version 5.* An online questionnaire designed to facilitate clini-

cian self-awareness, both generally (for all clinicians) and specifically to the practice of EMDR (eye movement desensitization and reprocessing).

http://www.hawaii.edu/hivandaids/Journal%20of%20Counseling %20and%20Development%20—%20Summer%201999.pdf
> Burke, M. T., Hackney, H., Hudson, P., Miranti, J., Watts, G. A., & Epp, L. (1999). *Spirituality, religion, and CACREP curriculum standards.* An online (.pdf) version of an article found in a past issue of the *Journal of Counseling & Development.* This article explores how the discussion of relevant religious/spiritual issues can be infused into the curriculum of a counselor education program.

Additional organizations that recognize the importance of religion/spirituality to the counseling process:

http://www.apa.org/divisions/div36/
> The American Psychological Association's Division 36: Psychology of Religion

http://www.aservic.org
> The Association for Spiritual, Ethical, and Religious Values in Counseling, a division of the American Counseling Association

http://www.gaps.co.uk/
> The Guild of Analytical Psychology and Spirituality

http://www.caps.net/
> The Christian Association for Psychological Studies

http://www.ahpweb.org/index.html
> Association for Humanistic Psychology

Summary

The importance of Competency 3, both in relation to the other competencies and to the ethical and professional practice of counseling, should be evident. In developing a metaphor for this chapter, I chose a tree: I have explored some of the roots of the problem (the rift between religion/spirituality and the practice of counseling), traveled up the trunk of self-awareness, and concluded with the leaves of sensitivity. It is my hope that this process will be of assistance in your work as a counselor.

References

American Psychiatric Association. (1994). *Diagnostic and statistical manual of mental disorders* (4th ed.). Washington, DC: Author.

Ardell, D. B. (1996). *The meaning of life and a life of meaning: The richer path to whole person well-being.* Retrieved January 15, 2001, from http://www.yourhealth.com/

Bergin, A. E. (1991). Values and religious issues in psychotherapy and mental health. *American Psychologist, 46,* 394–403.

Bishop, D. R. (1992). Religious values as cross-cultural issues in counseling. *Counseling and Values, 36,* 179–191.

Capuzzi, D., & Gross, D. R. (2003). Achieving a personal and professional identity. In D. Capuzzi & D. R. Gross (Eds.), *Counseling and psychotherapy: Theories and interventions* (3rd ed., pp. 23–40). Upper Saddle River, NJ: Merrill Prentice Hall.

Chandler, C. K., & Holden, J. M. (1992). Counseling for spiritual wellness: Theory and practice. *Journal of Counseling & Development, 71,* 168–175.

Chappelle, W. (2000). A series of progressive legal and ethical decision-making steps for using Christian spiritual interventions in psychotherapy. *Journal of Psychology and Theology, 28,* 43–53.

Constantine, M. G. (1999). Spiritual and religious issues in counseling racial and ethnic minority populations: An introduction to the special issue. *Journal of Multicultural Counseling and Development, 27,* 179–181.

Cortright, B. (1997). *Psychotherapy and spirit.* Albany: State University of New York Press.

Coster, J. S., & Schwebel, M. (1997). Well-functioning in professional psychologists. *Professional Psychology: Research and Practice, 28,* 5–13.

Dworkin, M. (2002). *The Clinician Self-Awareness Questionnaire in EMDR (Version 5).* Retrieved November 18, 2003, from http://www.emdrportal.com/clinical_applications_notes/DworkinQ_ver5.htm

Fukuyama, M. A., & Sevig, T. D. (1997). Spiritual issues in counseling: A new course. *Counselor Education and Supervision, 36,* 233–245.

Gendlin, E. T. (1978). *Focusing.* New York: Everest House.

Genia, V. (2000). Religious issues in secularly based psychotherapy. *Counseling and Values, 44,* 213–221.

Grimm, D. W. (1994). Therapist spiritual and religious values in psychotherapy. *Counseling and Values, 38,* 154–164.

Helminiak, D. A. (2001). Treating spiritual issues in secular psychotherapy. *Counseling and Values, 45,* 163–189.

Hickson, J., Housley, W., & Wages, D. (2000). Counselors' perceptions of spirituality in the therapeutic process. *Counseling and Values, 45,* 58–66.

Hinterkopf, E. (1994). Integrating spiritual experiences in counseling. *Counseling and Values, 38,* 165–175.

Ingersoll, R. E. (1994). Spirituality, religion, and counseling: Dimensions and relationships. *Counseling and Values, 38,* 98–111.

Karasu, T. B. (1999). Spiritual psychotherapy. *American Journal of Psychotherapy, 53,* 143–162.

Kelly, E. W., Jr. (1994). The role of religion and spirituality in counselor education: A national survey. *Counselor Education and Supervision, 33,* 227–237.

Kinnier, R. T. (1997). What does it mean to be psychologically healthy? In D. Capuzzi & D. R. Gross (Eds.), *Introduction to the counseling profession* (2nd ed., pp. 48–63). Boston: Allyn & Bacon.

McLennan, N. A., Rochow, S., & Arthur, N. (2001). Religious and spiritual diversity in counseling. *Guidance and Counseling, 16,* 132–137.

Meier, D. E., Back, A. L., & Morrison, R. S. (2001). The inner life of physicians and care of the seriously ill. *Journal of the American Medical Association, 286,* 3007–3014.

Merriam-Webster online. (2003). Retrieved October 24, 2003, from http://www.m-w.com/home.htm

Merwin, M. M. (2002). Let sleeping students lie? Using interpersonal activities to engage disengaged students. *College Student Journal, 36,* 87–93.

Murphy, B. C., & Dillon, C. (2002). *Interviewing in action: Relationship, process, and practice* (2nd ed.). Pacific Grove, CA: Brooks/Cole.

Myers, J. E., Sweeney, T. J., & Witmer, J.M. (2000). Counseling for wellness: A holistic approach to treatment planning. *Journal of Counseling & Development, 78,* 251–266.

Ott, M. J., Longobucco-Hynes, S., & Hynes, V. A. (2002). Mindfulness meditation in pediatric clinical practice. *Pediatric Nursing, 28,* 487–491.

Prochaska, J. O., & Norcross, J. C. (1999). *Systems of psychotherapy: A transtheoretical analysis* (4th ed.). Pacific Grove, CA: Brooks/Cole.

Richards, P. S., & Potts, R. W. (1995). Using spiritual interventions in psychotherapy: Practices, successes, failures, and ethical concerns of Mormon psychotherapists. *Professional Psychology: Research and Practice, 26,* 163–170.

Richardson, T. Q., & Molinaro, K. L. (1996). White counselor self-awareness: A prerequisite for developing multicultural competence. *Journal of Counseling & Development, 7,* 238–242.

Sacks, J. M. (1985). Religious issues in psychotherapy. *Journal of Religion and Health, 24,* 26–30.

Schwartz, S. E. (2003). Jungian analytical theory. In D. Capuzzi & D. R. Gross (Eds.), *Counseling and psychotherapy: Theories and interventions* (3rd ed., pp. 68–90). Upper Saddle River, NJ: Merrill Prentice Hall.

Tacón, A. M., McComb, J., Caldera, Y., & Randolph, P. (2003). Mindfulness meditation, anxiety reduction, and heart disease: A pilot study. *Family and Community Health, 26,* 25–33.

Teasdale, J. D., Segal, Z., & Williams, J. M. G. (1995). How does cognitive therapy prevent depressive relapse and why should attentional control (mindfulness) training help? *Behaviour Research and Therapy, 33,* 25–39.

Tuck, I., Pullen, L., & Wallace, D. (2001). A comparative study of the spiritual perspectives and interventions of mental health and parish nurses. *Issues in Mental Health Nursing, 22,* 593–605.

Vacarr, B. (2001). Moving beyond polite correctness: Practicing mindfulness in the diverse classroom. *Harvard Educational Review, 71,* 285–295.

Vaughan, F., & Wittine, B. (1994). Psychotherapy as spiritual inquiry. *ReVision, 17*(2), 42–48.

Walsh, R. (1999). *Essential spirituality.* New York: Wiley.

Weinstein, C. M., Parker, J., & Archer, J. (2002). College counselor attitudes toward spiritual and religious issues and practices in counseling. *Journal of College Counseling, 5,* 164–174.

Williams, E. N., Judge, A. B., Hill, C. E., & Hoffman, M. A. (1997). Experiences of novice therapists in prepracticum: Trainees', clients', and supervisors' perceptions of therapists' personal reactions and management strategies. *Journal of Counseling Psychology, 44,* 390–399.

Wilson, S. A., & Weis, D. (1995). Enhancing cultural self-awareness: Use of drawing. *Nurse Educator, 20,* 8–9.

Worthington, E. L., Kurusu, T. A., McCullough, M. E., & Sandage, S. J. (1996). Empirical research on religion and psychotherapeutic processes and outcomes: A 10-year review and research prospectus. *Psychological Bulletin, 119,* 448–487.

Young, J. S., Cashwell, C., Wiggins-Frame, M., & Belaire, C. (2002). Spiritual and religious competencies: A national survey of CACREP-accredited programs. *Counseling and Values, 47,* 22–33.

Zinnbauer, B. J., & Pargament, K. I. (2000). Working with the sacred: Four approaches to religious and spiritual issues in counseling. *Journal of Counseling & Development, 78,* 162–171.

Chapter 5

Spiritually and Religiously Sensitive Counselors

Michele Kielty Briggs and Andrea Dixon Rayle

Competency: *The professional counselor can demonstrate sensitivity and acceptance of a variety of religious and/or spiritual expressions in client communication.*

*C*urrently, the United States is made up of the most culturally and ethnically diverse group of individuals in its entire history (Sue & Sue, 2003). Individuals in the United States practice religious and spiritual traditions that are equally as diverse (Fukuyama & Sevig, 1997; Miller, 2003). For counselors, these realities present new and challenging clients and client expectations as well as create the need for spiritual and religious competence in their clinical counseling work (Faiver, Ingersoll, O'Brien, & McNally, 2001; Kelly, 1995; Miller, 1999).

The significance of spirituality and religiosity is evidenced by the continually increasing sale of spiritually oriented books based in Eastern and Western traditions (Carrigan, 1995) as well as by the fact that the majority of people in the United States practice a religion of some sort (Richards & Bergin, 2001). Spirituality and religion are a significant part of many individuals' lives, and many Americans are becoming involved in multiple forms of spiritual expression, including less formal and more global expressions of spirituality (Gallup & Lindsay, 1999). Over the course of recent years, the counseling profession has responded to the call for religious and spiritual competency within counselor training and counseling practice. To adequately address spiritual and religious concerns in counseling, it is imperative that counselors develop skills to respond to diverse spiritual and/or religious beliefs and practices using a well-informed balance of support and challenge. The fifth competency supports the need for counselor sensitivity: The professional counselor can demonstrate sensitivity and acceptance of a variety of religious and/or spiritual expressions in client communication. Competency 5 urges all counselors to not only state that they are unbiased and accepting of clients' diverse worldviews but also exhibit this sensitivity and acceptance in all of their counseling interactions and interventions.

The overall goal of this chapter is to further understand how to address Competency 5 in the counseling process. This goal is addressed by reviewing the following:

- a framework for counselors by which to conceptualize client spirituality
- guiding principles for spiritually sensitive counselors' behavior and orientation
- a summary of three major worldviews that may be held by clients
- typologies of religious and spiritually based clients and client issues
- relevant counseling approaches and techniques for counseling issues with spiritual and/or religious overtones or undertones
- caring responses to spiritual roadblocks
- relevant ethics

Spirituality Framework

In working with clients and in training counselors, we have found it helpful to start with a working definition of spirituality and religiosity. First, the similarities and differences between the spirituality and religiosity are reviewed, and then a thematic framework is introduced.

Religiosity and Spirituality

Most researchers consider the concepts of religiosity and spirituality to be intimately connected, and most counselors consider the experiences of spirituality and religion related even though many counselors do not address religious or spiritual issues in their work with clients. Uncertainty about addressing spiritual and/or religious issues may be due to the classic conflict existing between the scientific and objective view of psychology versus the inexplicable nature of spirituality (Prest & Keller, 1993). Beliefs that spiritual issues should only be considered within religious settings (Thayne, 1997) and feelings of incompetence in handling spiritual and religious issues in counseling on the part of many counselors (Roberts, Kiselica, & Fredrickson, 2002) also may contribute to counselor reticence related to addressing spirituality.

Counselors who do not have a clear conceptualization of religion and spirituality may have trouble addressing related issues in an appropriate and sensitive manner. Thus, beginning with a clear conceptualization is important. Religion and spirituality do share some qualities; however, as the delineation between the two concepts is understood better, the two are viewed less as synonymous. Spirituality is the deep sense of oneness, wholeness, and connectedness an individual has with the universe, the infinite, and a transcendent force (Kelly, 1994; Pargament, 1997). The experience of spirituality allows individuals to define and understand occurrences in their lives and provides them with a sense of meaning and purpose in their lives and existences. Most often, religion is viewed as a subcomponent of spirituality, which includes a faith system that adheres to one of the major religions of the world (e.g., Buddhism, Christianity, Islam, Judaism) and the rituals, creeds, and traditions that are connected with that religion (Kelly, 1994;

Miller, 2003; Richards & Bergin, 1997). Both spirituality and religion incorporate a sense of transcendence, a belief in something "greater than" ourselves; however, religion is viewed as a more social process and spirituality is considered a more personal, internal process (Pargament, 1997).

Themes of Spirituality

In a study about spirituality and tragedy, Briggs, Apple, and Aydlett (2004) conceptualized spirituality using a four-theme model drawn from literature reviews completed by Westgate (1996) and Howden (1992). We found it helpful to use these four themes to recognize common elements of spirituality relevant for clients of all backgrounds. As counselors review these themes, they might imagine using these terms with nonreligious clients or consider conceptualizing explicit religious concerns using this language when appropriate. The four themes include meaning and purpose in life, inner resources, transcendence, and positive interconnectedness.

Meaning and purpose in life is the process of searching or engaging in events or relationships that promote a sense of personal worth, hope, and reasons for living (Howden, 1992). Often, finding meaning and purpose in life is considered to be the motivating force behind living (Frankl, 1988). Creating a sense of meaning and purpose in life includes engaging in personal experiences that are unique to each individual in specific ways that change throughout time and across situations (Marseille, 1997). Meaning in life may be found in relationships with self, others, and/or a Divine, or in vocation, nature, hobbies, life challenges, or other aspects of daily living.

Drawing on *inner resources* means using an internal orientation to discover one's identity and personal empowerment, knowing and relying on one's inner strength, being at peace with oneself and the world, and going inside oneself for guidance (Howden, 1992). Using inner resources might involve practices such as centering prayer, breathwork, yoga, journaling the inner voice, meditation, self-awareness exploration, and so on.

Achieving *transcendence* requires moving outside one's ego to maintain deep connections to the self, others, nature, and the cosmos (Maslow, 1971). Transcendence includes the shifting of one's "locus of centricity" beyond the self to others and the universe (Chandler, Holden, & Kolander, 1992). Practices relevant to transcending the self might include group experiences like rituals, ceremonies, or counseling, as well as meditation, praying for others, or community activism. In a preliminary study about the effect of 9/11, Briggs et al. (2004) found that transcendence scores were higher among those exposed to images of 9/11 than for those who were not; thus, it seemed that experiencing an external tragedy might increase the need to go beyond the self to maintain a deeper connectedness.

Finally, *positive interconnectedness* involves having a healthy sense of relatedness to self, others, and all life, including the universe or a universal being (Howden, 1992). Positive interconnectedness often includes involvement in supportive relationships (Banks, 1980; Maslow, 1971). A sense of positive interconnectedness could be achieved through engaging in caring relationships, participating in community activities (which can include spiritual or religious community activities), and communicating lovingly with others and/or a universal being. Counselors may find that many clients experience positive interconnectedness through involvement with spiritual or religious groups such as churches, synagogues, mosques, study groups, meditation partnerships, and other spiritual practice-based groups. Numerous studies in the medical field indicate that individuals participating in religious communities report better overall physical and emotional health (Plante & Sherman, 2001).

Certainly, counselors will encounter religious and spiritual clients and issues in counseling, and they need professional competencies to guide their work. Counselors must not only be attentive of working definitions of religion and spirituality but also embody qualities that convey sensitivity to a wide variety of spiritual and religious expressions.

Guiding Principles for Spiritually Sensitive Counselors

For counselors to demonstrate sensitivity and acceptance of a variety of religious and/or spiritual expressions, counselors are expected to honor the importance of diverse expressions both personally and within the counseling relationship. Kelly (1995) asserted, "The in-depth center of the human relationship is a personal–relational sphere of *spiritual depth*" (p. 88) and "A counselor's personal affirmation of spirituality . . . clearly coincides with—indeed, enhances—the in-depth humanness of the counseling relationship" (p. 90).

Kelly (1995) outlined characteristics that spiritually sensitive counselors should demonstrate in the counseling relationship and emphasized that an open spiritual stance (i.e., encouraging spiritual connectedness and refraining from seeking to influence client beliefs) on the part of the counselor enhances the counseling relationship. Characteristics embodied by spiritually sensitive counselors, according to Kelly, include benevolent connectedness, unconditional and hopeful openness, and transcendent meaningfulness. These characteristics allow clients to experience the themes of spirituality, noted above, in the context of a caring relationship. In order for clients to feel safe in the counseling relationship, genuine interest and commitment to working within the client's chosen framework is vital (Ingersoll, 1994). Thus, avoiding using the relationship to influence client spiritual beliefs is important. Instead, counselors may view the relationship itself as a model of positive spiritual connection.

Benevolent connectedness connotes that the counseling relationship is a partnership between the counselor and client that promotes healing, acceptance, and emotional bonding. The counselor seeks to affirm ways in which spirituality connects the client with self, others, and the counselor. In essence, the counseling relationship involves a sense of positive interconnectedness between clients and counselors that has a spiritual quality, even if spirituality is not explicitly discussed.

Unconditional and hopeful openness allows for a positive outlook on the client's future through trust in the possibility of transformation and meaning-making for the client as a result of the work done in the counseling relationship. Instillation of hope, when clients gain hope by becoming inspired or encouraged directly or indirectly throughout the course of therapy, is a key therapeutic factor noted by Yalom (1995). The commitment shared between the counselor and client to work on difficult issues along with a shared faith in the fruitfulness of the counseling process might be considered elements of a sacred relationship.

Transcendent meaningfulness is another way in which themes of spirituality can be embodied in the counseling relationship. Simply participating in a relationship in which the classic Rogerian qualities of genuineness, unconditional positive regard, and empathy are experienced can allow the client to share meaning in a world in which he or she may sometimes feel insignificant. Transcending the self and engaging in a challenging yet accepting relationship can help provide a sense of personal worth.

Throughout the rest of the chapter, client worldviews, orientation, and issue typology with respect to spirituality and religion are reviewed. These concepts can help guide counselors' decisions with respect to spiritually sensitive interventions. Regardless of the ultimate choice made throughout the course of therapy, it is crucial for counselors who identify themselves as "spiritually sensitive" to embody the aforementioned qualities in the counseling relationship.

Summary of Three Major Worldviews

"Authentic spirituality is inherently a movement toward a keener awareness of the in-depth existential ground of self-reflective freedom in which positive human development occurs" (Kelly, 1995, p. 91). Looking at spirituality as a global vehicle for personal reflection, awareness, and growth may help counselors and clients find common ground for addressing spirituality. Still, it is important that counselors understand clients' cultural and religious influences so that they gain a better empathic understanding of the clients' way of making sense of the issues in their lives and in the world around them. Culture, religion, and spirituality are often intertwined, and their influence may be interconnected (Miller, 2003).

According to Richards and Bergin (1997), most religious and spiritual beliefs fall into three major categories. These categories include Western, Eastern, and naturalistic/scientific. In short, the *Western* mind-set contends that there is an all-knowing, loving God (capitalized here to connote a monotheistic representation) or a Supreme Being who created the world; humans are creations of God and they have a free will; there is a divine purpose of life as well as an afterlife and one must obey God's will; and there are laws and commandments set forth by God. The *Eastern* view embraces the ideas that there is not one god but perhaps many helping deities that are not all-powerful; there may or may not be a human soul and that humans choose paths that do or do not lead to harmony and enlightenment; the purpose of life is enlightenment and harmony, and one must attain these for peace or to exit the cycle of birth and rebirth; there are a variety of moral paths; and there may or may not be an afterlife, including an overall merging with the universe. Finally, according to Richards and Bergin, the *naturalistic/scientific* perspective affirms that there is not a god or a supreme being and the universe is governed by natural forces;

evolution processes are responsible for human life, and human consciousness is the result of physiological and biological factors; there is no inherent purpose in life—it is invented by humans; there are no spiritual realities and no absolute ethical or moral guidelines, although such guidelines may be useful; and there is no life or existence after death.

Clearly, a plethora of religions and beliefs systems and their variations exist under the first two worldviews. It is not the aim of this chapter to cover these. However, if counselors are aware of the basic belief systems that exist, they can better assist their clients along their journey toward healing. Some counselors might determine that nonreligious clients are not spiritual and therefore approaching issues from a spiritual perspective is useless. Such counselors may wish to revisit the general themes of spirituality or consider an alternative viewpoint. For example, some people who consider themselves to be agnostic (one who believes that it is impossible to know whether there is a god) may be some of the most spiritually oriented people because they are often open to the mystery of life and are able to embrace uncertainty and multiple possibilities (Weil, 1951). Therefore, broaching the topic of spirituality may be appropriate while using global language such as that provided through the use of the four themes at the beginning of this chapter.

Suppose a crisis counselor was responding to a tragedy such as 9/11 or a terrible accident resulting in the loss of a child. In working with the affected survivors and working through the spiritual issues connected to the loss, such as making sense of why the event happened, the counselor could start by ascertaining the client's spiritual/religious worldview. Because there are countless variations on these worldviews, the counselor would have to take on the role of student while learning about each client's perspective. Responding appropriately and sensitively requires the skills discussed above.

Using the example of the tragic death of a child, a client with a Western worldview may see the event as "God's will," believe that the victim is in a better place, and communicate directly with their god about their conflicted feelings concerning the loss. They may even wonder why their god allowed this to happen. Another client from an Eastern perspective may view the loss as a natural part of the life cycle while trusting that the person will either continue and "merge with the universe" or be reborn into another life. They may feel that the person's soul has been released, that there was no higher purpose for the event, and that it was not necessarily a personal plan intended for the victim. A client coming from a naturalistic/scientific standpoint might see the event as a random, unfortunate act that has no meaning behind it. This client may believe that the victim is simply gone and that the victim's life is over. A client who is blending worldviews using an agnostic stance may believe that there is an unknown reason for the tragedy, that the victim may or may not go on in another form, and that meaning can be found within each survivor over time. As a counselor, consider the following questions:

1. How might you respond to the clients described above? How would your responses be similar or different?

2. How can you honor the clients' perspectives when they vary from your own?
3. How would you best facilitate healing for each of the above clients, given their expressed worldview?
4. What are some of the ways each worldview could enhance or detract from psychological well-being?

Religious and Spiritually Based Clients and Client Issues Typologies

Even after ascertaining the client's primary worldview, counselors may wonder when it is appropriate to respond to overt or covert spiritual and/or religious expressions and they might be confused about if or when to bring spirituality/religion into the counseling session. Kelly (1995) provided some helpful guidelines about assessing client issues and client problems as related to spirituality and religiosity.

Client Orientation

For counselors to "meet the client where the client is," which is a guiding principle for spiritually sensitive counselors, it is important to gauge the client's religious or spiritual intensity. Kelly's (1995) taxonomy can be a helpful beginning. Miller (2003) noted that basic counseling responses are appropriate for all of the following categories, whereas religiously oriented responses may be appropriate for the first four categories but not for the second four. Counselors may find clients from the Eastern and Western worldview perspectives in all of the categories, whereas Categories 6–8 may include more clients with the naturalistic/scientific stance.

1. *Religiously committed* clients exhibit a high level of religious conviction that strongly influences the way they see the world and conceptualize and address problems. For example, such a client may follow the literal text of religious scripture and use it to guide daily life.
2. *Religiously loyal* clients are influenced by religious norms that are congruent with their culture. Their families, communities, culture, and religion are intertwined and share guiding beliefs and principles. For example, a culturally Jewish client may adhere to basic principles of the Jewish religion, consider culture and religion inseparable, while not viewing himself or herself as particularly religious.
3. *Spiritually committed* clients may value spiritual themes such as meaning, inner resources, positive interconnectedness, and transcending the self but do not identify with a particular religion. A spiritually committed client may be a person who self-describes as "spiritual but not religious" and sees spirituality as an open stance to others and a universal kindness.
4. *Religiously and spiritually committed* clients do not express a religious or spiritual orientation, but as counseling progresses, they

demonstrate an openness to the possibility that spirituality or religion may be helpful for them. For example, a client in this category may have lost a spouse to cancer, and although the client has not considered the role of spirituality or religion before, he or she is now wondering about meaning and illness and is seeking answers about making peace with death as a part of life.

5. *Superficially religious* clients state a religious affiliation but do not have an intrinsic experience of religion or spirituality. An example of this type of client may be someone who attends religious services for social purposes only.

6. *Religiously tolerant and indifferent* clients can tolerate others' religious perspectives, beliefs, and practices, but they do not embrace religion in their own lives at all. For example, a client who sees a religious saying on the counselor's wall may acknowledge its helpfulness for others but may see it irrelevant to his or her own life.

7. *Nonreligious* clients see religion as unnecessary and reject the merits of religion outright. Using the example from Example 6 above, a nonreligious client may state that the religious quote is just an excuse to escape the painful realities of life.

8. Clients who are *hostile to religion* are antagonistic to others who see the merits of religion. This hostility may be based on a rationalistic viewpoint or a psychologically detrimental pattern that is present in other aspects of the client's life. The latter must become a therapeutic issue, whereas the former can signal the counselor to simply leave religion and spirituality out of the session.

Counseling Issues Orientation

While it is important to understand the religious and spiritual paradigm of the client, it is also useful to consider the type of issue presented by the client. Counselors must make intentional decisions about how to approach an issue presented by clients. Kelly (1995) identified four major types of client issues. Counselors may find some degree of overlap between client orientation and issues orientation. For example, religiously committed clients may be more likely to present with a predominantly spiritual/religious issue or problem than clients who are hostile to religion. Thus the first type of client issue is the *predominantly or specifically spiritual/religious issue or problem.* The client presents these issues as mainly spiritual or religious in nature. One such issue might include a client who is considering pursuing a religious vocation.

Nonspiritual/nonreligious issues/problems with a significant spiritual/religious component are issues that are not seen by the client as particularly spiritual or religious in nature but they are affected by spirituality or religion. For example, a client who lost a friend in the 9/11 attacks may not perceive the loss as triggering spiritual or religious concerns for themselves, but they might be trying to make sense of the religious component of the terrorists' motives.

Nonspiritual/nonreligious issues/problems with a potential connection to the spiritual/religious dimension do not have an innate connection to spirituality or religion, but by their very nature, they have the potential to evoke questions about spirituality or religion. Illness, death, and family changes are examples of situations that may evoke concerns about spirituality or religion. Finally, *nonspiritual/nonreligious issues/problems with little apparent close connection with the spiritual/religious dimension* might include problems related to work, self-concept, relationship difficulties, and so on.

Once a counselor identifies the type of counseling problem and is aware of the client's orientation regarding spirituality and religion, he or she will want to determine whether to incorporate a base of spiritual or religious interventions. If counselors suspect that clients are using spirituality or religion to avoid facing difficult therapeutic concerns, counselors can refocus the sessions on "problem areas" of clients' lives, such as relationships, work conflicts, or self-worth. When counselors do choose to focus on spirituality or religion, there are guidelines they can follow to examine the effectiveness of their decision. According to Kelly (1995), the following are some of the conditions that should be met before counselors can ethically incorporate spiritual and/or religious responses and questions into the counseling process: The client is aware that there are several potentially helpful angles from which to address a problem and that a spiritual or religious approach is one way; the client is encouraged to explore spiritual expressions that are congruent with his or her beliefs and values, not the counselor's; the counselor does not feign expertise in beliefs or practices and makes appropriate referrals when needed; the counselor focuses on the most effective therapeutic tools for the client and does not "push" specific religious or spiritual beliefs; the counselor assists the client in reviewing the pros and cons of chosen spiritual approaches; and the counselor "drops" issues of spirituality and/or religion if the client does not want them to be a part of therapy.

Relevant Counseling Approaches and Techniques

To be a spiritually sensitive counselor, as indicated in Competency 5, the counselor must view counseling as a genuine encounter between two human beings, a journey of personal transformation, and a process in which the counselor takes on both learning and facilitating roles. Counselors may respond to clients who want to incorporate spirituality into the session by challenging them to look at what is missing in their lives and to discover what they really want and to help them explore how their religious/spiritual practices can aid them in their quest. Wilber (2000) noted the importance of spiritual experience for growth and healing to take place. Counselors can incorporate both *process* and *experience* into the counseling session.

Throughout the counseling process, counselors will use various techniques and skills in their counseling work to actively demonstrate sensitivity to and acceptance of their clients' religious and spiritual beliefs and practices. On a basic level, it is important to verbally and nonverbally encourage, validate, and inspire clients to be open about their religious and spiritual forms of expression. Counselors can help clients explore ways of finding meaning and purpose and clarify clients' values and beliefs by being open to listening and learning from clients about their religious and/or spiritual practices. Counselors may also consider taking a course or completing readings about diverse religious and spiritual traditions and customs.

After counselors have demonstrated a basic-level sensitivity and acceptance, they can utilize counseling techniques that foster experiencing spirituality, such as religious/spiritual life review and reauthoring of life story, personal or directed journaling, and art therapy (e.g., drawing, sculpture, graphs). General spiritually centered interventions suggested by Miller (2003) include bibliotherapy, meditation, relaxation, or imagery, and rituals. Miller also suggested using prayer, sacred writings, or religious practices with clients for whom it is appropriate. These counseling tools demonstrate counselors' openness and willingness to learn about the client and what is most meaningful in their lives, while integrating meaningful religious/spiritual expressions into the client's actual experience in counseling.

Before delving into the aforementioned techniques, counselors may want to determine their approach to religious and spiritual issues brought forth by the client. Kelly (1995) defined four specific approaches that counselors take toward spiritual and/or religious issues. Counselors can consider their "typical" approach with clients, and they may want to discuss situations in which each approach would be most appropriate. The first style noted by Kelly is a *deferring approach*. This is when the counselor decides to step away from or disregard spiritual or religious information or emphases brought to the session by the client. A counselor may do this, when, for example, a client tries to use the session to evangelize or tries to mask relevant relationship issues concerning power and responsibility behind religious jargon. An *invalidating approach* is intentionally used to dispute or confront harmful or destructive beliefs or practices, such as the intent to kill another or commit suicide based on a religious conviction. Counselor ethics are crucial in reporting harmful intents. Less drastic examples may be self-harmful beliefs, such as, "If I were more faithful this tragedy would never have happened." Sensitive responses for situations like this are included in the next section. The third approach, a *reworking approach*, involves reworking spiritual or religious beliefs that have become problematic for clients. For example, clients who adhere rigidly to beliefs, negatively apply beliefs to their lives, or take beliefs out of context may need assistance in finding a more workable approach. Kelly (1995) stated, "Reworking approaches involve a *rethinking/reexperiencing* process in which the counselor facilitates the client's reflective talking about spiritual and religious beliefs and practices in a therapeutically safe environment" (p. 197). Finally, an *encouraging approach* assists clients whose beliefs and practices are functioning in a developmentally appropriate and healing-enhancing manner apply and enhance their spiritual and/or religious beliefs and practices. For example, a client who has begun to experience the calming benefits of meditation may be given a particular meditation to practice in session or at home and may be encouraged to examine the benefits of the spiritual practice on other aspects of his or her life, such as in relationships and in work.

Consider the following case scenario. If you were Lilia's counselor, what counseling approaches and techniques would be most helpful? Using Kelly's

(1995) description of approaches, which of the following would you most likely use: deferring, invalidating, reworking, or encouraging?

Lilia is a 29-year-old biracial woman who lives in the southeastern United States. She was raised by a Euro American mother who identifies herself as an Evangelical Christian and a father who is a Native American "spiritual traditionalist" who gains strength from the Great Spirit. Lilia grew up attending church with her mother, and she thinks of herself as a Christian woman who relates with a monotheistic god. She says that the god she believes in is an all-powerful, all-loving being. Lilia presented in counseling struggling with her sexuality and her attraction to women. Through the process of counseling, Lilia came to accept her sexuality and she decided to come out to her friends and family. Some reacted positively. Others, such as her mother, reacted negatively, stating that because of her "sinfulness," she would no longer be welcome in their church. Lilia was angry and confused. Because she felt chastised by her childhood religion, she began experimenting with alternative forms of religious and spiritual expression. She has considered returning to her Native American spiritual roots. Lilia hoped that others would accept that her lesbianism is not a choice, but a way of life, and that she could maintain a strong sense of spiritual connectedness and support with others throughout her struggle.

Caring Responses to Spiritual Roadblocks

While spiritual and religious beliefs and practices can contribute to overall mental health and well-being in positive ways, such as helping individuals experience forgiveness (Carone & Barone 2001), reduce anxiety, experience meaning in life, and cope with stress (Plante & Sherman, 2001), such beliefs and practices also can be carried out in ways that cause psychological suffering. Specifically, when highly religious individuals use religious beliefs and practices to deny or repress difficult and intense feelings such as sadness and anger or to attribute all control and responsibility for life events on external forces, problems such as depression, anxiety, and lower personality functioning can result (Bergin, Masters, & Richards, 1987; Carone & Barone, 2001; Genia & Shaw, 1991).

Although there are many benefits associated with spirituality and religion, certain beliefs or practices may hamper psychological well-being. Helminiak (2001) cautioned counselors that challenging or rejecting pathological aspects of clients' religious beliefs can be a crucial therapeutic step. Counselors aiming to demonstrate sensitivity to clients' diverse spiritual and religious beliefs and practices might be confused about when challenging clients is appropriate. They may be seeking for a balance of support and challenge in the relationship but are unsure about when it is appropriate to challenge their clients in a caring manner. In this section, indications of clients whose well-being may be "off balance," owing to spiritual or religious approaches, are considered. We also review steps counselors can take to respond sensitively to these roadblocks.

Recognizing Challenging Tendencies in Clients

How can counselors recognize potentially harmful patterns? First, they may want to look for themes of repression, denial, or abandonment of personal responsibility in the client's thinking about life issues from a religious or spiritual viewpoint. James Hillman (1975), Jungian analyst, psychiatrist, and expert on the integration of psychological and spiritual issues, noted that depression is often seen as the "great enemy" by Western Christian believers (p. 98). He stated that such individuals are more likely to suppress and deny depression and other dark emotional states and engage in the "light fantasy," which involves "hoping against despair" (p. 98) instead of embracing or being true to one's difficult emotions. Facing these difficult emotions is the key to positive personal and spiritual growth (Hillman, 1975). Helen Luke (1987), Jungian therapist and author, cautioned against emotional suppression and reliance on external loci of control by stating that the only valid cure for despair involves the acceptance of real suffering. She noted that trying to climb out of difficult feelings lays the foundation for future despair, because transformative soul growth cannot occur by engaging in denial and refusing to go within oneself for internal examination. O'Connor (2002) noted that individuals who have experienced personal losses, such as death, divorce, or loss of a job, are more likely to be dealing with true depression rather than a "dark night of the soul," referring to a darkness most often associated with their relationship with a Higher Power. Thus, treating psychological depression solely with religious antidotes may prove to be detrimental.

Ken Wilber, founder of the Integral Institute and author of several books assimilating spiritual practice and psychological insights, affirmed the ability of people to integrate matters of matter, body, mind, spirit, and soul. He did, however, recognize the pathologies that can emerge as one moves through different levels of awareness, including matter, body, mind, soul, and spirit. For example, according to Wilber's complex model, spiritual roadblocks such as escapism, repression, or denial, if not recognized and dealt with, can become ingrained at the lower levels of consciousness, such as in the mind, and remain in the psyche (Wilber, 2000). Wilber himself recognized the tendency to fall back on unhelpful tendencies such as denial and repression when faced with a personal tragedy. After learning of his wife's possible recurrence of breast cancer in his book *Grace and Grit*, Wilber exclaimed,

> It has to be cancer, is all I thought at that moment. What else could it be? The doctor will explain. The doctor . . . can go jump in the lake. Damn! Damn! Damn! Where was the denial and repression when I really needed it? (p. 179)

Through his somewhat sarcastic remark, Wilber seemed to be recognizing the desire to lean on these defenses. In spite of his wish that the treacherous situation would disappear, Wilber made a choice to take responsibility for his deepest and most difficult emotions. In the account of his wife Treya's illness, Wilber in fact decided to face the tragic circumstances of her illness with determination and honesty. The result was indeed a sorrowful loss, but an intact soul and an unfragmented psyche.

In addition to the phenomenon of denial or repression of feelings, overreliance on forces outside of oneself for assistance and comfort (i.e., maintaining an external locus of control or extrinsic religiosity) can result in harmful resignation or powerless submission (McCandless, 1991). Attributing *all* life outcomes and processes to "God's will" can serve as a personal resignation of responsibility and self-efficacy (York, 1989). Relying on a Universal or Higher Power for strength while taking responsibility for one's actions and reactions is a more empowering approach (Pargament, 1997).

Second, counselors may consider some of the markers of religious pathology identified by Lovinger (1996). These markers include strictly adhering to religious principles, using religion as an escape from difficulties, taking too much or too little responsibility, changing places of worship frequently, thoughtlessly and enthusiastically adhering to religion, and using scriptures to guide all aspects of life without consideration of the context.

Responsive Steps

Because religious or spiritual beliefs and practices can contribute to better or worse overall well-being, dealing with related beliefs and practices in the counseling relationship can be overwhelming and confusing for counselors. Managing personal biases throughout the process of providing caring and sensitive challenging responses is important. The following steps can assist counselors in doing so.

According to Briggs and West (2001), there are several steps counselors can take upon recognition that a client is implementing his or her religious beliefs in an unhealthy manner. These steps can be categorized into phases of affirming, assessing, confronting, and connecting.

First, to maintain a sense of trust and positive connectedness with clients, counselors can work to *affirm* clients. Foremost, counselors should respect clients as individuals by listening to them in a nonjudgmental manner, regardless of the counselor's own beliefs (York, 1989). Counselors should affirm the positive role of religion/spirituality in clients' lives (Ingersoll, 1994). Encouraging expression of feelings, regardless of the intensity or perceived incongruence, is important (McCandless, 1991). In addition, counselors may want to especially affirm beliefs and practices that seem to strengthen clients' self-esteem (Peterson & Nelson, 1987). For example, a counselor could say to a client who relies heavily on external forces, "When you take an active role in making meaningful decisions in your life, I notice that your feelings of despair and loneliness seem to lessen. Let's talk about this." Asking clients to remember a time when their religious beliefs and practices gave them a deep sense of meaning and purpose in life (e.g., looking for the exception) and encouraging them to connect their religious beliefs with accompanying feelings are additional methods of affirmation and positive self-discovery (Peterson & Nelson, 1987).

Assessing the contribution of clients' beliefs and practices to overall psychological well-being is a difficult task. Counselors should be careful to examine their own judgments about religious matters that enter into the counseling session. It is important to refrain from labeling clients' beliefs as pathological in the assessment process (Storr, 1997). Keeping in mind this caution, counselors may find it useful to ask if clients' religious beliefs or practices (a) seem to build barriers or bridges between people, (b) strengthen or weaken a basic trust in and relatedness to others and the universe, (c) help or hinder inner freedom and responsibility, (d) facilitate the movement from guilt to forgiveness, (e) emphasize love or fear, or (f) encourage the denial or acceptance of reality. Counselors may wish to engage clients in discussion of these questions in the assessment phase (Clinebell, 1972; Peterson & Nelson, 1987).

After counselors determine that a sense of trust has been established in the counseling relationship throughout the stages of affirmation and assessment, counselors can gently and responsibly *confront* clients' self-destructive beliefs. Counselors should work through clients' defenses gradually, remembering to affirm the ways in which religious beliefs and practices are working for the client (York, 1989). In the confronting phase, counselors who are knowledgeable about clients' religious/spiritual orientation, either through their own studies or through information provided by clients, may point out contradictions in the beliefs of clients and actual religious teachings. Using vocabulary that is congruent with the client's worldview is helpful in conceptualizing and confronting issues (Ingersoll, 1994). Eriksen, Marston, and Korte (2002) provided an example of working with a conservative, Christian client for whom only positive emotions were deemed acceptable to express because of their adherence to the Biblical scriptures "perfect love casts out fear" (1 John 4:18) and "rejoice always" (Phillipians 4:4). Eriksen et al. suggested that the client's desire to reach these emotional states described in the religious scriptures could be affirmed while reminding the client that Jesus, the religious figure in this case, experienced emotions like anger and sadness and that the God of the Old Testament even expressed jealousy and rage. The authors suggested providing clients with a realistic time frame for working through negative emotions while striving toward the end goals of joy and peace.

When clients are able to point out their own self-harmful, negative thinking, counselors can more easily help them restructure these thoughts. Throughout the confronting experiences, counselors should remember that arguing with clients' beliefs and practices is not helpful. Instead, focusing on personal problem solving with the client will be more beneficial (Carone & Barone, 2001). For example, counselors working with clients who tend to repress or deny emotions by using religious explanations might want to examine how doing so affects aspects of clients' lives such as intimate relationships, social functioning, feelings of self-worth, and job functioning.

Finally, *connecting* with positive support systems is an important step for clients whose religious beliefs or practices are roadblocks to their overall psychological well-being. Having a sense of positive interconnectedness with a spiritual community in addition to friends and family members is a significant aspect of overall spiritual well-being (Westgate, 1996). Counselors also may encourage clients' involvement with religious support persons such as religious leaders who foster healthy and affirming beliefs and attitudes (Peterson & Nelson, 1987; York, 1989). Finally, counselors may help clients work through difficult relationship issues (Storr, 1997), which can cause problems relating positively to a Higher Power and others.

Pertinent Ethics

Because counselors should only practice in areas in which they have professional competence and training (American Counseling Association [ACA], 1995), it may become necessary to refer clients to individuals such as spiritual healers or leaders who have a deeper understanding of clients' religious or spiritual framework (Ingersoll, 1994). At the same time, counselors are ethically required to respect their clients' differences, understand how their own values and beliefs influence the counseling process, and refrain from imposing their values onto clients (ACA, 1995). Thus, simply not agreeing with clients' religious backgrounds is not a legitimate reason for automatic referral or limitation of topics covered in counseling. In light of ethical and professional considerations, counselors should provide as much support as possible for the integration of psychological and religious/spiritual issues in the counseling process while working toward maximizing the mental health of clients.

According to the ACA's ethical standards, counselors do not discriminate on the basis of age, color, culture, disability, ethnic group, gender, race, religion, sexual orientation, marital status, or socioeconomic status, and they attempt to increase their personal awareness, sensitivity, and skills with regard to counseling diverse client populations (ACA, 1995, Standards A.2 and E.5b, 1995). ACA and the Council for Accreditation of Counseling and Related Educational Programs (CACREP; 2001) have embraced spirituality and religion as issues of diversity that counselors must be prepared to work with in their clinical positions. Finally, the *Diagnostic and Statistical Manual of Mental Disorders* (4th ed., text revision; American Psychiatric Association, 2000) includes the diagnosis "Religious or Spiritual Problem" as a possible focus for therapeutic attention.

These highly important standards in the field of professional counseling have set the stage for counselors' ethical considerations when counseling clients from all religious and/or spiritual backgrounds. First and foremost, counselors are expected do no harm to their clients (ACA, 1995) and are taught to exhibit appropriate empathy and understanding when counseling all clients (CACREP, 2001). Specifically related to this competency, all practicing counselors are not to discriminate based on the variety of religious and/or spiritual expressions in clients' communication according to the ethical codes of ACA. Therefore, counselors should be open and accepting of clients' religious and spiritual concerns and expressions, and exhibit appropriate empathy and sensitivity to clients concerning these and other issues. Competency 5 can be better applied in counseling when professional counselors have (a) gained *knowledge* about a variety of religious and spiritual expressions their clients might communicate (anything from Buddhism, Christianity, and Judaism to nontraditional medicine ways or Shamanism); (b) focused on their own *awareness* of personal preferences in relation to religion and spirituality and how they affect their personal lives; and (c) gained actual counseling skills for demonstrating sensitivity and acceptance for clients' various religious and spiritual expressions. This sensitivity of professional counselors is demonstrated through their professional ethics and counseling competence with respect to religious and spiritual beliefs and practices, and ultimately begins at the training level and should be carried out into the profession through continuing education and training.

Case Study

Consider the following case study and determine Rae's worldview, religious/spiritual orientation, and issues orientation. Then discuss how you would ensure that addressing spirituality/religion would be effective.

Rae was a woman in her 40s who was participating in a women's counseling group facilitated by the first author. During the last session, Rae, who had previously acted as a supportive member for the other women in crisis, began to reveal the impetus for her joining the group. She informed the group members that her son had been killed less than a year ago in a neighborhood shooting and that she had been able to hide this from the group up until this point in time because she was "fine and free of pain." She asserted that she did not grieve and would not need to because her son was in a "better place." In fact, Rae emphasized that her friends were coming to her for consolation related to her own son's death because she was a strong, religious woman with unwavering beliefs. However, Rae did reveal that her relationship with her spouse had been crumbling because of her insistence that her husband rely more on his faith and exhibit less anguish over the loss of their son. Rae exhibited several signs of psychological distress such as appearing to dissociate from what was going on around her and crying during times of more benign discussion, such as vocational issues, that did not typically elicit emotional responses from other group members. She often became emotional and gave advice to the other women about how they could make their lives better in the midst of their problems. Rae stated that she had been a member of a supportive church community and that several church members offered her and her family support during this time of crisis. However, Rae turned down their offers because she felt she and her Higher Power could handle this on their own. Rae's pastor was concerned about her shutting out the community.

The following are some questions for reflection and discussion:

1. Considering the types of worldviews presented, which worldview does it seem that Rae espouses?
2. Using Kelly's (1995) taxonomy, which types seem most like Rae?
3. What kind of "counseling issues orientation" was presented in this case study?
4. Using the various responses and techniques covered in this chapter, formulate spiritually and religiously sensitive responses and share them with a partner.

Recommended Reading

It may be useful for counselors and counselors-in-training to explore not only readings focused on religious and spiritual traditions but also readings concerned with the incorporation of these various expressions into counseling work. Below are several recommended readings for counselors who are seeking to provide ethical and culturally sensitive counseling with religious and spiritual clients and to better understand their own spiritual and religious beliefs.

Abels, S. L. (2000). *Spirituality in social work practice: Narratives for professional helping*. Denver, CO: Love.

Earhart, H. B. (1993). (Ed.). *Religions and traditions of the world*. San Francisco: Harper.

Faiver, C., Ingersoll, R. E., O'Brien, E., & McNally, C. (2001). *Explorations in counseling and spirituality: Philosophical, practical, and personal reflections*. Belmont, CA: Wadsworth/Thomson Learning.

Frame, M. W. (2003). *Integrating religion and spirituality into counseling: A comprehensive approach*. Pacific Grove, CA: Brooks/Cole-Thomson Learning.

Fukuyama, M. A., & Sevig, T. D. (1999). *Integrating spirituality into multicultural counseling*. Thousand Oaks, CA: Sage.

Miller, G. (2003). *Incorporating spirituality in counseling and psychotherapy*. Hoboken, NJ: Wiley.

Sperry, L. (2001). *Spirituality in clinical practice: Incorporating the spiritual dimension in psychotherapy and counseling*. Ann Arbor, MI: Taylor & Francis.

Web Sites of Interest

The following Web sites may be useful to counselors seeking to better understand various forms of religious and spiritual expressions clients may reveal:

http://www.explorefaith.org
   Explore Faith

http://www.apa.org/divisions/div36/
   Psychology of Religion (Division of the American Psychological Association)

http://www.mindspirit.org
   Psychotherapy and Spirituality Institute

http://www.religioustolerance.org
   Religious Tolerance

http://www.spiritweb.org
   Spiritweb

http://wri.leaderu.com
   World Religions Index

Summary

This chapter has focused on Competency 5 of the spirituality competencies. Throughout the chapter, counselors have been exposed to a spiritual framework, guiding principles for spiritually sensitive counselors, three major worldviews, typologies of religious and spiritually based clients and client issues, relevant counseling approaches and techniques, caring responses to spiritual roadblocks, and relevant ethics. By conceptualizing clients' spiritual and religious orientation responsibly and responding to clients' spiritual and religious expressions using appropriate techniques and approaches, counselors should be able to identify themselves as spiritually and religiously sensitive professionals.

References

American Counseling Association. (1995). *ACA code of ethics and standards of practice*. Alexandria, VA: Author.

American Psychiatric Association. (2000). *Diagnostic and statistical manual of mental disorders* (4th ed., text revision). Washington, DC: Author.

Banks, R. (1980). Health and spiritual dimensions: Relationships and implications for professional preparation programs. *Journal of School Health, 50,* 195–202.

Bergin, A. E., Masters, K., & Richards, P. S. (1987). Religiousness and mental health reconsidered: A study of an intrinsically religious sample. *Journal of Counseling Psychology, 34,* 197–204.

Briggs, M. K., Apple, K. J., & Aydlett, A. E. (2004). The role of spirituality in world crisis: Examining the events of 9/11. *Counseling and Values, 48,* 174–182.

Briggs, M. K., & West, M. A. (2001). *When religion gets in the way: Maximizing client mental health while managing personal biases.* Unpublished manuscript.

Carone, D. A., & Barone, D. F. (2001). A social cognitive perspective on religious beliefs: Their functions and impact on coping and psychotherapy. *Clinical Psychological Review, 21,* 989–1003.

Carrigan, H. (1995). Reading is believing: Religious publishing toward the millennium. *Library Journal, 120,* 36–40.

Chandler, C. K., Holden, J. M., & Kolander, C. A. (1992). Counseling for spiritual wellness: Theory and practice. *Journal of Counseling & Development, 71,* 168–175.

Clinebell, J. (1972). *The mental health ministry of the local church.* Nashville, TN: Abingdon Press.

Council for Accreditation of Counseling and Related Educational Programs. (2001). *Accreditation and procedures manual.* Alexandria, VA: Author.

Eriksen, K., Marston, G., & Korte, T. (2002). Working with God: Managing conservative Christian beliefs that may interfere with counseling. *Counseling and Values, 47,* 48–68.

Faiver, C., Ingersoll, R. E., O'Brien, E. M., & McNally, C. (2001). *Explorations in counseling and spirituality.* Pacific Grove, CA: Brooks/Cole.

Frankl, V. (1988). *The will to meaning.* New York: Meridian.

Fukuyama, M. A., & Sevig, T. D. (1997). Spiritual issues in counseling: A new course. *Counseling and Values, 36,* 333–344.

Gallup, G., & Lindsay, D. M. (1999). *Surveying the religious landscape: Trends in U.S. beliefs.* Harrisburg, PA: Morehouse.

Genia, V., & Shaw, D. G. (1991). Religion, intrinsic–extrinsic orientation, and depression. *Review of Religious Research, 32,* 274–283.

Helminiak, D. A. (2001). Treating spiritual issues in secular psychotherapy. *Counseling and Values, 45,* 163–189.

Hillman, J. (1975). *Revisioning psychology.* New York: Harper & Row.

Howden, J. W. (1992). Development and psychometric characteristics of the Spirituality Assessment Scale (Doctoral dissertation, Texas Woman's University). *Dissertation Abstracts International, 54*(1-B), 166.

Ingersoll, R. E. (1994). Spirituality, religion, and counseling: Dimensions and relationships. *Counseling and Values, 38,* 99–111.

Kelly, E. W. (1994). The role of religion and spirituality in counselor education: A national survey. *Counselor Education and Supervision, 33,* 227–237.

Kelly, E. W. (1995). *Spirituality and religion in counseling and psychotherapy: Diversity in theory and practice.* Alexandria, VA : American Counseling Association.

Lovinger, R. J. (1996). Considering the religious dimension in assessment and treatment. In E. P. Shafranske (Ed.), *Religion and the clinical practice of psychology* (pp. 327–364). Washington, DC: American Psychological Association.

Luke, H. (1987). *Old age.* New York: Parabola Books.

Marseille, J. (1997). The spiritual dimension in logotherapy: Viktor Frankl's contribution to transpersonal psychology. *Journal of Transpersonal Psychology, 42,* 55–71.

Maslow, A. H. (1971). *Farther reaches of human nature.* New York: Viking.

McCandless, J. B. (1991). The church confronting adult depression: A challenge. *Counseling and Values, 35,* 104–113.

Miller, G. (1999). The development of the spiritual focus in counseling and counselor education. *Journal of Counseling & Development, 77,* 498–501.

Miller, G. (2003). *Incorporating spirituality in counseling and psychotherapy: Theory and technique.* Hoboken, NJ: Wiley.

O'Connor, M. (2002). Spiritual dark night and psychological depression: Some comparisons and considerations. *Counseling and Values, 46,* 137–148.

Pargament, K. I. (1997). *The psychology of religion and coping.* New York: Guilford Press.

Peterson, E. A., & Nelson, K. (1987). How to meet your clients' spiritual needs. *Journal of psychosocial nursing and mental health services, 25,* 34–39.

Plante, T. G., & Sherman, A. C. (Eds.). (2001). *Faith and health : Psychological perspectives.* New York: Guilford Press.

Prest, L. A., & Keller, J. F. (1993). Spirituality and family therapy: Spiritual beliefs, myths, and metaphors. *Journal of Marital and Family Therapy, 19,* 137–148.

Richards, P. S., & Bergin, A. E. (1997). *A spiritual strategy for counseling and psychotherapy.* Washington, DC: American Psychological Association.

Richards, P. S., & Bergin, A. E. (2001). *Handbook of psychotherapy and religious diversity.* Washington, DC: American Psychological Association.

Roberts, S. A., Kiselica, M. S., & Fredrickson, S. A. (2002). Quality of life of persons with medical illnesses: Counseling's holistic contribution. *Journal of Counseling & Development, 80,* 422–432.

Storr, A. (1997). Commentary on "Spiritual experiences and psychopathology." *Philosophy, Psychiatry, & Psychology, 4,* 83–85.

Sue, D. W., & Sue, D. (2003). *Counseling the culturally diverse: Theory and application* (4th ed.). New York: Wiley.

Thayne, T. R. (1997). Opening space for clients' religious and spiritual values in therapy: A social constructionist perspective. *Journal of Family Social Work, 2*(4), 13–23.

Weil, S. (1951). *Waiting for God.* New York: Putnam.

Westgate, C. E. (1996). Spiritual wellness and depression. *Journal of Counseling & Development, 75,* 26–35.

Wilber, K. (2000). *Grace and grit: Spirituality and healing in the life and death of Treya Killam Wilber.* Boston: Shambhala.

Yalom, I. D. (1995). *The theory and practice of group psychotherapy* (4th ed.). New York: Basic Books.

York, G. Y. (1989). Strategies for managing the religious-based denial of rural clients. *Human Services in the Rural Environment, 13,* 16–22.

Chapter 6

Religious/Spiritual Life Span Development

Geri Miller

Competency: *The professional counselor can describe her or his religious and/or spiritual belief system and explain various models of religious or spiritual development across the life span.*

The religious/spiritual belief system and the development of the individual, be it the client or the counselor, can be difficult to pinpoint and assess. First, what are the beliefs and development, and how does one assess them? This struggle with definition and assessment can be resolved readily and simplistically by "locking on" to one theoretical framework and applying a formula definition of beliefs and development to each individual. The other extreme is to become lost in a sea of definitions and assessment guidelines or instruments. A second difficulty with spiritual beliefs and development assessment is that it is extremely culture-bound. Factors such as gender, age, geography, ethnicity, and health affect one's spiritual development in a complicated, interactive manner. It can be easy to neglect addressing the individual's cultural framework or become lost in the numerous factors involved in that cultural framework.

This chapter attempts to find a balance between these extremes by discussing ways to assess religious/spiritual beliefs and developmental theories within a culturally sensitive structure. The first part of this chapter emphasizes the competency as it relates to counselor self-assessment, specifically examining the impact of one's belief system in treatment settings. The second part of this chapter emphasizes how life span development issues can affect the client's religious/spiritual views. Applied examples and resources are presented at the end of the chapter.

Competency and Self-Assessment of Religious/Spiritual Beliefs

Impact of Beliefs

When counselors assess their religious/spiritual beliefs, they are engaged in a process of coming to know what they believe. This self-knowledge facilitates their identification of these beliefs' impact on their professional behavior. Before discussing ways counselors can identify their concepts, I explore briefly some of our profession's founders' beliefs.

Early in the development of counseling as a practice, science challenged religion for the role of cultural "truth-holder." The works of Freud and others painted religion in a negative view. For example, Freud believed that a mature person would abandon religion (Wulff, 1996) and that the person needed to face the world on his or her own, rather than relying on a god who was based on neurotic projections of the father from childhood (Rizzuto, 1998). Therefore, from Freud's perspective, people needed to accept their fate and believe in science (Rizzuto, 1998). While West (2000) stated that Freud may have needed to take this stance to establish psychoanalysis as a science within the cultural context of his time, Freud and others may have also had their own struggles with religion.

Consider that Freud may serve as an example of the impact of a counselor's personal perspective on developing professional views. Rizzuto (1998) analyzed Freud from a psychodynamic perspective. In this analysis, Rizzuto stated Freud's negative, pessimistic view of religion stemmed from his own personal issues with religion and described Freud as a parentified child in his family of origin who could not depend on his parents psychically, thus resulting in a role reversal of parent and child. Rizzuto proposed that because of this role reversal, Freud's parental projections were played out with his image of God. Therefore, Freud had no choice but to become a "godless Jew," an atheist, as he described himself (Rizzuto, 1998, p. 252). Yet Rizzuto stated, "in spite of his compelling need to reject religion, he could not stop thinking about it" (p. 252). From this view, Freud did with God what he accused others of doing: placing neurotic projections from one's childhood onto God.

This analysis of Freud's religious/spiritual beliefs may cause us to wonder how very differently the counseling profession's perspective on religion may have developed if originators of treatment theory had viewed religion in a positive light rather than a pathological one. The example of Freud emphasizes the importance of examining how a counselor's religious/spiritual views can affect counseling practice. As counselors, we need to assess our religious/spiritual beliefs and then work within our biases (as we would any type of countertransference) to enhance the welfare of the client.

In general, many people do not receive information about religions other than the one in which they were raised (Eck, 2001). Thus, as counselors, our reactions to our clients may come from a relatively narrow knowledge and experience base. Worthington (1989) stated that therapists are generally not as religiously oriented as their clients, and, as a result, their ability to work with religious clients could be hindered by a lack of understanding. Even counselors who have learned about religious or spiritual perspectives other than one(s) within which they were raised or exposed may still have limited perspectives. In addition, counselors may struggle with their own biases given the context of current events and struggle to maintain a neutral therapeutic stance. An example of the latter emerged in my 9/11 disaster mental health counseling work with the American Red Cross at the New York City Pier 94 site. I had a client whisper to me in a crowded lobby, "I am Muslim." That disclosure, depending on my own countertransference on a Muslim client, could have strongly negatively affected my work with the client. By being aware of, and working with, my own reactions, I was able to focus on the client's self-care in the midst of negative stereotypes so prevalent for the client.

Counselors also need to examine how they incorporate spirituality in life span development. Is it one aspect of wellness or is it at the core of wellness? Chandler, Holden, and Kolander (1992) described spirituality as a part of humanness that is natural to all human beings. They stated that spiritual health is at the core of wellness: It exists within the intellectual, physical, emotional, social, and occupational aspects of the person—aspects that interact with and are related to one another. They argued that (a) spiritual health helps people maintain changes they make in their life span development, (b) spiritual wellness is a "balanced openness to or pursuit of spiritual development" (Chandler et al., 1992, p. 172), and (c) spiritual development involves taking spiritual experiences (transcendent experiences that increase knowledge and love) into one's life, resulting in spiritual transformation.

Myers, Sweeney, and Witmer (2000) also viewed spirituality at the core of wellness, which they defined as the highest health and well-being a person can achieve. In their model, they defined spirituality as the core life task wherein there is the awareness of a power that transcends the material and results in a sense of connection with the world. From this core of spirituality emerges the second task of self-direction, which consists of sense of worth, sense of control, realistic beliefs, emotional awareness and coping, problem-solving and creativity, sense of humor, nutrition, exercise, self-care, stress management, gender identity, and cultural identity. These, in turn, are connected to the remaining three life tasks of work and leisure, friendship, and love.

Both theoretical arguments place spirituality at the core of lifestyle development. This perspective stresses the importance of the counselor assessing his or her own spiritual perspective and that of each of his or her clients.

Self-Assessment Perspective

How do we assess ourselves accurately in terms of our religious and spiritual perspectives? First, we need to realize that our own spiritual development is a *spiral* one that is not linear or clearly defined by phases/stages (Tisdell, 2003). The spiral shape of our spiritual development is due to the tendency we have to return to old experiences and make new meaning of them (Tisdell, 2003). In response to this fluid framework, assessment of our religious/spiritual views needs to be ongoing because we both accumulate new knowledge (about ourselves, others, life, religious/spiritual views, etc.) *and* have new experiences as we live. Our views will shift and change as we "spiral back" and make new meaning out of old knowledge or old experiences.

Second, our development is also a fluid one because of interactions between the past, present, and future as it relates to our religious/spiritual views. Our religious/spiritual bias may be based on perspectives we learned in our childhood, affecting how we live in the present and how we move to a more authentic identity in the future (Tisdell, 2003). Examination of our current views requires that we look both at their origins and how these origins affect our present clinical work and potentially our future work.

Third, Tisdell (2003) stated that not only life transitions such as birth and death affect us spiritually, but also dreams and activities involving meditation, nature, art, music, and storytelling can affect us in terms of our thoughts and emotions. Therefore, as we assess ourselves with regard to spiritual/religious views, we need to be aware of how current life transitions and experiences may be causing us to revisit or re-create past experiences that once again affect our present and future thoughts, emotions, and behaviors.

In addition, an assessment of one's own religious/spiritual perspective requires the examination of spiritual beliefs and development within a cultural context. Washburn (2003) stated that gender differences and values connected to the earth are core to examining spiritual perspectives culturally. One's religious/spiritual perspective is inherently embedded within a cultural context because spirituality involves affect, cognition, and unconscious processes that are heavily connected to culture (Tisdell, 2003). Tisdell suggested that projections on to religious/spiritual symbols are connected to cultural memory. Therefore, as we assess ourselves in terms of beliefs and development, we need to use a multicultural framework. One such framework is ADDRESSING (Hays, 2001). In this framework, the acronym breaks down as follows:

> **A**ge and generational influences
> **D**evelopmental and acquired **D**isabilities
> **R**eligion and spiritual orientation
> **E**thnicity
> **S**ocioeconomic status
> **S**exual orientation
> **I**ndigenous heritage
> **N**ational origin
> **G**ender

This framework can be used by the counselor on both self and client as a way of organizing and prioritizing the impact of cultural factors. The counselor can use the following checklist (see Exhibit 6.1) to determine if this area has been, or needs to be, addressed in the assessment, and if so, what needs to be done. Such a checklist would enhance the competency of the counselor by allowing for a culturally sensitive assessment of self and client. While this checklist can be filled out separately for the counselor and client, it can be helpful for the counselor to keep the checklist for self and compare it with each client checklist to examine potential barriers and bridges in the counseling process.

Assessment, then, needs be done with sensitivity to the spiral development of the individual's spirituality: the interaction between the individual's past, present, and future religious/spiritual development, and the impact of life transitions and experiences on the individual's religious/spiritual development. These aspects need to be viewed within the context of the cultural fabric of the individual's life. Conducting an assessment with this sensitivity provides an opportunity for

Exhibit 6.1
Assessment Areas

Assessment Areas	Possible Areas to Be Explored
1. Age and generational influences Age _____	

2. Developmental and acquired Disabilities
    _____Yes: Type: _____
                Originated when:
 	
                Cause: _____
 	
    _____No	

3. Religion and spiritual orientation
    Religion of childhood:
 	
    Current religious affiliation:
 	
    Brief summary of spiritual/religious
    perspective:	

4. Ethnicity:_____	
5. Socioeconomic status: _____	
6. Sexual orientation: _____	
7. Indigenous heritage: _____	
8. National origin: _____	
9. Gender: _____ Male _____ Female	

the counselor to examine with increased clarity his or her biases and counter-transference related to religion and spirituality.

Internal Bias and Countertransference

Miller (2003) discussed how potentially powerful an impact countertransference and internal bias can have on the counseling session. These biases may arise from personal or professional experiences ranging from positive to negative. They can emerge when counselors and clients are from similar or different religious backgrounds or when existential life themes arise in the client's story that are pertinent to the counselor personally.

The assessment process can be affected when the counselor has an extreme focus with regard to religious issues (too much or too little). According to Miller (2003), these issues can emerge in the treatment process when counselors:

- avoid addressing religious concerns,
- [have] negative reactions to the topic of religion,
- [have] positive reactions leading to an urge to "convert" clients, or
- [engage in] inappropriate disclosure or intervention. (p. 27)

Miller (2003) made some suggestions on working with countertransference. First, counselors need to examine any discomfort they feel in themselves when exploring the religious/spiritual dimension with a client in terms of the counselor's own values, philosophy, or spiritual beliefs. Second, the counselor may want to process the discomfort with a trusted colleague or supervisor in the context of the following questions:

1. Can I continue to work with this client given my own countertransference issues?
2. Do I *want* to continue to work with this client?
3. In working with this client, what limits will I set on how I will address this concern in counseling?
4. In working with this client, how much of my own struggles with these religious views do I need to share?
5. If I decide I cannot work with this client, who will I refer the client to for counseling? How will I bring up the referral with the client? (p. 56)

West (2000) recommended that counselors minimize countertransference issues by a variety of means. On a personal note, he suggested that counselors examine their views, positive and negative, about religion and spirituality, experience a religion that is different, and be actively involved in one's own spiritual development. Professionally, he suggested that counselors be familiar with counseling literature related to the topic, be familiar with assessment issues and spiritual development models, learn counseling approaches that implicitly or explicitly involve a religious/spiritual approach, understand how counseling and spirituality are alike and different, and obtain supervision focused on this area.

Life Span Developmental Theories

Examining the religious and spiritual development of the client requires both knowledge and sensitivity, as the following statement by psychoanalyst Erich Lindemann explained:

> These are young people who suddenly have become quite a bit older; they are facing possible death, or serious limitation of their lives; and they will naturally stop and think about life, rather than just live it from day to day. A lot of what they say will be reflective—and you might respond in kind. It would be a mistake, I think, to emphasize unduly a psychiatric

point of view. If there is serious psychopathology, you will respond to it, of course; but if these children want to cry with you, and be disappointed with you, and wonder with you where their God is, then you can be there for them—and help all of us here in the hospital. (in Coles, 1990, p. 101)

While this quote specifically addresses children with serious illness, it has broader application and shows the necessity for the counselor to have knowledge of mental health issues that may be present in a client, yet be able to view these sensitively within the context of the client's stage of life development. All of these developmental factors weave together to create a cultural context of the client's religious/spiritual perspective that require careful, thoughtful assessment. As the above quote so eloquently describes, a client's life situation may significantly impact the client's religious/spiritual life, thereby requiring a sensitive counselor assessment of the client's religious/spiritual development.

Religious/spiritual life span developmental theories have evolved from different theoretical perspectives. These perspectives have served as bridges between spirituality/religion and therapy (Miller, 2003). One theoretical perspective is descriptive, focusing on the inner life of the client to effect change; three individuals who expressed this perspective were James, Jung, and Allport. James (1985) saw religion as core to life, and Jung, responding to James's influence, viewed religious traditions as helping people develop themselves (*Carl Gustav Jung [1875–1961]*, 2001). Until individuals became middle-aged, Jung (1958, 1958/1973) viewed humans as "deeply involved in ego concerns, in rational order, and in logical systems of religion" (Worthington, 1989, p. 567). Upon reaching middle age, Jung believed humans to be more open to religious experiences stemming from a desire for balance and wholeness (Worthington, 1989). Allport (1950) followed Jung's view while adding a humanistic-existential perspective. From Allport's perspective, religion was considered a source of strength to help people effect change. Like James and Jung, Allport saw individuals' religious beliefs as emerging from different needs (companionship, values, meaning) and expressing themselves in different forms. While Allport (1950) stayed with the descriptive perspective, he went further than James and Jung, developing a model of religious sentiments (Worthington, 1989).

Washburn (2003) presented a transpersonal model that encourages a blend between two transpersonal perspectives, *structural-hierarchical* and *spiral-dynamic*, that have at times been at odds with one another. The *structural-hierarchical* perspective has emphasized a hierarchy of abilities and capacities that are organized in a hierarchical fashion. In this view, human beings develop spiritually within basic structures. By contrast, the *spiral-dynamic* perspective looks at submerged life forces that can emerge at a higher level. Washburn (2003) argued that both are important to the spiritual perspective and are both needed to understand overall development. Yet, Washburn stated that the *spiral-dynamic* perspective, with which he most closely aligned, does better at describing transcendence. In this perspective, the dynamic potential of the individual is not locked to a specific stage but is present during development and can emerge at developmental points resulting in a transformation of the individual. These dynamic potentials are critical throughout life and unfold in a spiral path so that the whole psyche becomes integrated.

Five models (Allport, Piaget, Rizzuto, Erikson, and Fowler) are briefly summarized in this section. While these models are helpful to describe an individual's stage of personal growth, it is important to remember that people do not develop spiritually in a linear fashion but, as mentioned before, in a spiral fashion. Therefore, while the models can be used to understand someone's developmental stage, the counselor needs to make a stage-level "diagnosis" with a great amount of flexibility. Although each of these models involves both the individual and others to some degree, they are organized in terms of an emphasis on the individual (Allport and Piaget) or the individual-in-relation to others (Rizzuto, Erikson, and Fowler).

Individual Emphasis

Allport's Religious Sentiment Stage Model

Worthington (1989) described Allport's three-stage model of religious sentiments (emotions affected religious beliefs, which affected behavior). The three stages were (a) believing what we are told, (b) doubting what we have been told, and (c) living with the ambiguity of what we have been told (a fluctuation between faith and doubt). Mature faith involves more faith than doubt. Allport assessed religious maturity in the individual in terms of these components: well-differentiated, dynamic, directive, comprehensive, integral, and heuristic. Kelly (1995) summarized Allport's theory of the mature religious person as follows:

> *Well-differentiated*: Religious views are based on a cognitively critical process of knowledge and experience that become organized into a religious framework.
> *Dynamic*: Religion has helped with personal and social development.
> *Directive*: The person's actions match their beliefs in caring for others.
> *Comprehensive*: The person has the tendency to address the meaning of life.
> *Integral*: Science information and humanity harms are taken in by the person.
> *Heuristic*: The person can change views and develop as new information or experience requires integration.

The counselor can use this developmental model to determine both the client's level and type of religious maturity of the client. Such an assessment can assist the counselor in understanding the relative strengths and weaknesses of the client's religious/spiritual development resources in addressing their life struggle(s). For example, the counselor may see the client as struggling with the comprehensive aspect as it relates to his or her career ("What is the meaning of my life's work?") and yet being very strong in the directive aspect because he or she has chosen work that reflects caring for others (e.g., being a minister). In counseling, the counselor may view the comprehensive dimension as an area of vulnerability that needs to be addressed while drawing on the strength of the directive component.

Piaget's Cognitive-Development Stage Model

Religious aspects of the individual evolve as cognitive abilities develop (Worthington, 1989). Elkind's (1970, 1978) work on cognitive development is summarized by Kelly (1995) as follows:

> Piagetian theory forms a basis for understanding how object permanence,
> symbolic representation, logical thinking, and formal operational thought
> are involved in increasingly advanced cognitive abilities for representing
> the presence of an unseen God, symbolizing objects of faith, thinking
> about religious questions, and conceptualizing the complex interactions
> between religious faith and life experiences. (p. 68)

These cognitive-development stages and their related spiritual focus can be
organized as follows (Worthington 1989): object permanence (infancy—presence of an unseen God), symbolic representation (early childhood—symboliz-
ing objects of faith), logical thinking (late childhood—thinking about religious
questions), and formal operational thought (adolescence—conceptualizing the
complex interactions between religious faith and life experiences).

The counselor assessing the client's religious/spiritual development needs to
assess the cognitive development of the client. While these stages are formatted
here within the context of age (infant, late childhood, adolescence), the counselor can potentially use these stages flexibly to better understand the individual's
cognitive development in relation to religious/spiritual beliefs. For example, a
client may be middle-aged and yet struggling with religious/spiritual questions
that are more representative of late childhood cognitive development. With this
client, the counselor may need to realize the cognitive aspect of the religious/
spiritual beliefs that may be affecting the life struggle issues(s) of the client. For
example, the client may be 45 years old and yet grappling with basic questions of
her religion (e.g., "Do I need to attend church each Sunday in order to be a
good servant of God?") and not addressing religious concerns that might be
more "age-appropriate" in attempting to apply her religious views to her life.

Individual-in-Relation to Others

Object Relations

Rizzuto (1979) examined development from an object-relations perspective.
Here the relationship to an object is based on the client's inner perspective.
How does the object meet the need of the client? Once this object is incorporated into the individual, it is called an *introject*. Rizzuto's view was that one's
perception of God was a reflection of primary introjects. The person's perception of God, then, was the "amalgation of the mental models of his or her
primary attachment figures" (Hall & Gorman, 2003, p. 2). Therefore, Western individuals each have a picture of God regardless of their belief because
they have had some attachment figures who represent God for them. It is
possible this perception of God could then change as the individual absorbed
new experiences or the attachment figures are viewed differently. An extension
of this view is presented by Hall, Brokaw, Edwards, and Pike (1998), who
suggested that one's relationship with God is a reflection of one's relationships
with other human beings.

The counselor can use the theory of object relations as it relates to perceptions of God and how that plays out in relationships with others. By understanding the client's view of God or view of his or her primary attachment
figures, the counselor can understand the other. For example, by coming to
understand the client's view of the relationship with his or her parents, the

counselor can form a tentative hypothesis of how the client views his or her relationship with God and how these relational perspectives evidence themselves in the client's relationship with others. An understanding of these projections by the client on God and others can facilitate the counselor's understanding on when and how to intervene on the life struggle(s) of the client.

Erikson's Psychosocial Stage Model

Erikson (1964, 1968) also examined the roles religion can play in human development. These roles, as summarized by Kelly (1995), are

- Fostering a faith that supports a child's sense of trust and hope, in contrast to religious faith that instills fear.
- Building up a system (ideology) of values, sometimes manifested in religious tradition, that adolescents may relate to in their expanding search for personal identity.
- Promoting a sense of universalism to undergird the generative care of adulthood.
- Contributing to older adults' formulation of a mature sense of the meaningful and integral wholeness of life. (p. 69)

The counselor can use the understanding of these four roles of religion in a client's life to determine how religious/spiritual frameworks are strengths or weaknesses for the client in addressing counseling issues. Specifically, what is the role of faith, values, universality, and meaning in the client's life as it relates to religious/spiritual concerns?

Worthington (1989) reviewed how Erikson's theory applies to religious development. He indicated that the stages of psychosocial development can assist us, as counselors, in seeing how religious themes can merge with developmental stages, such as formation of identity, intimacy, growth/decline, and moral development. Worthington's application of these psychosocial stages to religious/spiritual development are in italics: Trust versus Mistrust (first year of life, *the basis of faith is the development of hope*), Autonomy versus Shame and Doubt (1–3 years, *a healthy ego develops*), Initiative versus Guilt (3–6 years, *a sense of purpose is present*), Industry versus Inferiority (6–12 years, *a sense of adequacy develops*), Identity versus Role Confusion (12–18 years, *commitment to faith is possible*), Intimacy versus Isolation (18–35 years, *self-imperfections are faced and self-forgiveness experienced*), Generativity versus Stagnation (35–55 years, *increased altruism and religious legacy*), and Integrity versus Despair (65 years to death, *life is present-focused and future-hopeful*).

The counselor can use these stages of development to determine what a client may be facing in terms of his or her life struggle(s). For example, a 65-year-old client may look at a past choice, such as an extramarital affair, with a religious/spiritual focus that is more present-based than a 30-year-old client addressing the same life struggle in therapy from a perspective of self-forgiveness.

Fowler's Stages-of-Faith Model

Fowler (1981, 1991) developed a stages-of-faith model that can assist the counselor in understanding an individual's religious/spiritual development stage. Fowler described the following six stages of faith (as cited in Miller, 2003, pp. 141–142).

Intuitive-projective (3–7 years): This stage focuses on imagination when the child can be affected by the faith of adults around them. Fowler described this stage as one filled with fantasy and imitation that is uninhibited by logic. At this stage, adults can influence the child's spiritual development through example, mood, action, and story. The imagination can result in feelings and images that last a long time. For example, death, sex, and taboos related to them first come into the child's awareness at this stage.

Mythical-literal (7 to puberty): This stage is when the person takes in the beliefs and symbols of their religious community in a literal way. Symbols are taken literally here. An order is placed on the imagination of the previous stage resulting in a linear, coherent story that provides a child with meaning. Drama and myth give the understanding to the experience, and there is an emphasis on reciprocity and justice.

Synthetic-conventional (puberty to adulthood): The person is involved in interpersonal faith but tends to conform to beliefs and values of their community with an emphasis on authority. Here the experience expands from family to include school/work, peers, and religion. Faith unifies one's values and information resulting in a sense of identity and perspective. Here the person is affected by others' expectations/judgments but does not have an independent view. Beliefs and values have not been reflected on or examined in depth.

Individuative-reflective (young adulthood): There is more personification of beliefs, symbols, and meanings, and one is committed to these meanings. The person becomes responsible for his or her own views and ways of living by facing tensions such as being an individual or being defined by belonging to a group. Symbols become translated into meaning where the self and perspective are deeper.

Conjunctive: A person tries to integrate opposites, sees a community that is inclusive, and exerts self in conjunction with beliefs. One reclaims and reworks oneself by listening to the deep voices of self-recognition of the social unconscious. Self and perspective are more open to change because of the awareness of paradox and contradiction while the individual attempts to unify opposites.

Universalizing: The focus is on loving others at a universal level and goes beyond one's specific faith. These people are generous, free, loved, actualized, trusting of the future, and trying to make the spiritual present in the present moment.

By determining the client's stage of faith, the counselor can understand what issues are related between the life struggle(s) and religious/spiritual perspective in terms of strengths and weaknesses. For example, a common problem in the young adulthood phase involves struggling with the meaninglessness of life and how religious/spiritual practices no longer provide the meaning they once did.

Use of the Models

The counselor can use these developmental models to determine a client's stage of general spiritual development (use Exhibit 6.2 as a tool for applying these models). Worthington (1989) stated that stage development theories are useful with children but that one ought to be aware that the religious development of adolescents and adults may be better described by the use of transitional or crisis models.

Another consideration is for the counselor to use these developmental models in a flexible manner within a cultural context. For example, Tisdell (2003)

Exhibit 6.2
Five Theories and Stages of Development

Theory and Stage of Development	Notes
Allport's mature religious characteristics	
Dynamic	
Directive	
Comprehensive	
Integral	
Heuristic	
Well-differentiated	
Piaget	
Object permanence	
Symbolic representation	
Logical thinking	
Formal operational thought	
Rizzuto	
View of God	
View of attachment figures	
Impact on relationships	
Erikson	
Trust vs. mistrust	
Autonomy vs. shame & doubt	
Initiative vs. guilt	
Industry vs. inferiority	
Identity vs. role confusion	
Intimacy vs. isolation	
Generativity vs. stagnation	
Integrity vs. despair	
Fowler	
Intuitive-projective (3–7 years)	
Mythical-literal (7–puberty)	
Synthetic-conventional (puberty to adult)	
Individuative-reflective (young adult)	
Conjunctive	
Universalizing	

focused on the last four stages of Fowler's model from a spiral development perspective within a cultural context. During adolescence (Stage 3), it is normal for people to question their faith, and this questioning can continue into adulthood. In this process, people may leave their childhood religion either temporarily or permanently. For example, life experiences, such as realizing one is gay or lesbian, might facilitate such a change.

Worthington (1989) outlined life span religious issues that individuals may experience. In childhood, the individual has to deal with death, self-discipline, development of a God image, and school interactions. During adolescence the person faces issues with identity, sex, and alcohol/drug use. In young adulthood, issues emerge in relation to work, being single or married, and being a parent. Middle adulthood brings issues around themes of personal power/career, care/family, and inferiority/personal reflection. Finally, older adulthood incorporates factors such as retirement, autonomy, and death. The counselor can use these issues in a developmental religious/spiritual assessment with regard to stages of life. Transitions, particularly during adolescence and adulthood, may need to be carefully assessed for the presence of these issues. How the transitions "play out" with regard to religious/spiritual practice will vary in relation to the type of transition, the individual, and the meaning of that transition for the individual within his or her cultural context.

Tisdell (2003) pointed out that even people who choose not to return to their formative religion may use certain familiar rituals during critical transitional times. For example, they may find comfort and meaning in a religious ritual for death even though they do not practice their religion in its entirety. Tisnell proposed that this tendency is because it is a part of their cultural identity. A person may spiral back to attain one of these aspects during a developmental process. Such a developmental spiraling back may be a result of what Marty (2000) described as five common characteristics of religions: (a) focus on life's meaning and purpose, (b) provide a sense of community, (c) provide guidelines on how to live, (d) find truth through myth and symbol, or (e) use rituals and ceremonies to assist with life transitions. Individuals may be drawn to a religion as a result of their stage of religious/spiritual development or their transitional life experiences, attempting to match the characteristics of the religion with the need they are experiencing.

Assessing with a sensitivity to the context of cultural characteristics is difficult because there is a need for measures to be more culturally sensitive (Hill & Pargament, 2003). However, until sensitive measures can be implemented, the counselor can use a framework such as ADDRESSING (discussed earlier) to best assist assessment and treatment of the client.

These five models provide the counselor with a qualitative, flexible assessment approach to the religious/spiritual development of the client. This approach can assist the counselor in accurately evaluating the area of the problem that overlaps between a client's life struggle(s) and his or her religious/spiritual views. An accurate assessment (as discussed more fully in chap. 8) facilitates the determination of effective intervention. The counselor, then, by understanding the client's religious/spiritual development, can facilitate healing in the client. In turn, the counselor can use the same approach, as discussed earlier in this chapter, to increase the effectiveness of therapy.

Case Studies

Case Study 1

The counselor has a client who uses language rich in Judeo-Christian terminology (i.e., "miracle," "heaven/hell," "baptized by fire"), yet they have never discussed the religious/spiritual views of the client. The client's presenting problem has been a concern, in midlife, over death issues. The client recently lost several friends and family members through both unexpected and expected deaths. The counselor is concerned about raising the topic of religion/spirituality because the counselor typically does not do so in sessions and is currently facing some health concerns and dealing with aging parents. You may wish to discuss the following questions with another counselor or counselor-in-training:

1. Should the counselor bring up the religious/spiritual perspective in session?
2. If you believe the counselor should, how would you recommend that he or she prepare to raise such concerns in terms of consultation with other professionals and personal processing of the countertransference?
3. What countertransference issues do you see arising in this situation?
4. What would you recommend the counselor do in the future to minimize possible countertransference?

Case Study 2

A client comes to counseling who is 45 years old, female, and recently diagnosed with breast cancer. She is an African American client who had been having marital problems for the last 2 years of her 10-year, second marriage. She has three children who live with her and who have no contact with their birth father. Her second husband has adopted the children. She is a devout Christian and tells you that faith has sustained her for many years, but since her recent diagnosis, she has felt a loss of connection with God.

Answer the following questions:

1. Which model might you find most helpful in your work with her?
2. Where might you diagnose her with the developmental models?
3. How might you use the ADDRESSING framework in your work with her?

Recommended Reading

Fukuyama, M. A., & Sevig, T. D. (1999). *Integrating spirituality into multicultural counseling.* London: Sage.
> This book provides an overall perspective on the incorporation of spirituality within a multicultural context.

Hays, P. (2001). *Addressing cultural complexities in practice: A framework for clinicians and counselors.* Washington, DC: American Psychological Association.
> This book elaborates on the framework of ADDRESSING, which can be used to ensure that multicultural complexities are addressed in the counseling process.

Miller, G. (2003). *Incorporating spirituality in counseling and psychotherapy: Theory and technique.* Hoboken, NJ: Wiley.
> This book provides specific exercises throughout the text that can be used by counselors to examine their religious/spiritual beliefs. In addition, there are exercises that focus on assessment and treatment with cultural sensitivity.

West, W. (2000). *Psychotherapy and spirituality.* Thousand Oaks, CA: Sage.
> This book provides overall suggestions for the incorporation of spirituality in counseling and has excellent suggestions for reducing bias and countertransference.

Worthington, E. L. (1989). Religious faith across the life span: Implications for counseling and research. *The Counseling Psychologist, 17,* 555–612.
This article is an overview of different developmental theories with an emphasis on developmental issues from a religious perspective.

Zinnbauer, B. J., & Pargament, K. I. (2000). Working with the sacred: Four approaches to religious and spiritual issues in counseling. *Journal of Counseling & Development, 78,* 162–171.
This article provides four orientations that can assist the counselor in finding an effective approach to cross-cultural counseling.

Web Sites of Interest

The following are Web sites that may assist a counselor in expanding his or her knowledge of different religions:

Judaism
http://www.zipple.com
http://www.4judaism.4anything.com/
http://www.jewsforjudaism.org

Christian Based
http://www.christianitytoday.com
http://www.suite101.com/welcome.cfm/christian_women
http://www.christianity.net.au

Church of Jesus Christ of Latter-Day Saints (Mormons)
http://www.mormons.org
http://www.lds.org

Jehovah's Witness
http://www.jehovahs-witness.com
http://www.watchtower.org
http://www.jw-media.org

Black Christian Churches
http://www.churchfolk.com
http://www.ame-today.com

African American Islam
http://www.noi.org
http://www.geocities.com/mikailtariq
http://www.islam.org/mosque/Intro_Islam.htm

Islam
http://www.islamworld.net
http://www.addawah.com
http://www.isprin.com

Zoroastrianism
http://www.zoroastrianism.com

Sikhism

http://www.sikhs.org
http://www.sikhnet.com
http://www.srigurugranthsahib.org

Native American Religions

http://www.native-american-online.org
http://www.press-on.net

Hinduism

http://www.indiadivine.com

Shintoism

http://www.jinja.or.jp/english/index.html
http://www.egroups.com/group/shintoml

Jainism

http://www.jainnet.com
http://www.jainsamaj.org
http://www.jainworld.com

Buddhism

http://www.tricycle.com
http://www.livingdharma.org/index.html
http://www.members.tripod.com/~lhamo

Confucianism

http://www.thespiritualsanctuary.org/Confucianism/Confucianism.html
http://www.chineseculture.about.com

Taoism

http://www.taorestore.org
http://www.clas.ufl.edu/users/gthursby/taoism/index.htm

Summary

The purpose of this chapter has been to highlight the importance of understanding self and others as religious and/or spiritual beings from a developmental framework. The highlight of the chapter has been a summary and overview of five major models of spiritual or religious development and, in some instances, comparisons between these developmental models. Case studies are provided to encourage further exploration and reflection.

References

Allport, G. W. (1950). *The individual and his religion: A psychological interpretation*. New York: Macmillan.

Carl Gustav Jung (1875–1961). (2001). Retrieved November 29, 2001, from http://www.kirjasto.sci.fi/cjung.htm

Chandler, C. K., Holden, J. M., & Kolander, C. A. (1992). Counseling for spiritual wellness: Theory and practice. *Journal of Counseling & Development, 71,* 168–175.

Coles, R. (1990). *The spiritual life of children*. Boston: Harper/Collins.

Eck, D. (2001). *A new religious America*. San Francisco: Harper.

Elkind, D. (1970). The origins of religion in the child. *Review of Religious Research, 12,* 35–42.

Elkind, D. (1978). *The child's reality: Three developmental themes*. Hillsdale, NJ: Erlbaum.

Erikson, E. H. (1964). *Insight and responsibility*. New York: Norton.

Erikson, E. H. (1968). *Identity: Youth and crisis*. New York: Norton.

Fowler, J. W. (1981). *Stages of faith*. New York: HarperCollins.

Fowler, J. W. (1991). Stages in faith consciousness [Special issue: Religious development in childhood and adolescence]. *New Directions for Child Development, 52,* 27–45.

Hall, T. W., Brokaw, B. F., Edwards, K. J., & Pike, P. L. (1998). An empirical exploration of psychoanalysis and religion: Spiritual maturity and object relations development. *Journal for the Scientific Study of Religion, 37,* 305–315.

Hall, T. W., & Gorman, M. (2003, August). Relational spirituality: Implications of the convergence of attachment theory, interpersonal neurobiology, and emotional information processing. *Psychology of Religion Newsletter,* 1–12. (Reprint of paper presented at the 110th Annual Convention of the American Psychological Association, Chicago, IL)

Hays, P. (2001). *Addressing cultural complexities in practice: A framework for clinicians and counselors*. Washington, DC: American Psychological Association.

Hill, P. C., & Pargament, K. I. (2003). Advances in the conceptualization and measurement of religion and spirituality: Implications for physical and mental health research. *American Psychologist, 58,* 64–74.

James, W. (1985). *The varieties of religious experience: A study in human nature*. Cambridge, MA: Harvard University Press. (Original work published 1902)

Jung, C. G. (1958). *The undiscovered self* (R. F. C. Hull, Trans.). New York: Mentor Books.

Jung, C. G. (1973). *Answer to Job* (R. F. C. Hull, Trans.). London: Routledge & Kegan Paul. (Original work published 1958)

Kelly, E. W. (1995). *Spirituality and religion in counseling and psychotherapy: Diversity in theory and practice*. Alexandria, VA: American Counseling Association.

Marty, M. M. (2000). *Education, religion, and the common good*. San Francisco: Jossey-Bass.

Miller, G. (2003). *Incorporating spirituality in counseling and psychotherapy: Theory and technique*. Hoboken, NJ: Wiley.

Myers, J. E., Sweeney, T. J., & Witmer, J. M. (2000). The wheel of wellness counseling for wellness: A holistic model for treatment planning. *Journal of Counseling & Development, 78,* 251–266.

Rizzuto, A. M. (1979). *The birth of the living god*. Chicago: University of Chicago Press.

Rizzuto, A. M. (1998). *Why did Freud reject God?* New Haven, CT: Yale University Press.

Tisdell, E. J. (2003). *Exploring spirituality and culture in adult and higher education*. San Francisco: Jossey-Bass.

Washburn, M. (2003). Transpersonal dialogue: A new direction. *Journal of Transpersonal Psychology, 35,* 1–19.

West, W. (2000). *Psychotherapy and spirituality.* Thousand Oaks, CA: Sage.

Worthington, E. L. (1989). Religious faith across the life span: Implications for counseling and research. *The Counseling Psychologist, 17,* 555–612.

Wullf, D. M. (1996). The psychology of religion: An overview. In E. P. Shafranske (Ed.), *Religion and the clinical practice of psychology* (pp. 71–112). Washington, DC: American Psychological Association.

Chapter 7

Religion and Spirituality in a Cultural Context

Mary A. Fukuyama, Farhad Siahpoush, and Todd D. Sevig

Competency: *The professional counselor can describe religious and spiritual beliefs and practices in a cultural context.*

We know very little about the mysteries of the human soul.
—Imman Bilal Hyde
(personal communication, July 26, 2003)

$\mathcal{W}$e welcome the opportunity to contribute to this timely compilation of knowledge related to developing competencies in counseling with spiritual and religious values. Although it is a topic to which we have devoted much thought and energy, it is also an area that challenges us at a deep level. We want to be accurate in our approach to this topic and, at the same time, respectfully acknowledge that there is much that we do not know. The question of how to discuss the mystery of religion and spirituality and the complexity of culture in a concise and comprehensive way is the task to which we set ourselves in this chapter.

We conceptualize religion, spirituality, and culture as intertwined and interrelated. Religion and spirituality exist within cultures, and it is likely that few cultures exist without some expressions of religion and spirituality. One way to imagine the interrelationships of religion, spirituality, and culture is to see them as overlapping circles. In some cases, the overlap of the three may be minimal, and in some cases, there may be only one circle (e.g., the Island of Bali is seen as a spiritually and religiously infused culture).

We propose a metaphor to help understand the connections between religion, spirituality, and culture. Artress (1995) suggested that religion is a container and spirituality the essences held within. Using this metaphor, we visualize a vessel holding water, resting on the earth. The vessel represents religion, the water spirituality, and the earth the surrounding culture—and people (individuals and groups) comprise all three.

In this metaphor, we suggest that the earth provides a foundation for cultural expressions of religion and spirituality. The boundary between the vessel of religion and the larger culture, however, has various degrees of permeability and interchange. One might imagine that an ecological system exists, such as in nature, with each contributing to the other, like clouds, rain, and the ocean. The shape and designs of the vessel may reflect cultural and religious nuances (e.g., places of worship have various architectural styles, such as a Protestant church steeple or the Tori gate of a Shinto shrine). In addition, the experiences and expressions of spirituality (the essences held within) may take on varying dimensions of color, texture, and sensual qualities mediated by cultural beliefs and practices (e.g., incense burning at a Buddhist temple; the excitement of gospel music from an African American church).

We view religion and spirituality through a multicultural or pluralistic lens, that is, many or multiple worldviews that include universal concepts. Our focus is primarily on the religious and cultural diversity found in the United States, which is admittedly quite vast. Religious pluralism has increased through immigration patterns over the past 100 years (Hoge, 1996), and contemporary figures would place the number of religious groups in the United States at over 2,100 (Creedon, 1998).

We see the United States as a nation built on *both* religious and cultural diversity. The United States was founded originally by seekers of religious freedom. The separation of church and state was an important principle to avoid the imposition of one church or religion over all others, as was the case in England. Another principle at play in the 1700s was a focus on religious diversity. But, at that time, diversity meant different forms of Protestantism. Over the past 250 years, however, the United States has not "caught up" with the heavy influence of immigrants' religious and spiritual traditions. There remains a strong emphasis on Protestantism in American cultural norms. Thus, tensions have developed without a "template" in which to incorporate an expanded sense of religious and cultural diversity.

The purpose of this chapter is to elucidate a discussion of religion and spirituality by taking cross-cultural and multicultural perspectives. We propose to do the following: (a) highlight key words—religion, cult, spirituality, culture, and worldview; (b) present several universal approaches to understanding culture and religion; (c) explore religion as cultural diversity, including culture-specific examples; (d) discuss dimensions of power and privilege that affect engagement on religious/spiritual/multicultural issues; (e) propose that multicultural and spiritual values are synergistic for multicultural and spiritual growth; and (f) conclude with implications for counseling and training.

Definitions

In this section, we highlight definitions of key words: religion, cult, spirituality, culture, and worldview. In addition, we refer the reader to chapter 2 (Competency 1) for comprehensive descriptions of religion and spirituality.

Religion

Paul Tillich (1964) described religion as the depth dimension of human existence:

> Religion is the aspect of depth in the totality of human spirit. . . . [This] means that religious aspects point to that which is ultimate, infinite, unconscious in man's [*sic*] spiritual life. Religion, in the largest and most basic sense of the word, is ultimate concern. (p. 7)

In addition, religion is viewed as a social institution. Holm (1977) described religion as made of seven elements: belonging, belief, worship, festivals, rites and customs, sacred writings, and codes of ethics. Swindler and Mojzes (2000) provided a definition that encompassed the "four C's": creed, code, cult, and community. Their description follows:

> Religion is an explanation (creed) of the ultimate meaning of life and how to live (code and community structure) accordingly, which is based on the notion of the transcendent with whom the believers have a relationship (cult). Because religion is an explanation of the ultimate meaning of life, it provides a code of behavior in the fullest possible sense, including all the psychological, social, and cultural dimensions of human life, and is hence a way of life for humans. The way of life that religion tries to provide is not, however, just a more or less acceptable way of life. It is an attempt, on the basis of its "explanation" and experience, to put forth the best way of life. (p. 41)

Religiousness has been described as having an intrinsic or extrinsic orientation (Allport & Ross, 1967). Individuals who are intrinsically oriented see religious activities as an end in itself and may incorporate religion on a daily basis. Those who are extrinsic in their orientation use religion or religious affiliation as a means to other ends such as social status or personal gratification.

It is clear that these definitions of religion are comprehensive and inclusive. It would be difficult to separate culture from a religiously identified person. Religion is woven into cultural identities, ethnicity, and group memberships, and it significantly contributes to the phenomenon known as ethnocentrism, that is, the belief that one's cultural view is the *right* one. Although religion has been important for nurturing a spiritual life, increasing numbers of Americans are claiming spirituality outside of organized religion (Chandler, Holden, & Kolander, 1992).

Cult

According to Webster's dictionary, the Latin roots of *cult* mean "to cultivate" and "to worship"; thus, cult refers to "a community or system of religious worship and ritual" (*Webster's II New Riverside University Dictionary*, 1988, p. 335). However, this word has been used pejoratively to cast dispersion on religious groups that are "different from the mainstream." This phenomenon has been described by other terms, such as new religious movements (see http://religiousmovements.lib.virginia.edu), marginal religions, intense group belief systems (see Kelly, 1995), and charismatic group psychology (Galanter, 1996). Kelly (1995) summarized the characteristics of cults as follows.

> Typical characteristics of most cults are intensely shared and bonding beliefs, often involving religious expectations about a dramatic world change, and a high degree of group cohesiveness and social regimentation within an authoritarian structure, headed by a charismatic leader and requiring members' sharp separation from nongroup members. (p. 24)

Although there are troubling psychological processes that can be attributed to cults, it is important to consider the positive and negative effects overall for participation in any religious group. A process of discernment is needed to understand if participation in religious activities is nourishing or damaging to the person.

Spirituality

Some of the dimensions that have been identified as spiritual in the counseling literature range from esoteric mysticism to matters of everyday living. Other authors have emphasized certain spiritual values, including meaning and purpose in life, a sense of mission and goals, awareness of the sacred, helping others, and striving toward making the world better (Elkins, Hedstrom, Hughes, Leaf, & Saunders, 1988). We also acknowledge the definition of spirituality provided by the Association for Spiritual, Ethical, and Religious Values in Counseling (as defined in chap. 2, p. 13) as comprehensive and useful for counselors.

Culture

Culture has been described as "patterns of beliefs, behaviors, and values that are maintained by a group of interacting people" (see video lecture by Bennett, 1996). Culture may be described as being both objective and subjective. Objective culture refers to institutions, systems, artifacts, kinship, and knowledge; subjective culture refers to behavior, communication styles, verbal and nonverbal competencies, and cultural values. Intercultural communication experts cite the cultural context as an important variable for understanding one another. A high-context culture relies heavily on the context for meaning, whereas a low-context culture (like the United States) relies primarily on words. Cross-cultural misunderstandings frequently occur between people who represent this cultural difference, that is, what is said verbally versus what is implied in the communication by contextual factors (see Stewart & Bennett, 1991).

Everyone has culture, and cultural identities include such sociodemographic features as race/ethnicity, language, religion, social class, physical abilities, sexual orientation, age, nationality, and more. The trend in multicultural counseling training is to focus on race and ethnicity as the defining variable in culture (such as Asian Americans, Euro Americans, African Americans, etc.); however, culture can be understood in many other ways.

Jackson and Vontress (2003) suggested that culture is defined by four core variables: biology (universal aspects of being a human), ecology (the environment), nation (laws, customs, country), and region. They cautioned counselors-in-training not to stereotype clients on the basis of race/ethnic cultural generalizations. The same could be said about overgeneralizing on the basis of religion. A cultural generalization is a "hypothesis of probability to be like the mainstream of a group," whereas a stereotype is applying a cultural generalization to all members of a group (Bennett, 1996). Thus, counselors are encouraged to "check out" their hypotheses rather than make assumptions.

Worldview

Religion and spirituality fit quite naturally into the concept of worldview. *Worldview* is a term widely used in the multicultural counseling literature as a way of describing how individuals or groups organize complex cultural information. Worldviews are composed of attitudes, values, opinions, concepts, and philosophies of life construed through the lenses of our cultural upbringing. Stated more broadly, worldview is "how a person perceives his/her relationship to the world (nature, institutions, other people)" (Sue & Sue, 1990, p. 137).

Universal Approaches to Understanding Culture and Religion

From anthropology, the study of culture entails both universal (etic) and culture-specific (emic) approaches. These approaches have been discussed in application to multicultural counseling (Fukuyama, 1990; Locke, 1990), and we include both perspectives in this chapter. Similarly, Holm (1977) suggested that there are two approaches to the study of religion. The first is living in the culture of a particular religion and getting detailed knowledge about it; the second is a comparative, cross-cultural approach. However, by studying only one religion the individual may get an incomplete picture of other religions. According to Holm (1977, p. 2), for example, "Christians think that religion necessarily involves a belief in a Supreme Being, a form of congregational worship and a set of creedal statements. Theravada Buddhism is one religion that does not conform to this pattern."

The Kluckhohn Model

One universal approach to culture borrowed from anthropology is the Kluckhohn model for worldviews. This approach provides a structure for understanding values and a way to conceptualize religious and spiritual practices within a cultural context (Ibrahim, 1985, 2003; Kluckhohn & Strodtbeck, 1961). While *all* cultures have *all* of the values suggested by this model, each culture *emphasizes* different dimensions of these values. These values dimensions are not an either-or choice; they exist on a continuum.

The five values dimensions found in the Kluckhohn model are (a) *human nature* (humans may be good, bad, mixed, and this may or may not be changeable—mutable or immutable), (b) *relation of humans to nature* (humans are subjugated by, in harmony with, or have mastery over nature), (c) *activity orientation* (life is oriented around doing, being, or becoming), (d) *time orientation* (the focus is on the past, present, or future), and (e) *relational* (the emphasis is on the individual or group, which may be collateral or lineal). These five dimensions may be used in analyzing the subcultures of specific religious groups. Each dimension is discussed further and applied to selected religious/spiritual phenomena.

The first dimension, *human nature*, is included in many theological belief systems. For example, some conservative or traditional Christian religions emphasize "original sin"; that is, humans are born "bad" or in need of salvation. Other interpretations of Christian tenets have emphasized that humans are born essentially "good" or with "original blessing" (see Fox, 1983). Religions often explore conflicts between good and evil or the human journey toward wholeness or enlightenment.

The second dimension, *relation of humans to nature*, provides a framework for conceptualizing spiritual beliefs in relation to both the natural and supernatural worlds. It can also be used to describe a dimension of locus of control, or empowerment. For example, "it's in God's hands" defers decision making to a Higher Power. In another example, the *Santeria* tradition, a person might believe that gods and goddesses influence all of life's actions and that prayer and sacrifices are necessary to ensure harmonious relationships (Gonzalez-Wippler, 1992; Nunez, 1995).

The third dimension, *activity orientation*, also reflects both cultural and religious values and beliefs. Calvinism (early Protestant Christian) emphasized good works or "doing" as an avenue to God. Some Hindu yoga traditions view physical labor as a means to higher spiritual consciousness. Other traditions may emphasize being in the present moment as the way to enlightenment (Buddhism). New Age spirituality focuses on the "becoming" or personal growth aspect of spiritual development.

The fourth dimension, *time orientation*, also reflects cultural and religious values. For some faith traditions, ancestor worship may be important (West African Yoruba or Shinto, an indigenous Japanese tradition), whereas others may focus on future salvation over present-moment concerns.

The fifth dimension, which focuses on interpersonal *relationships*, may emphasize the individual over the group (individual salvation) or may emphasize the importance of communal worship and community service.

Often these dimensions are expressed in a variety of ways within groups, as demonstrated by the following culture-specific examples (again, we caution against overgeneralizing from this information; these descriptions are for "flavor"). (a) Puerto Rican elders may emphasize service to others, communal worship, participation in rituals, and devotion as important to their spiritual practices. (b) Native American spiritually focused individuals may emphasize communion and relationships with all aspects of nature (animals, plants, minerals, rivers, and mountains). (c) Fundamentalist Christians may be concerned with individual salvation and the life hereafter. (d) Vipassana Buddhist practitioners may be focused on developing consciousness through meditation, with an emphasis on present-moment awareness.

The Western-trained counselor is likely to hold a worldview that emphasizes mastery, doing, future time orientation, and individualism (Katz, 1985). It is important for the multicultural counselor to be able to understand clients' worldviews, in particular clients' beliefs around spirituality (i.e., belief in higher power), their relationship to the supernatural or transcendent, and their religious histories.

We suggest that spirituality alludes to universal qualities and religion refers to the culture-specific expressions of spirit. However, religion is both culture specific (e.g., Mexican Catholic) and extends beyond specific cultural boundaries (e.g., universal Catholic), which is referred to as being *transcultural*. Religion is one of many ways in which culture is embodied and transmitted, and it also embodies values and traditions that transcend cultural boundaries. For instance, one of the reasons Protestant Christianity is becoming popular in Africa is that it provides social support for people as they migrate from country to country looking for work. In another example, although Judaism has heritage, language, and rituals that connect people throughout the globe (transcultural), a 20-year-old Jewish woman in Miami may have little in common *culturally* with a 20-year-old Jewish woman from the Ukraine.

The Perennial Philosophy: A Universal Approach to Religion

Just as we are interested in the commonalties between cultures, we want to explore the commonalities found between world religions. We now discuss a universal approach to religion. The universal qualities that are common to all theological systems have been described by a "perennial philosophy" that extracts universally agreed-on concepts about the nature of spirituality from the major world religions. This conceptual framework is based on the work of Huston Smith (in Cortright, 1997). The framework defines the nature of God or Higher Power from both Western and Eastern perspectives and describes different levels of identity and existence.

From a Western perspective (e.g., Hebrew, Christian, and Islamic monotheistic traditions), God is a Personal Divine, theistic or theistic-relational in nature. Fundamental to this worldview is that the individual seeks a relationship with the Divine through spiritual practices such as love, devotion, witness, or service. In contrast, in the Eastern traditions (e.g., Hinduism, Buddhism), God is known as the Impersonal Divine, or nondual in nature. Nonduality refers to the unity or completeness of reality despite differences or polarities. Religions such as Buddhism, Advaita Vedanta, and Taoism emphasize the illusory nature of self and "the existence of a formless, nameless, impersonal spiritual reality which is ultimately revealed as the ground of being" (Cortright, 1997, p. 27). The goal is to merge the individual into the Impersonal Divine, and this is accomplished through spiritual practices such as meditation, karma yoga, or devotion. In the mystical traditions, the emphasis is the inclusive or connecting dimension of spirituality; that is, there is no separation of self from the Divine.

Both Eastern and Western religions include the personal and impersonal dimensions, and the differences that exist are a matter of emphasis. Another way of expressing this concept is to say that God is both immanent (personal and present) and transcendent (impersonal and beyond our understanding).

The perennial philosophy also included four levels or dimensions of human identity and four levels of existence. Humans identify with being a body, mind, soul, and spirit (see Cortright, 1997, p. 28). Spirit here refers to identification with the Divine that is eternal and transcends subject–object duality, that which is "Ultimate." The soul is our spiritual nature, which is unique to each person and transcends the birth/death cycle. For example, according to the Hindu tradition, the soul reincarnates or returns to the earthly plane.

Finally, the four levels or dimensions of existence include (a) the terrestrial plane, which is observed and measured by the five senses; (b) the intermediate plane, which refers to psychic, subtle energies, the domain of spirits (e.g., entities), and unconscious archetypes (e.g., Jung); (c) the celestial plane that contains the personal Divine, theistic-relational traditions, God, and Divine beings; and (d) the infinite plane, which is depicted by the Impersonal Divine, nothing but Oneness, Divine Unity, without form, beyond all distinctions (Cortright, 1997).

This framework helps to explain various spiritual phenomena. For example, disembodied spirits or spirit guides are thought to be on the intermediate plane, whereas angels and other Divine figures are on the celestial plane. In this schema, all of the diverse ways of spiritual naming and worship have credibility. Some cultural worldviews accommodate these dimensions of existence more readily than others, for example, as seen in the prevalence of magic realism in Latin American literature (see Allende, 1986).

If we combine both of the above universal approaches to culture and religion, the following questions may be useful to explore a specific religious worldview: What is the nature of humans, God, and the relationship between them? What is spiritually intrinsic to humans? How does one relate to the transcendent? How does nature and community life itself interact with these realities? How are spiritual practices influenced by concepts of time and space, and activity level? What is the relative importance of the individual versus group membership?

Religion as Cultural Diversity

Similarities and Differences Across Cultures

Nielsen (1983) considered the cross-cultural parameters of religion and concluded that religion should be explained as a process, a relationship, and a symbol system: "Religion is human involvement with sacred sanction, vitality, significance, and value. This involvement is mediated through symbolic processes of transformation. Religion is expressed in and transmitted by cultural traditions that constitute a system of symbols" (p. 7).

Cultural diversity exists within and between religious organizations (e.g., each mainstream denomination typically has membership that represents a range of conservative to liberal values). Religious denominations may have racial and ethnic diversity, also, such as found in African Methodist Episcopal, Spanish-speaking Catholic, or Korean Baptist congregations. As another example, there is a marked difference between Irish Catholicism and Latin Catholicism, the former being more focused on sin and guilt (M. Flanagan, personal communication, November 7, 2002). In addition, regional cultural nuances are blended with core belief systems. For example, Roman Catholicism in the American Southwest has incorporated customs from Native American traditions; *Santeria,* a religion common in the Caribbean, includes a combination of West African *orishas* and Catholic saints.

Just as there are differences between religions, cross-cultural comparisons show that there are commonalties; for example, religious guidance can be found in all world religions. In Judaism, *Halacha* means the way to live according to Torah. In Christianity, the Greek New Testament calls it *Hodos*. Islamic tradition calls it *Shari'a*. Hinduism has the three *Margas* (the way of knowledge, work, and love). In Buddhism, the way refers to the *Noble Eightfold* path. In Taoism, the *Way of the Tao* is central. In Japan's Shinto, *To* means "the way."

Churches historically have played important roles in social group dynamics. For example, the African American church has been seen as a refuge from racism and a place for healing (Frame, 1996; Frame, Williams, & Green, 1999). But for other cultural groups, the church has been the oppressor, such as in the case of New England Protestant missionaries who proselytized in Hawaii in the mid-1800s. Interestingly, in the late 1990s, the president of the United Church of Christ formally apologized to the Native Hawaiians for damages inflicted by their ancestral missionaries.

Much can be learned about a religion, its beliefs, and practices through tracing the original stories that gave it birth. These stories are sometimes referred to as myths (and sometimes referred to as the "absolute truth"). We do not intend to debate the credibility of these stories but offer here some brief examples of contrasting religious worldviews based on myths. Myths tell of people's beliefs, practices, and worldview. They carry in them the heroes, the models, and ideals. People imitate and follow their heroes and aspire to be like them. People, their heroes, and leaders are closely connected to the stories of their origins, as God is considered to be the highest authority.

A Comparison of the Hindu and Hopi Creation Myths: Mahalakshmi and Spider Woman

A comparison of the Hindu and Hopi creation myths shows remarkable and surprising similarities and reveals what these traditions consider to be feminine and its jurisdiction. Keep in mind that these two cultures are situated halfway around the world from each other. Both myths begin in the same way; there was nothing but the two: the God and the Goddess.

In the Hopi myth, the two are Tawa and Spider Woman, and they control the "Above" and "Below." Between the Above and Below "lay shimmering only the Endless Waters" (Leeming, 1990, p. 37). Tawa and Spider Woman decide there should be creation and then divide themselves. From the division of Spider Woman comes Huzruiwuti, the Goddess of Wealth. She also proclaims, "I am Kokyanwuhi . . . I am the mother of all that shall be." Later they, Tawa and Spider Woman, sit together and think of creation of Earth in the middle of the Above and Below.

This is exactly the way the Hindu creation myth begins. In the beginning there are Vishnu (God) and Mahalakshi (Goddess). There is nothing but the Cosmic Water on which the two are sitting (Bhkativedanta, 1972, p. 22). They decide to create and begin to expand or emanate different forms for each phase of creation that is to take place. The expansions of each are numerous. For Mahalakshmi, a few are known as Lakshmi, Devi, Durga, Shakti, Prakriti, Isha, and Shri (Bhkativedanta, 1972, p. 18). Lakshmi means wealth as well as good fortune. She is also propitiated as the supreme mother (Bhkativedanta,

1972, p. 37). In Devi-Mahtmayam (see Coburn, 1991) we see the following passage: "Through her [Devi] is created the entire three-tiered universe" (in Bhkativedanta, 1972, p. 35). The footnote tells us that in the Hindu tradition the universe is divided into three regions: Heaven, Earth, and lower regions. Earth is in the middle.

Another similarity between these myths is found in the reason why Spider Woman and Mahalakshmi create. In the Hopi myth Tawa says: "I am light. I am life" (Leeming, 1990, p. 37). Spider Woman says: "I receive light and nourish life." Later she says that she gives form to the thoughts of Tawa; she actualizes his thoughts. This is not much different from the Hindu version in which Vishnu awakes from his dream and looks at Mahalakshmi. This glance, or ray of light, from his eyes agitates or inspires her to move and create.

In the Hopi myth we see that the Goddess (Spider Woman) is depicted as being wise and having "all seeing eyes" (Leeming, 1990, p. 38). In other words she knows everything, she is omniscient, and she knows how to use that knowledge. She divides the creatures into groups, leads them to a place to build their homes, and tells them of their duties for a happy life. She is the leader, organizer, and law giver. She "cradled them [the forms of creatures] in her warm young bosom" (Leeming, 1990, p. 37). She is the nourishing and protecting mother. She later again assures everyone that she is the protector and helper (along with Tawa), and she demands obedience (Leeming, 1990, p. 39). To be wise, to give law, to lead, and to organize were considered feminine, in addition to qualities of nourishment and protection.

We return to the Hindu myth. The Goddess (Devi) is addressed thus in the beginning of Mahatmayam: "You are the Goddess, the supreme mother. By you everything is supported, by you everything is created; by you it is protected" (Bhkativedanta, 1972, p. 37). She is addressed as the personality of knowledge and intelligence: "You are the great knowledge [knowledge supreme] . . . . You [are] intelligence" (Bhkativedanta, 1972, p. 35). She is the knowledge that liberates. How she (Durga) protects is elaborately delineated in many places in the Mahatmayam (Bhkativedanta, 1972, pp. 49–51). It is said, "No accident befalls men who have resorted to you for those who have resorted to you have truly entered a refuge." She is knowledge, intelligence, and protection. And she is the queen ruler of all rulers (Bhkativedanta, 1972, p. 37). Also, she is the Vedas (the scripture) and she is the law (Bhkativedanta, 1972, p. 49). The Vedas give a detailed account of the different classes of people, the qualities and duties of each group, and the qualities of different animals and creatures. This all parallels what occurs in the Hopi myth.

In sum, we see that knowledge, intelligence, law, protection, refuge, creativity, power, and energy are the domain of the feminine. We add here a few more qualities considered by the Hindus to be feminine. These may be thought of as extensions of the above discussion and may help to expand our vision of what is considered to be feminine in the two cultures. They are considered as the Goddess abiding within every creature and are as follows: consciousness, memory, patience, modesty, tranquility, loveliness, activity, and contentment (Bhkativedanta, 1972, pp. 53–54).

Consider for a moment if this creation myth were the dominant story in the United States (in contrast with the Judeo-Christian story of the expulsion of

Adam and Eve from the Garden of Eden). Although we are a culturally and religiously diverse nation, the "dominant paradigm" continues to be Judeo-Christian, with the emphasis on Christian. For example, national holidays tend to include Christmas; the weekly "day of rest" tends to be Sunday (whereas Fridays and Saturdays are days of worship in Islam and Judaism, respectively); and school/university calendars are set exclusively around a Christian calendar (although in most universities, there are policies around "accommodating" to other calendars). Feminist thinkers have challenged the patriarchal structures of Judeo-Christian traditions, and the roles of women in the church continue to evolve (Anderson & Hopkins, 1992). These challenges to historic values and the patriarchal system have created tensions and power struggles in many areas. We consider these issues in the next section.

Power and Privilege

Religion is a mirror for patriarchal social structures, and men traditionally have been privileged in terms of leadership roles in the church and by masculine images of God. Even to this day, various denominations struggle over the issue of ordination of women as clergy. Just as masculine values have influenced organized religion, they have influenced spiritual practices, such as meditation and monastic practices. Carol Flinders (1999) exposed this conflict between masculine privilege and feminist principles in her poignant recollections of what it was like for her to belong to a spiritual (Eastern-style meditation) community. She identified four characteristics of meditation that created dissonance for her: to be silent, to humble oneself ("unseat the ego"), to resist one's desires, and to turn inward (enclosed community). She reflected,

> Formulated for the most part within monastic contexts, they cancel the basic freedoms—to say what one wants, go where one likes, enjoy whatever pleasures one can afford, and most of all, to *be* somebody—that have normally defined male privilege. . . . Women, on the other hand, have not been in a position to renounce these privileges voluntarily *because they never had them in the first place.* (Flinders, 1999, p. 84)

In contrast, Flinders pointed to the following feminist principles that at first glance appear to conflict with spiritual practice: to find your voice, to know who you are, to reclaim your body, and to move freely in the world. Although these two worldviews may seen contradictory, Flinders recommended that the resolution of these differences lies in the ability for women (and men) to make choices: for example, to be heard and to be silent, to know yourself and to transcend yourself, to appreciate being "in-body" and in the world, and to practice detachment. In addition, Flinders saw the feminist movement as "a resistance movement based in spirituality" (p. 324). She also saw the similarities between the modern feminist movement and women mystics of medieval cloisters.

> Paradoxically, feminism is currently performing for contemporary women many of the same functions Christianity did, quite inadvertently, for medieval women. It insists upon women's right and capacity to choose, it celebrates the acts of courageous decisive women, and it fosters feminine community. (p. 135)

The issue of individual and systemic privilege occurs in multiple ways. On an institutional level, it prevents the entry of minority religions and customs and traditions into the cultural norms or ways of being/thinking, and ultimately prevents them from being fully validated. On an individual level, all of us— whether we are in a privileged group or not—are socialized into thinking and believing that minority ways are "lesser than." Privilege supports the dichotomy of "us-them" and the belief that "my way is the right way."

However, most religions and spiritual traditions of the world also have as a central component the breaking down of such barriers. Concepts such as "love thy neighbor" imply crossing boundaries. The result then can be a clash of belief systems. Ways of handling the clash include both oppressive and more inclusive ways. Oppressive ways, for example, take the position that "one way is the right way" or the "way that should be accommodated." More inclusive ways, for example, try to find multiple ways of being or acting, or finding one way that "encompasses" all that are affected. Being multicultural and having multicultural beliefs can help address this dissonance to move away from the false dichotomies. Spiritual beliefs also can help one "travel" among and between cultures and traditions. We suggest that such conflicts can be mediated by multicultural and spiritual values, which is discussed next.

Multicultural and Spiritual Values

First, we make a distinction between cultural values and moral values. *Cultural values* typically refer to social constructs that may vary along a continuum, such as individualistic versus collectivistic cultures. For example, in the United States, we tend to value the individual over the group. Most Latin American cultures value the group (family) over the individual. In this case, we have cultural differences; neither is inherently right nor wrong. Thus, the concept of cultural relativism is "it depends on the cultural context." This line of thinking is different from *moral values,* which inherently implies a right–wrong distinction. Sometimes religious values are used to reinforce cultural norms, such as viewing "the man as head of the household" as sacrosanct. Sometimes, religious leaders are critical of cultural relativism because it does not uphold a particular morality (right vs. wrong). Dealing with value differences (both cultural and moral) can sometimes present ethical dilemmas. For example, addressing an issue in a strict, nonrelativistic manner implies there is a very clear line (e.g., abortion is a "black-or-white issue"). Addressing an issue in a culturally sensitive and relative manner, in which the individual situation is taken into account, implies a line may be there, but it may be a bit wider and not as clear (e.g., abortion is a moral issue that needs to be approached with compassion and care).

Engaging in multicultural training may be enhanced by spiritual values (Fukuyama & Sevig, 1999). Cross-cultural experiences have the potential to contribute toward an expansion of one's worldview and deepening of faith. Knowledge of differing worldviews has a twofold effect: "I have a clearer idea of who I am now, because I know who I am NOT" and "Even though we are different, we are also similar" (e.g., we worship God, even though God is called different names). In realizing these connections, a feeling of separateness is gradually lessened. A paradoxical effect of clarifying and softening cultural boundaries happens simultaneously.

Concurrently, experience has shown that people struggle with the dilemmas of understanding the meaning of diversity and multiculturalism. Cultural conflicts are stressful, and a multicultural society is more likely to be dynamic, challenging, and changing. This is true for the United States as a nation and also for the world community as globalization becomes a reality. It is clear that unlearning racism, confronting internalized oppression, truly valuing difference, and taking risks to build alliances are formidable and painful tasks. Fortunately, spiritual qualities can assist the process of multiculturalism (see Table 7.1). The interaction of faith, creativity, patience, humor, flexibility, and the ability to detach or let go of one's point of view (even momentarily) will assist the process of becoming multiculturally skilled. Feelings of love and compassion for humanity ("we are all connected") increase the chances of working through difficult cultural differences. A reciprocal cycle of learning can yield benefits to both the multicultural and spiritual seeker. Thus, we suggest that multicultural learning fosters spiritual evolvement and that spiritual evolvement strengthens the multicultural learning process.

Implications for Counseling and Training

How does one begin to discuss religious and spiritual concerns in the classroom, in supervision, and in counseling? Certainly a prerequisite for disclosure

Table 7.1
Comparison of Spiritual and Multicultural Values

Spiritual Values	Multicultural Values
Connectedness with others	Cultural similarities
Contact and conflict with reality	Cultural differences
Compassion and love	Understanding and empathy
Relationship outside of self	Movement from ethnocentrism toward cultural pluralism
Social justice	Dealing with issues of oppression, advocacy
Faith	Flexibility and patience
Grace, intimacy, creativity	Commitment and humor
Sacredness and mystery	Tolerance for ambiguity
Detachment	Observational skills
Paradox	Bicultural and multicultural skills

Note. From *Integrating Spirituality Into Multicultural Counseling,* by M. Fukuyama & T. Sevig, 1999, p. 75. Copyright © 1999 by Sage Publications, Inc. Reprinted with permission.

is creating a safe space. There is good reason for the adage "Never discuss politics or religion in polite company." It does not take long for values differences to become evident. In our collective experience in teaching and training on multicultural issues, we generally begin with a discussion of "how can we make it safe to talk about spiritual/religious issues?"

When asked, counseling students have specifically mentioned the following:

- To not feel judged.
- To not be pressured to convert to a particular belief system or practice.
- To have permission to be ignorant about various religions.
- To have the freedom to be nonreligious.
- To have the freedom to be religious.
- To feel respected—concern for the personal as private (confidentiality and "permission to pass" on personal sharing).

We suggest that these concerns apply equally to clients, but due to the power differential in the therapy relationship, it is incumbent on the counselor to establish a feeling of safety. The more the counselor has worked through their issues on this topic, the easier it will be to engage the client.

Although various instruments and measures have been developed to assess or measure religiosity and spirituality (see Friedman & MacDonald, 2002; Hill & Hood, 1999), and assessment was discussed in detail in chapter 3, we have found the following questions useful as a general guide for exploring religious and/or spiritual backgrounds.

1. What are some of your earliest memories of religion, church, synagogue, or perhaps absence of religion?
2. What, if any, were your early images of God?
3. What are your earliest memories of non-ordinary reality, a higher power, some mystery in the universe, or other meaningful spiritual or transpersonal experiences?
4. What were sources of authority, values, and power?
5. What is your experience of transcendence?
6. What resistance or barriers exist that prevent you from connecting with sources of spirituality?
7. Where are you now on your spiritual journey?
8. How have your experiences with religion, spirituality or the transpersonal shaped the attitudes and values that inform your counseling work? (Fukuyama & Sevig, 1999, p. 9)

There has been some discussion in the field of multicultural counseling on the effectiveness of working with the sacred in counseling when the counselor holds particular worldviews or values orientations. Zinnbauer and Pargament (2000) suggested that there are four worldviews related to religious beliefs and values: the *rejectionist* (antagonism against religion), the *exclusivist* (religious absolutism), the *constructivist* (beliefs are constructed by the individual; it is all relative), and the *pluralist* (recognizes spiritual absolute with multiple interpretations). The most compatible orientations are constructivist and pluralist. The least compatible are rejectionist and exclusivist. Religious mental health professionals need to examine their values to determine when they will work best on matters of mental health, cultural diversity, and religious beliefs and when it is better to refer, as discussed more fully in chapter 9.

Religion and culture frequently influence how people define themselves and their spiritual experiences. Because there is a strong overlay of individualism and free choice in Western psychology, it is natural for mental health professionals to imagine that individuals will seek their own spiritual paths based on personal preferences and values. Individualism is not necessarily universally valued, however, nor does everyone "individualize" their religious ideologies. Some people may never question their religion of birth. Because we (the authors) are trained as therapists (not as theologians), we tend to gravitate toward psychological approaches to spirituality and imagine it as a developmental process.

In fact, the concept of development or growth over a life span, in and of itself, may be a culturally bound concept. The idea that people grow spiritually is a concept based on individuation and human development, which are constructs associated with Western civilization. If one looks at world cultures from an anthropological point of view, only two "mainstreams" have embraced the concepts of growth and development: Far Eastern philosophies that originated in China and influenced modern Korea and Japan, and philosophies that originated in Mesopotamia that became Greco-Roman, European, and then "Western culture." Many other cultures, including sub-Saharan Africa, Native American, or Australian Aboriginal, have not been oriented around the concept of growth or making progress (May, 1998, in Fukuyama & Sevig, 1999, p. 24).

When a counselor opens to religious and spiritual process in therapy, the issue of having "words to express" what one feels is frequently a challenge. Finding words to describe spiritual and religious experiences is not easy. That is why poetry, metaphors, music, and the arts are frequently used to represent phenomena that hold strong emotions and meaning. The use of metaphors has been suggested to describe spiritual experiences, such as one's relationship with God or a Higher Power.

In this case, a metaphor uses a familiar, concrete, descriptive image or phenomenon to describe an abstract concept, for example, "I am on a spiritual journey" or "My soul is like a wave in the ocean." A metaphor makes concepts or experiences that are difficult to understand more manageable or accessible. Some even claim that the sacred cannot be described except through metaphors (Griffith & Griffith, 2002).

Although it is helpful to find a metaphor that speaks to one's experience, metaphors also limit one's worldview. They both enable or elaborate on a theme, and also restrict or constrain one's understanding; for example, God as Father, God as Mother, and God as Lover—each has its own connotations.

Just as there are individual metaphors of meaning, there are cultural metaphors that are reinforced through social institutions and cultural customs. Investigating cultural metaphors is one avenue for understanding worldview. The metaphors of the hoop or medicine wheel or spider web describe variations on Native American cosmology. The struggle of good versus evil has been depicted by words such as the *evil empire*. Spirituality has been described as being a river, wellspring, mountain, or tree of life. God has been described as being like a judge, king, rock, fortress, or cloud of unknowing. In these cases, the unknown or life mysteries are put into known and familiar words.

Griffith and Griffith (2002) suggested that some metaphors for spirituality may limit a client's perceptions, and that by changing metaphors, new avenues for healing or growth may open. "Whether a metaphor is useful or not depends upon whether it can fulfill the purpose for which it was intended and whether its usage carries any unsought, adverse consequences" (p. 66). The therapist or counselor may engage in a dialogue with a client to elaborate the meanings and implications of held metaphors, to broaden to multiple metaphors, or to seek alternative metaphors. For example, the metaphor of the journey implies movement, progress, and change. Perhaps the journeyer needs to rest sometimes, to stop and be still. As a case in point, consider the contrasting images of the Buddha sitting in meditation and Jesus carrying the cross. Other types of metaphors related to spirituality include journey, trial, warfare, and *jihad* or holy war (see Schreurs, 2002).

From the Islamic tradition, the *jihad* or holy war was justified in self-defense during the times of the Prophet Mohammed. At the same time, the Prophet said that the greatest war was the "war within"—the struggle of the ego for control and the need to surrender to the will of God. The word *Islam* means "submission." Although the media portrays radical Islamic fundamentalists as violence-prone, the Islamic faith is based on the values of peace and harmony.

An area of significance for counselor training as well as clinical work is consideration of *religious wounding*. Religious wounding occurs when religious structures directly hurt or restrict people's authentic selves (Fukuyama & Sevig, 1999). Wounding can happen on both an overt or a covert level, intentionally or unintentionally. Sometimes the wounding takes place in the context of child abuse by religiously oriented parents. Other social issues have been subjected to moral judgment by organized religion, including abortion, sexuality, and divorce, and negative judgments can contribute to religious wounding. Sexism in the church has been seen as detrimental to women's experiences of spirituality. Reilly (1995) suggested that masculine models of God and religious language has excluded the feminine and women from full participation in the church. Similarly, men have been restricted from experiencing spontaneous spirituality because they have been conditioned to always be "in control" and not to openly express emotions (Kivel, 1991). Frequently, religious wounds are retained in the unconsciousness. Judy (1996) recommended that people "make peace with our religion of origin, because it was the first window into the vastness of the universe" (p. 301).

Training counselors to be competent in dealing with religious and spiritual issues requires personal reflection on some of these issues. For example, students who have had negative experiences with religion may avoid addressing it in therapy. In addition, students with specific religious values may avoid dealing with some therapeutic issues. A training case study of such a situation is discussed next.

Case Study

Some counseling students who hold conservative religious values are uncomfortable with the prospect of counseling lesbian, gay, or bisexual (LGB) clients, because it conflicts with their religious (moral) beliefs about what constitutes an "acceptable lifestyle" (i.e., married heterosexual). This issue may come up in a practicum placement or in a multicultural counseling course. If the trainer follows an inclusive training model, becoming aware of heterosexism and homophobia is expected as part of training. Students would not be allowed to exempt themselves from learning about the effects of this social oppression anymore than learning about the effects of racism or other forms of social oppression. Additionally, working through an LGB sexual orientation may be a vehicle for spiritual growth rather than condemnation for some clients (Fortunato, 1982). The struggle for self-worth and identity of LGB people has been connected with their spiritual life (Ritter & O'Neill, 1996). Obviously, this is a complex training issue. Here are some questions for discussion and reflection:

- What is the ethical thing to do when a student says that he or she cannot work with LGB issues because of religious beliefs?
- Do these beliefs also restrict students from working with nonmarried sexually active heterosexuals?
- Can a student differentiate homophobic social conditioning from religious values?
- How should a trainer or educator handle a situation when a student's religious worldview clashes with a multicultural worldview?

Recommended Reading

Cornett, C. (1998). *The soul of psychotherapy: Recapturing the spiritual dimension in the therapeutic encounter.* New York: The Free Press.

Fadiman, A. (1997). *The spirit catches you and you fall down: A Hmong child, her American doctors, and the collision of two cultures.* New York: Farrar, Strauss & Giroux.

Kaschak, E. (Ed.) (2001). *The invisible alliance: Psyche and spirit in feminist therapy.* Binghampton, NY: Hawthorne Press.

McBride, J. (1996). *The color of water: A Black man's tribute to his White mother.* New York: Riverhead Books.

Smith, H. (1991). *The world's religions: Our great wisdom traditions.* New York: Harper SanFrancisco.

Web Sites of Interest

http://www.awesomelibrary.org/Classroom/Social_Studies/Multicultural/Religious_Diversity.html)
    The Awesome Library

http://www.unesco.org/most/rr1.htm
    MOST Clearing House on Religious Rights, UNESCO (United Nations Educational, Scientific and Cultural Organization)

http://www.religioustolerance.org/
Ontario Consultants on Religious Tolerance

http://www.pluralism.org/about/mission.php
The Pluralism Project, Committee on the Study of Religion, Harvard University

http://religiousmovements.lib.virginia.edu/
The Religious Movements Homepage, The University of Virginia

Summary

In a best-case scenario, the counselor who engages in an active learning process in multicultural counseling will include religion and spirituality in the cultural context of therapy. The intersection of feminism, spirituality, and multiculturalism in counseling can be an energizing and creative space (Funderburk & Fukuyama, 2001). Other chapters in this book address the exploration of self-awareness for the counselor as he or she explores the boundary of the sacred in psychotherapy. We recommend continuing education on this topic, and the World Wide Web is a rich resource (see Web sites listed above).

We began this chapter with a quote about the mysteries of the human soul. It is natural for humans to gravitate toward religious belief systems and social organizations that make sense and are familiar, that work for them. Each culture has forms that make sense within that culture. As the United States becomes more culturally diverse, we suggest that two phenomena are happening: There are increasing numbers of people who participate in fundamentalist churches, in part as a response to rapid social change; and there is more blending of religious and spiritual beliefs and practices as cultures have more contact. Wherever counselors find themselves on this continuum, they will need to know themselves and be as open as possible when engaging clients who represent a wide range of religious, spiritual, and cultural perspectives.

References

Allende, I. (1986). *The house of spirits.* New York: Bantam Books.

Allport, G., & Ross, J. (1967). Personal religious orientation and prejudice. *Journal of Personality and Social Psychology, 5,* 432–433.

Anderson, S. R., & Hopkins, P. (1992). *The feminine face of God: The unfolding of the sacred in women.* New York: Bantam Books.

Artress, L. (1995). *Walking a sacred path: Rediscovering the labyrinth as a spiritual tool.* New York: Riverhead Books.

Bennett, M. (1996). *Better together than apart—Intercultural communication: An overview* [Videotape]. (Available from Intercultural Resource Corporation, 78 Greylock Rd., Newtonville, MA 02160).

Bhkativedanta, A. C. (1972). *Srimad Bhagavatam* (Vol. 1, 30 vols.). Los Angeles: ISKCON.

Chandler, C. K., Holden, J. M., & Kolander, C. A. (1992). Counseling for spiritual wellness: Theory and practice. *Journal of Counseling & Development, 71,* 168–175.

Coburn, T. B. (1991). *Encountering the goddess: A translation of the Devi-mahatmya and a study of its interpretation.* Albany: State University of New York Press.

Cortright, B. (1997). *Psychotherapy and spirit: Theory and practice in transpersonal psychotherapy.* Albany: State University of New York Press.

Creedon, J. (1998, July/August). God with a million faces. *Utne Reader,* 42–48.

Elkins, D. N., Hedstrom, L. J., Hughes, L. L., Leaf, J. A., & Saunders, C. (1988). Toward a humanistic-phenomenological spirituality: Definition, description, and measurement. *Journal of Humanistic Psychology, 28,* 5–18.

Flinders, C. L. (1999). *At the root of this longing: Reconciling a spiritual hunger and a feminist thirst.* New York: Harper Collins.

Fortunato, J. E. (1982). *Embracing the exile: Healing journeys of gay Christians.* New York: Harper & Row.

Fox, M. (1983). *Original blessing.* Santa Fe, NM: Bear & Co.

Frame, M. W. (1996). Counseling African Americans: Integrating spirituality in therapy. *Counseling and Values, 41,* 15–28.

Frame, M. W., Williams, C. B., & Green, E. L. (1999). Balm in Gilead: Spiritual dimensions in counseling African American women. *Journal of Multicultural Counseling and Development, 27,* 182–192.

Friedman, H. L., & MacDonald, D. A. (2002). *Approaches to transpersonal measurement and assessment.* San Francisco: Transpersonal Institute.

Fukuyama, M. A. (1990). Taking a universal approach to multicultural counseling. *Counselor Education and Supervision, 30,* 6–17.

Fukuyama, M. A., & Sevig, T. D. (1999). *Integrating spirituality into multicultural counseling.* Thousand Oaks, CA: Sage.

Funderburk, J., & Fukuyama, M. (2001). Feminism, multiculturalism, and spirituality: Convergent and divergent forces in psychotherapy. *Women and Therapy, 24*(3/4), 1–18.

Galanter, M. (1996). Cults and charismatic group psychology. In E. P. Shafranske (Ed.), *Religion and the clinical practice of psychology* (pp. 269–296). Washington, DC: American Psychological Association.

Gonzalez-Wippler, M. (1992). *The Santeria experience.* St. Paul, MN: Llewellyn.

Griffith, J. L., & Griffith, M. E. (2002). *Encountering the sacred in psychotherapy.* New York: Guilford Press.

Hill, P. C., & Hood, R. W. (1999). *Measures of religiosity.* Birmingham, AL: Religious Education Press.

Hoge, D. (1996). Religion in America: The demographics of belief and affiliation. In E. P. Shafranske (Ed.), *Religion and the clinical practice of psychology* (pp. 21–41). Washington, DC: American Psychological Association.

Holm, J. (1977). *The study of religions.* New York: Seabury Press.

Ibrahim, F. A. (1985). Effective cross-cultural counseling and psychotherapy: A framework. *The Counseling Psychologist, 13,* 625–638.

Ibrahim, F. A. (2003). Existential worldview counseling theory: Inception to applications. In F. D. Harper & J. McFadden (Eds.), *Culture and counseling: New approaches* (pp. 196–208). Boston: Allyn & Bacon.

Jackson, M. L., & Vontress, C. E. (2003, July). Reader's viewpoint: Where has culture in counseling gone? *Counseling Today, 7,* 10.

Judy, D. H. (1996). Transpersonal psychotherapy with religious persons. In B. W. Scotton, A. B. Chinen, & J. R. Battista (Eds.), *Textbook of transpersonal psychiatry and psychology* (pp. 293–301). New York: Basic Books.

Katz, J. H. (1985). The sociopolitical nature of counseling. *The Counseling Psychologist, 13,* 615–624.

Kelly, E. W. (1995). *Spirituality and religion in counseling and psychotherapy: Diversity in theory and practice.* Alexandria, VA: American Counseling Association.

Kivel, P. (1991). Men, spirituality, and violence. *Creation Spirituality, 7*(4), 12–14, 50.

Kluckhohn, F. R., & Strodtbeck, F. L. (1961). *Variations in value orientations.* Evanston, IL: Row, Peterson.

Leeming, D. A. (1990). *The world of myth.* Oxford, England: Oxford University Press.

Locke, D. C. (1990). A not so provincial view of multicultural counseling. *Counselor Education and Supervision, 30,* 18–25.

Nielsen, N. C. J. (1983). *Religions of the world.* New York: St. Martin's Press.

Nunez, L. M. (1995). *Santeria: A practical guide to Afro-Caribbean magic.* New York: Spring.

Reilly, P. (1995). The religious wounding of women. *Creation Spirituality, 11*(1), 41–45.

Ritter, K. Y., & O'Neill, C. (1996). *Righteous religion: Unmasking the illusions of fundamentalism and authoritarian Catholicism.* New York: Haworth Pastoral Press.

Schreurs, A. (2002). *Psychotherapy and spirituality: Integrating the spiritual dimension into therapeutic practice.* Philadelphia: Jessica Kingsley.

Stewart, E. C., & Bennett, M. J. (1991). *American cultural patterns.* Yarmouth, ME: Intercultural Press.

Sue, D. W., & Sue, D.(1990). *Counseling the culturally different: Theory and practice* (2nd ed.). New York: Wiley.

Swindler, L. J., & Mojzes, P. (2000). *The study of religion in an age of global dialogue.* Philadelphia: Temple University Press.

Tillich, P. (1964). *Theology of culture.* New York: Oxford University Press.

Webster's II new riverside university dictionary. (1988). Boston: Houghton Mifflin.

Zinnbauer, B. J., & Pargament, K. I. (2000). Working with the sacred: Four approaches to religious and spiritual issues in counseling. *Journal of Counseling & Development, 78,* 162–171.

Chapter 8

Use of Spiritual and Religious Beliefs in Pursuit of Clients' Goals

Alan Basham and Mike O'Connor

Competencies: *The professional counselor is sensitive to and receptive of religious and/or spiritual themes in the counseling process as befits the expressed preference of each client.*

The professional counselor uses a client's religious and/or spiritual beliefs in the pursuit of the client's therapeutic goals as befits the client's expressed preference.

This chapter focuses on the use of a client's beliefs as a means of helping her or him reach therapeutic goals. Working within the expressed religious or spiritual belief system of the client to help resolve problems or to alleviate suffering necessitates counselor consideration of several important issues. These include the beliefs of the client, the depth of conviction and personal values emerging from religious belief, the nature of the presented problem, the beliefs of the counselor, and the formation of a working alliance to support the use of religious and spiritual beliefs in the counseling process. We begin by addressing these issues, then describe a number of specific techniques that can be used based on the client's beliefs. We present case examples to illustrate both the importance of counselor understanding of the client and appropriate use of techniques. We conclude with a list of follow-up resources.

Basic Premises

The following are five basic ideas or concepts that underlie effective use of client beliefs in counseling. We discuss each of these below.

Premise 1

A client's belief about truth, meaning, and reality is a construct of the mind. Such beliefs may emerge from personal religious conviction, from life experience, and from trusting the instruction of others whose beliefs and cosmology the client may adopt. This simple idea that the mind is busy creating its own perception of reality is one of the central tenets of constructivism. Gladding (2001) defined constructivism as "a philosophy that proposes that reality is subjective in nature, a reflection of observation and experience, not an objective entity" (p. 30). From the constructivist perspective, each person actively creates her or his subjective understanding of experience and of the world rather than passively receiving some objective reality. In other words, "To know is to construct, not to find" (McAuliffe & Eriksen, 1999, p. 268). Clients are not born with their view of the world or beliefs about themselves, life, cosmology, or theology. Instead, as they move through life stages and events, religious and spiritual beliefs may be introjected from the teachings of significant others, co-constructed in discourse with other seekers, or derived from individual reflections. Regardless of how it is attained, the client's worldview both reflects and contributes to the formation of personal reality and meaning.

Some components of one's belief system are individual and emerge from the individual's unique experiences and perceptions. Some are the result of identification with and internalization of an established system of belief such as a religion. This latter form of acquisition is the result of social constructionism, which Shapiro and Ross (2002) defined as "the idea that the way people experience themselves and their situation is 'constructed' through culturally mediated social interactions" (p. 96). Among these social interactions, of course, are the religious aspects of one's culture.

Why is this understanding of the constructed nature of reality important? Because effective counseling requires a working alliance based on mutual respect, because the expression of this genuine respect is dependent on understanding, and because what is to be understood by the counselor is the unique way of looking at life and its problems constructed by the client. Georgia (1994) stressed that when assisting clients from different faith backgrounds, counselors must of necessity be aware of and understand the clients' beliefs and spiritual practice. Therefore, our first premise is that skilled use of spiritual and religious beliefs in counseling is based on understanding the client's beliefs, and that those beliefs and values are uniquely constructed in the mind of the client.

Premise 2

Integrating spiritual and religious components into the counseling process requires the creation of a working alliance with the client (Kelly, 1995) characterized by genuine respect for the client and a relationship of "benevolent connectedness" (p. 92). This therapeutic alliance is formed between client and counselor to the degree that the client perceives the counselor to be warm, caring, trustworthy, and nonjudgmental (Egan, 1998; S. D. Miller, Duncan, & Hubble, 1997; W. R. Miller & Rollnick, 1991). The client who believes he or she is valued, accepted, and safe is far more likely to work with the counselor to accomplish her or his therapeutic goals than is one who feels objectified and judged (S. D. Miller et al., 1997). S. D. Miller et al. stressed the importance of this concept when they summarized the research indicating that the working alliance between counselor and client has a greater impact on therapeutic outcomes than does the therapeutic modality chosen by the counselor.

Premise 3

To build a working alliance with the client, the counselor must communicate respect for the client's religious values and beliefs. Respect does not mean that the counselor must share the same worldview or hold the same beliefs as the client. It does mean that the importance of the client's religious beliefs and their role in the creation or resolution of the client's problems must be recognized, validated, and treated with respect by the counselor. This respect is especially important when working with clients who have deeply held religious beliefs and values convictions (Helminiak, 2001; G. Miller, 2003). Watts (2001) summarized the issue well:

> [T]he importance of attending to clients' spirituality in counseling and psychotherapy cannot be overemphasized. Spirituality is a vital area for counselors to understand because clients' spiritual beliefs typically provide the value system by which they view themselves, others, and the world. . . . [I]f clients perceive counselors as devaluing or ignoring the importance of their spirituality in the therapeutic process, they may become reluctant to share those beliefs or terminate counseling. (p. 211)

How a counselor responds to the religious beliefs of the client has much to do with whether or not they will form a genuine working alliance. As mentioned briefly in chapter 7, Zinnbauer and Pargament (2000) described four approaches that counselors can take in response to religious and spiritual issues in counseling. The *rejectionist* approach is to deny the reality of the sacred or supernatural elements of belief that are foundational to most world religions. Religion is seen in this case as irrational, as a method of psychological defense against the existential realities of life, and as necessarily contributing to the disturbance of the client. The rejectionist approach has contributed substantially to the mistaken perception among many religious people that psychology in all its forms rejects the validity of religion and human spirituality, leading to an understandable distrust of the secular counseling profession.

The *exclusivist* counselor takes the opposite approach, upholding the belief in a particular religious or spiritual reality accompanied by absolute values, certainty of the counselor's own religious paradigm, and belief that there is only one path to spiritual truth. Just as the rejectionist may seek to dismantle or modify religious belief to help the client be more "rational," the exclusivist counselor is respectful of the client's views only to the degree that they match those of the counselor. Exclusivist counselors are more likely than others to limit their practice to clients from their own religious orientation or to try to influence the beliefs of other clients until they are correct in the eyes of the counselor.

A third counselor approach is *constructivist* in nature. The constructivist counselor's personal position could be theistic, agnostic, or atheistic. Counselors constructing their own reality may conclude the existence of God, an afterlife, supernatural forces and beings, or not, depending on their unique spiritual journey, religious discourses with others, and the conclusions they reach. To the constructivist counselor, psychological problems indicate that the client's constructs are breaking down or are inadequate to help her or him cope with emerging problems in life. The counselor seeks to enter the worldview of the client and to work within that worldview to help the client develop new, modified, or strengthened constructs with which to encounter personal difficulties. The constructivist counselor does not have a preconceived investment in the final beliefs of the client. It is important only that the beliefs arrived at be meaningful, derived from a "thickened" rather than a limited or thin narrative (White, 2000), and functional for the client without being oppressive to others. The flavor of the counselor's intervention is respectful curiosity regarding the client's story, belief systems, and how they contribute to the authoring of her or his story (Monk, Winslade, Crocket, & Epston, 1997).

The final approach to helping clients with religious and spiritual issues is that of the *pluralist*. In contrast to all three other approaches, the pluralist position accepts that religious or spiritual truth exists and that there are many possible interpretations of and paths to that truth (Zinnbauer & Pargament, 2000, p. 167). The pluralist realizes that differences in religious and spiritual beliefs are to be expected and will not necessarily limit therapeutic progress. Because of this openness, the pluralist is able to work with clients from many different spiritual and religious orientations. Because religion is a part of culture, the pluralist works within a cross-cultural framework to respect the religious views of the client while appropriately including her or his own in the treatment process. As is the case when providing effective cross-cultural counseling, the counselor must be aware of her or his own beliefs and values, must become aware of and respect the beliefs and values of the client, and must work with the client in an accepting, supportive fashion to find the commonalities that will contribute to therapeutic success while accepting and valuing the differences (Guinee & Tracey, 1997; Sue & Sue, 2003).

To conclude our discussion of Premise 3, we believe that the most effective means of building a working alliance with clients from diverse spiritual and religious backgrounds entails either a constructivist or pluralist approach in a relationship marked by acceptance, warmth, compassion, and respectful interest and curiosity regarding the client's personal belief system.

Premise 4

What a person actually believes about religion or spirituality has little impact on her or his life unless the belief is deep enough to become a value and is thus manifested in behavior. Most people in the United States believe in the existence of God (Kelly, 1995). The difference between religious belief and religious values, however, is that values actually influence the decisions, behavior, and feelings of the client (Kelly, 1995; McCullough & Worthington, 1995). One way to understand the distinction between belief and values is to consider the different ways of being religious conceptualized by Allport and Ross (1967). Their model describes two approaches or orientations to religion: extrinsic and intrinsic.

Allport and Ross (1967) suggested that a person with an *extrinsic* orientation uses religious belief as a means to various ends, including explanations for existential dilemmas, security, acceptance into a community, self-justification, and reassurance of the adequacy of self. Extrinsic believers tend to hold their creeds lightly and to modify or selectively apply them to meet existing needs. An example of an extrinsic orientation is that of the faithful churchgoer who makes business contacts through church socializing, gains status in the church from teaching classes or holding a leadership position, and gains public credibility in the presentation of his moral, good citizen persona. Extrinsic religious belief should not be misunderstood as fake or insincere. It is, however, a part of the person's life primarily because of the benefits to self and well-being that it helps to produce.

In contrast, a person who holds an *intrinsic* orientation to her or his religious belief has deeply internalized the precepts of the religion, defers to the firmly held values of the religion to guide daily decisions and behavior, and incorporates the tenets of the religion in an ongoing assessment of her or his spiritual commitment and personal maturity. The intrinsically religious person does not just believe; he or she lives out the faith as the central motive for and purpose of life. For example, consider the woman who is financially successful but, in contrast to her society's material values, lives modestly and well within her means to give most of her income anonymously to help alleviate the poverty and suffering of others. Another example of intrinsic belief is the man who is grieving over an error in judgment that hurt another person's feelings. He is motivated to examine why he did what he did, not by embarrassment at making a mistake or by the fear of what others will think, but because of genuine sorrow over having been unloving to another person.

Batson and Ventis (1982) added a third approach to religion to Allport and Ross's (1967) original concept. They suggest that a person with a *quest* orientation approaches existential questions without attempting to simplify them or to arrive at comforting but incomplete answers. The person on a religious or spiritual quest understands that he or she will never fully understand the answers to life's most important questions but is unwilling to accept answers that seem simple, dualistic, or too easy. The person on a quest may or may not believe in a transcendent reality, but the person tends to enjoy questioning and seeking intellectually satisfying conclusions regarding major life issues. Spiritual questions for the questing person emerge from a longing to understand life and to develop wisdom more than from a desire to feel better, to solve a particular problem, or to have absolute answers.

A parallel to Allport and Ross's (1967) religious categorization of extrinsic and intrinsic is Wilber's (1997) more radical presentation of religion's two functions, translation and transformation, and their related spiritualities, translational and transformative.

> The first function—that of creating meaning for the self—is a type of *horizontal* movement; the second function—that of transcending the self—is a type of *vertical* movement (higher or deeper, depending on your metaphor). The first I have named "translation," the second, "transformation." (Wilber, 1997, p. 24)

Wilber identified the importance of each function. Translation provides meaning and legitimacy to the self and its beliefs that can prevent neurosis or even psychosis. With transformation, however, the very process of translation itself is challenged, uprooted, and ultimately rejected. With translation, the self (or subject) is given a new conceptualization about the world (or objects). Radical transformation, however, inquires into the very nature of this *self*. Wilber pressed his distinction further by asserting, "where translative religion offers *legitimacy*, transformative religion offers *authenticity*" (p. 26). Counselors working with clients presenting religious and spiritual concerns would do well to familiarize themselves with Wilber's ideas on this and related topics (Wilber, 1996, 1997, 1998).

G. A. Miller (1992) indicated that understanding the religious orientation of the client can help the counselor grasp the impact of religious belief on the mental health of the client. To this end, Kelly (1995) listed eight categories describing the degree to which spirituality and religion are central to the client's life. While these categories were described in detail in chapter 5, we discuss them briefly here. *Religiously committed clients* have a deeply held personal conviction about their religious beliefs—similar to Allport and Ross's (1967) notion of an *intrinsic* religious orientation. These beliefs shape the person's outlook and act as a source of values that he or she uses to make decisions and guide behavior. *Religiously loyal clients* hold beliefs that emerge from their family history or cultural origins. They are often connected to religious traditions by birth and may keep those traditions faithfully, although application of their religious beliefs to personal growth or problem solving may or may not occur. *Spiritually committed clients* are not affiliated with organized religion, but nonetheless possess a willingness to look within, a sense of belonging to the cosmos, an awareness of connectedness to the transcendent, and an altruistic desire to help create a better world. *Spiritually/religiously open clients* are not committed to any religion but are interested in the spiritual dimension as an avenue to problem solving and personal growth. Similar to Allport and Ross's extrinsic religious orientation, Kelly suggested that *externally religious clients* have an outward appearance of religious belief, but those religious expressions lack inner conviction and have little or no impact on personal values, thinking, or conduct. *Spiritually/religiously tolerant or indifferent clients* are accepting of the spiritual and religious beliefs of others but have no interest in including such beliefs in their own lives. *Nonspiritual/nonreligious clients* intentionally reject religious belief as unreal and as not essential for living well and understanding life. While they reject spirituality and religion, they are not necessarily hostile to them or to those who do believe. *Clients hostile to religion* not only reject religious belief but are actively opposed to religion, religious groups, and the impact of religion on society. It is clear that understanding which of these overlapping categories best describes the client is crucial to knowing whether and in what ways to integrate religious and spiritual belief issues into the counseling process.

Premise 5

Religious belief may be a part of the solution or be part of what is creating the presented problem or conflict (Bishop, 1995; Suyemoto & MacDonald, 1996). There is a long-standing distrust between some religious communities and the counseling profession, due not in small part to the antireligious stances of some major figures in the field (Beck, 1997). The religious client may distrust the counseling process until the counselor demonstrates respect and at least nominal support of the client's beliefs. Additionally, the client's religious beliefs may lead her or him to seek assistance with a goal that the counselor sees as self-limiting or harmful. For example, a fundamentalist Christian wife may seek assistance in being more submissive to her husband, whom the counselor discovers to be authoritarian and emotionally abusive. In this case, the client's belief that wives should obey their husbands no matter what and that such obedience can be used by God to mature their husbands confines her to a vulnerable position in which she may be psychologically or physically harmed. Conversely, the religious belief of that same couple that the Bible is literally true can provide a foundation for the effective use of contrasting biblical principles to champion mutual respect and shared kindness in their relationship. Thus, the religious belief that helps to create the problem also holds the key to resolution of their problem of marital conflict. Further examples of this premise regarding religious beliefs as both problematic and as resource are illustrated in the case studies presented later in the chapter.

Techniques

This section describes several techniques that a counselor can use to assist clients with spiritual and religious belief issues. Whether or not a given technique should be used depends on the nature of the client's beliefs, the client's openness to the technique, and the counselor's skill level.

Exploration

While formal assessment of a client's religious and spiritual views is important (G. Miller, 2003; Richards & Bergin, 1997), the counselor also can include gradual exploration of the client's beliefs as one of many topics during the initial stages of counseling. This interaction about the client's faith will help the counselor know what the client believes, how important that belief is, to what degree it is associated with the client's presented issues, and what techniques it may suggest for working with the client (Kelly, 1995; G. Miller, 2003). In addition, this exploration weaves acceptance of religious belief into the context of counseling and makes it a part of the working alliance. It is not necessary that the counselor hold the same religious convictions as the client, as long as the therapeutic process is respectful and encouraging of the client's beliefs (Worthington, Kurusu, Sandage, & McCullough, 1996).

The counselor's stance during this exploration should be that of "not knowing," in which the counselor is "guided by a curiosity" of what is unknown about the client and her or his life experience (Jankowski, 2002, p. 73). Using appropriate, respectful questions emanating from this not-knowing stance enables the counselor to understand the client, decreases the possibility of imposing the counselor's spiritual beliefs onto the client, and helps the client to feel heard and understood.

Here are a few examples of questions the counselor might ask initially to explore religious and spiritual issues with the client:

1. Do you have any spiritual or religious beliefs? Help me understand them.
2. How do your spiritual or religious beliefs affect or influence you?
3. Are there any religious practices you follow? What do you like about them and how are they helpful?
4. When you think about the problems or issues we are talking about together, what religious or spiritual convictions that you hold seem to apply?
5. Considering the problem or issue you've presented, what do you imagine _____ (Buddha, Jesus, Muhammad, the Jewish prophets, etc.) might have said about it?
6. Are you aware of any ways in which your beliefs may be contributing to the problem or helping to keep you stuck in it?

A thoughtful examination of these and similar questions will help the counselor understand both the nature and depth of the client's beliefs, provide the client with an opportunity to explore and disclose those beliefs, and enable the counselor to make therapeutically accurate decisions about which spiritual integration techniques to use.

Consultation and Referral

Sometimes a client will be affiliated with a particular religion whose doctrines and worldview have a substantial impact on the client's perception of self and of the problems presented in counseling. When the client is deeply committed to a given religion and the counselor is not, the counselor can often benefit from the guidance and support of clergy from that religion. If you are going to work with a number of clients from a given religion, it is a good idea to contact clergy in the area to create a positive working relationship in advance of needing their assistance. Faiver, O'Brien, and McNally (1998) described some characteristics of these "friendly clergy" (p. 218). They are experienced teachers and respected leaders in their particular religious traditions. They are aware of, supportive of, and knowledgeable about the value of counseling. They understand that not all personal problems can be readily resolved through the application of religion per se, no matter how sincerely practiced. It is important that these clergy not see counseling and psychology as antifaith or demean secular counseling (Faiver et al., 1998). Other referral resources include spiritual directors, often found in Roman Catholic and Episcopal traditions. Spiritual directors may or may not be ordained clergy, but they have seminary or institute training in the scriptures of their tradition and are specifically prepared to companion intentional seekers on their religious and spiritual journeys. (See the "Recommended Reading" section below for more information on spiritual direction.)

Working with friendly clergy and spiritual directors has a number of advantages. Counselors can ask questions about the meaning of particular religious practices or beliefs. Clergy and spiritual directors can shed light on the meaning of certain passages of scripture or other religious writing, including alternative interpretations or other passages that balance out a one-sided view held by the client. A friendly clergy can help the counselor understand whether the client's belief stance is normative for the religion or is extreme and defensive. Finally, a positive dialogue with clergy "can enhance the counseling work with future clients as well as create a possible bridge for religious leaders to refer clients for counseling" (G. Miller, 2003). Such dialogue also enables the counselor to refer clients whose questions are more specifically religious than psychological in nature, and might therefore be more readily answered by a competent member of the clergy (Wolf & Stevens, 2001) or a trained spiritual director. A more complete discussion of consultation and referral is presented by Faiver and Ingersoll in chapter 9 of this book.

Bibliotherapy

Bibliotherapy in the realm of spiritual and religious issues serves the same function as in secular therapy. It involves the use of recommended readings for the purpose of providing the client broader perspective on her or his issues. Readings may include sacred writings from the client's religion, novels and autobiographies about people who have faced similar religious and spiritual crises, and topical books that address the area of concern expressed by the client. Suggested readings should be compatible with the client's religious belief if possible (G. Miller, 2003; Richards & Bergin, 1997) or at least not openly critical of the client's religion. Often the appropriate readings can be suggested by a friendly clergy or spiritual director, who also may suggest some key passages in sacred writings for the client to consider. When the client examines the sacred writings of her or his religion in greater depth, information or guidance can emerge that sheds additional light on the issue at hand. However, counselors should realize that recommending *only* scripture from the client's tradition eliminates the possibility of helpful insights from supplementary texts, including biography. Biographies of spiritual or religious historic figures (Egan, 1998) and contemporary spiritual autobiographies (Leigh, 2000) are rich sources for discussion of the spiritual journey. Apart from biography, popular literature now teems with resources for women (Conn, 1989, 1996; King, 1992; Snow, 1994) and men (Carmody, n.d.; Keen, 1991; Leigh, 2000), to name a few.

A particular case in point is the use of bibliotheraphy with people experiencing spiritual "dark night" situations (Conn, 1989; Cronk, 1991; Dombrowski, 1992; O'Connor, 2002). The phrase *dark night of the soul* was coined by St. John of the Cross, a 16th-century Spanish poet, Carmelite reformer, and theologian who wrote three classic works about his own spiritual journey: *The Ascent of Mount Carmel, The Dark Night of the Soul,* and *The Spiritual Canticle* (see Kavanaugh & Rodriguez, 1973). In *Dark Night* in particular, he chronicled his progressive loss of former ways of knowing and relating with God. Using *night* as a metaphor, he described this privation, beginning with sensory losses at dusk, proceeding to a profound sense of abandonment and desolation at midnight, and evolving into the transforming consolation of God's love at dawn. Because classic dark night experiences involve loss of former relationship with the Divine, they presuppose a theistic orientation in the client and a resulting grieving of this loss. This grief can be distinguished from clinical depression (O'Connor, 2002), which may or may not also be present. Whether depression can be ruled out or treated if present, dark night clients often benefit from appropriate bibliotherapy. From this reading they can realize that people intentionally committed to a religious or spiritually based life have arid periods, even feelings of abandonment by God. These spiritual dry periods are to be expected. Such times may be seen as invitations to let go of some former beliefs about how their relationship with God should be and to open themselves to new invitations for a deeper relationship with the Divine, whose dimensions and characteristics may not yet be clear. Use of relevant readings with people in this deep place of spiritual transformation requires the respectful companionship of a spiritually oriented counselor familiar with such resources. One of the case studies presented later illustrates working through the dark night experience in counseling.

Journaling

Journaling has several benefits that can help clients develop understanding of the spiritual and emotional issues they have encountered. A major advantage of journaling is that the client can express her or his thoughts freely, without fear of the judgments of self or others (G. Miller, 2003). Journaling does not require perfect grammar, complete sentences, or even a logical train of thought. Spontaneous expression of whatever comes to mind, including drawing, poetry, singular ideas or key concepts that may be centered alone on a page, or the unrestrained expression of thought and feeling that flows from the pen, all combine to provide for the client a different and more complete picture of her or his own story.

Functionally, there is no one right way to journal. Some use a hardbound blank book, some write on their computer, and some carry a spiral notebook. Some journalers write occasionally, whereas some chronicle their thoughts, emotions, and experiences everyday. Some write at length once a day when they write. Others jot down thoughts and reflections as they occur throughout the day. Linder, Miller, and Johnson (2000) suggested writing after or between counseling sessions and discussing in session the insights and awareness that emerge through the journaling process. Over time, journaling also creates a personal history or chronology that contains far more of the client's life experience and identity than does a simple history of events and facts. Reading back over a journal that spans a significant period of time can be tremendously helpful for understanding oneself in context. Understanding where and who one is today is much easier if one knows where and who one has been.

Journaling also allows a form of what narrative therapists call *externalizing conversations* (Monk et al., 1997). When the client writes her or his story in the journal and steps back to view it with some counselor-aided distance and skillfully crafted "scaffolding questions" (White, 2000) that support client options for reframing, the client may discover alternatives to earlier limited self-perceptions, and perhaps even new perspectives on aspects of her or his faith tradition. The client can be invited to review core beliefs and values as indicated in the journal and note how he or she may have changed or how the beliefs and values may have changed over time. Such noted evolution in beliefs can suggest possibilities for alternatives to current beliefs that seem to have lost their meaning or value and that may be contributing to psychological disturbance in the client.

Creating a journal allows the writer an opportunity safely to focus her or his attention on self for a period of time. The client is able to reflect, to ponder, to wonder about things as the content emerges. Here clients gain greater trust in themselves and find personal inspiration (G. Miller, 2003). For example, a client who was struggling with his tendency to rely on intellectual defenses and to appear brilliant in the eyes of others was working in counseling on his desire to feel and to express his emotions more fully. Understanding the facts of his dilemma did little to change him until the day he spontaneously drew a certain picture in his journal. He drew a military combat tank with a tiny, helmeted person peering out of the turret hatch, with only his eyes and helmet exposed. On the side of the tank, the client printed the word *think*. His drawing was a pun, using the idea of a think tank (a place where problems are considered and solutions offered) to represent his own tendency to think about everything but not to allow feeling. He was able to see himself in a new but somewhat bitter-sweet light, as a frightened person who peered out at the world from within his mobile fortress of armored, defensive cognition, his think tank. This both amused and saddened him, and led to rapid progress in his efforts to engage the world with his emotions.

Meditation

Meditation is a major component of most world religions (Kelly, 1995), including Christianity (Schopen & Freeman, 1992). Unfortunately, the consensus in the United States today is that meditation is an Eastern, not a Western, tradition (Schopen & Freeman, 1992). In fact, both Eastern and Western spiritual traditions include some form of meditation, though there are some differences in the types of meditation practiced. Schopen and Freeman summarized the basic differences between Eastern and Western forms of meditation. Eastern meditation tends to be more about promoting freedom from ideas or cessation of concentrated thought. The purpose of this form of meditation is to achieve a state of mind that is free from concentration, ideas, and intrusive thoughts. The traditional Western form of meditation is more cognitive, dwelling on ideas or concentrating on a particular issue or focus. This contemplative state of mind is intended to provide clarity and insight about the issue being considered. Keating (1986), a contemporary Cistercian priest, monk, and abbot, has revived an ancient Christian meditation practice in his reintroduction of centering prayer. His works and those of Pennington (1986) offer a spiritually nourishing Western-rooted meditation practice.

Research indicates that meditation can create a variety of physical, psychological, and spiritual benefits for the client (G. Miller, 2003). These include relaxation, stress reduction, alleviation of discomforting emotions, and an increase in personal awareness. Schopen and Freeman (1992) included the following as benefits of meditation: the calming and focusing of attention for contemplation; changes in one's mental, emotional, and physical state; stress reduction; a clearer, more accurate perception of reality; and a means of self-therapy for the client between sessions. G. Miller (2003), Frame (2003), Kelly (1995), and Schopen and Freeman (1992) presented more detailed information about the use of various meditation techniques in counseling. One of the most widely used is guided imagery, in which the client achieves a state of calm through progressive muscle relaxation, then follows counselor verbal guidance as visualizations emerge in the mind (G. Miller, 2003). These visual images can contribute to a changing perspective, reduce stress and anxiety, or provide new avenues for exploration of the issues.

Prayer

McCullough and Larson (1999) defined prayer as "thoughts, attitudes, and actions designed to express or experience connection to the sacred" (p. 86). Prayer is reportedly popular in the Unites States. Frame (2003) quoted a 1993 Gallup poll indicating that "90% of Americans pray, 97% believe that prayer is heard, and 86% believe that prayer makes them better people" (p. 185). Prayer is practiced in many forms. McCullough and Larson (1999) identified five types of prayer: contemplative/meditative (opening to one's experience of the Divine), ritual (reciting written or memorized prayer), petitionary (making a personal request for self or others), colloquial (various forms of informal conversation with God), and intercessory (praying for others).

Counselors may encounter prayer in various ways. Frame (2003) suggested three major uses of prayer in therapeutic settings. First, clients may use prayer as an ancillary tool along with mental health treatment. Second, counselors may pray about or for their clients outside of the counseling session. Third, counselors may choose to pray with their clients in the counseling session when they deem it to be appropriate. Various research has documented the efficacy of prayer (Neighbors, Jackson, Bowman, & Gurin, 1983; Pargament, 1997; Poloma & Pendleton, 1991), though there are often qualifications offered by these researchers regarding its limited use, and only with selected clients. Butler, Gardner, and Bird (1998) described various effects of couples' using prayer as part of their counseling process and gave a cautious recommendation for its use with religious couples in conflict. Frame (2003) seconded the notion of Richards and Bergin (1997) that prayer should not be considered as a substitute for the professional competency and psychological health of the counselor.

We are quite equivocal regarding the use of prayer as a therapeutic intervention, but we include the topic here to give breadth to the presentation of techniques and to caution the counselor considering prayer. We agree with Kelly (1995) that using prayer in counseling is both problematic and controversial, especially in secular counseling. We are cautious about the use of prayer in session, as it can blur boundaries with the work of clergy and spiritual directors and can elicit negative transference (Richards & Bergin, 1997) from earlier adverse experiences with clergy. Kelly (1995) described other potential problems, including the intrusion of the counselor's religious values into the counseling process and the inappropriate blending of religious practice into scientifically based psychotherapy. In addition, the use of prayer itself may be an avoidance technique of the client (Kelly, 1990), who may attempt to rationalize away real problems by praying them away.

If prayer is to be used as part of the counseling process, we recommend the following guidelines:

1. Prayer is most appropriate when the counselor and client hold the same or very similar religious beliefs.
2. The idea of prayer should be initiated by the client, not the counselor, so the counselor's values are not imposed on the client.
3. If the counselor does not share the client's religious beliefs, and the client wants to pray during sessions, the counselor should either present an attitude of respect while the client prays or suggest that the client seek guidance for prayer from their clergy or spiritual director. This is an excellent way to rely on friendly clergy as a referral source.
4. The counselor should be attentive about whether or not the client's use of prayer is part of an attempt to avoid personal responsibility for problem resolution, or is a sincere, deeply felt connection to the transpersonal in which the client seeks guidance and comfort while confronting personal problems.
5. When a client chooses to pray during the session, it is important to talk with the client during the session about the purpose for and experience of the prayer.

Ritual

Clients bringing religious and spiritual issues provide rich opportunities for employment of ritual for therapeutic intervention. Denzin (1974) defined ritual as

> A conventionalized joint activity given to ceremony, involving two or more persons endowed with special emotion and often with sacred meaning, focused around a clearly defined set of social objects, and when performed confers on its participants, a special sense of the sacred and the out of the ordinary. (p. 272)

Among others, Jung (1933, 1968), Scotton, Chinen, and Battista (1996), Tart (1983), and Wynstrock (1995) have noted the healing power of ritual. Rituals, co-constructed with the client, can be grounded in the client's religious or spiritual beliefs and designed to promote client therapeutic goals. While a full discussion of various application of ritual as therapeutic interventions could be the subject of an entire text, a brief presentation will suffice here. Parker and Horton (1996) noted that rituals—both secular and religious—are part of our everyday lives. They provided a thoughtful discussion of various considerations designed to maximize the therapeutic impact of ritual, which include incorporating the five senses, creating sacred space and time for the event, and using potent symbolism and ritual actions. Germane to the therapeutic application of ritual, they identified three types of therapeutic ritual that can easily be connected with client religious and/or spiritual beliefs: liberation, transformation, and celebration.

Liberation rituals involve restoration through symbolic removal of or disengagement from some form of oppression, be it a toxic relationship with a person, place, institution, or even self. The goal is release. Such rituals contain an element of paradox in that they usually involve an act of destruction to effect healing. Liberation rituals regarding severing destructive relationships may involve selecting a meaningful location and the destruction of symbols of that relationship, various forms of grieving, and the inclusion of positive affirmations about self and one's future. Specific examples of this general scenario are limited only by the imaginations of the client and counselor working together. The case studies below include the use of an effective liberation ritual.

Transformation rituals may have elements of both liberation and celebration in them, though they can have a particular emphasis on life transition events—passages from one state to another. Religious examples include the seven sacraments of the Catholic Church and other Christian denominations, bar and bat mitzvah in the Jewish tradition, and related passage markers in all the world's major religions and indigenous spiritual traditions, including christening, puberty rites, marriage, ordination, and funerals. These are rites-of-passage events, rituals of initiation and formation wherein a new identity is affirmed, nurtured, and empowered. The goal is the cultural or societal confirmation of a new condition or state through relinquishing of a former way of living and being. Cultural or religious institution-sanctioned passages may or may not have the psychological impact that a client-developed counterpart may have. Couples designing their wedding ceremonies and writing their own vows are examples of the importance of ownership by the participants in the ritual. Other life transitions not necessarily institutionalized by religious or civil authorities may also be important opportunities for transformation rituals—losses of all kinds (including miscarriages, abortions, jobs) are powerful and potentially debilitating examples. Other examples evoking the entire emotional spectrum abound in family therapy literature (Frankl, 1993; Imber-Black, Roberts, & Whiting, 1988; Kaslow, 1993).

Celebration rituals often are associated with cyclic events of remembrance such as religious holidays, birthdays, and anniversaries of major occurrences, including life transition episodes. As with transformation rituals, many of these ceremonies are religious, cultural, or socially sanctioned events. Additionally, celebrants often wish to add their own unique contributions (ideas, symbols, speeches) to the event. Here again, counselors of religious or spiritually oriented clients may assist in the co-creation of personally meaningful and affirming celebrations by encouraging the client to explore and possibly enact some elements of their faith tradition's dimension regarding the event.

Ethical considerations regarding therapeutic use of ritual begin with respect for the client's cultural boundaries and beliefs. Whether the ritual expresses liberation, transformation, or celebration, counselor sensitivity to the client's religious and spiritual worldviews is essential. As noted in this chapter's earlier discussion on therapeutic alliance, trust and respect between client and counselor are fundamental to client change. Ritual work can be very powerful and ego-enhancing for the counselor as well as for the client. Consequently, when counselors participate in construction of therapeutic rituals, such questions as "Whose ritual is it?" and "Whose needs are being met?" must be asked. To ensure respect for client beliefs and boundaries, counselors would do well to bring an attitude of creative collaboration—power *with* rather than power *over* their clients—while facilitating construction of therapeutic rituals. Other counselor questions such as, "What symbols (locations, implements, or associations) can be incorporated to enhance the meaning and emotional nourishment of the ritual?" and "How will incorporation of ____ relate to the purpose of your ritual?" will help keep the counselor in a facilitating, collaborative rather than directive role.

Another prime consideration in application of ritual in therapy is relevance and meaningfulness (G. Miller, 2003). The client's connection between the ritual itself and the life circumstance being addressed is crucial to effective implementation of ritual in spiritually based client issues. The counseling questions in the previous paragraph also apply here regarding relevance. Another consideration is the possible overuse of ritual that can dilute its impact. Once again, the seductive power of effectively used ritual can be a temptation for overuse, with the accompanying consequences of using any therapeutic intervention too frequently.

A final thought on ritual concerns the importance of remembering the *individual* as well as her or his familial or social network. Some rituals may be appropriate only to the individual client and may be conducted by the client alone. In such cases, the counselor is the affirming party or "witness" via the necessary processing that occurs in the session(s) following the ritual enactment.

Case Studies

Spiritual Emergence From the Dark Night

On occasion, counselors will encounter clients who are experiencing what Grof and Grof (1989) and Bragdon (1990, 1993) called *spiritual emergence*. Brother David Steindl-Rast, a Benedictine monk, gives the following description:

> Spiritual emergence is a kind of birth pang in which you yourself go through to a fuller life, a deeper life, in which some areas of your life that were not yet encompassed by this fullness of life are now integrated or called to be integrated or challenged to be integrated. . . . Breakthroughs are often very painful. Often acute and dramatic breakthroughs (happen) on all levels: what we call material, spiritual, bodily—all levels. (Bragdon, 1993, p. 18)

When the pace of spiritual emergence quickens, the client may experience a spiritual emergency. Spiritual emergency may take many forms, from dark night experiences wherein they feel a profound loss of connection with their Higher Power, God, or Creator, to near or even apparent psychotic experiences. While this topic has been the subject of entire texts (Bragdon, 1990, 1993; Grof & Grof, 1989), the case presented here is limited to the experience of *dark night of the soul*, a term first coined by St. John of the Cross (Kavanaugh & Rodriguez, 1973), as described previously in the section on techniques.

Teresita, a 44-year-old devout Roman Catholic Filipina, wife of 23 years and mother of two daughters in college, established a trusting relationship with a counselor who had helped her and her family with a number of issues, including marital stresses and adolescent developmental transitions. She returned to counseling a year after successful resolution with her husband, Ramon, of some early empty-nest issues. Her reason for returning was a recent unpleasantly surprising development in her religious life. She tearfully reported to her counselor, "I can't find God anymore. I'm afraid I have done something terribly wrong. It's like He has abandoned me." She reiterated that all her life she had attended mass and participated in the sacraments regularly, said her rosary at least weekly, and generally had had "a very precious and satisfying relationship with Jesus." Her church committee work, once a source of much satisfaction in her relationships with God and fellow parishioners, now seemed like busywork. She longed for more meaningful connection with God. Her daily prayer routine became a chore, prompting feelings of guilt and sadness from her loss of connection with God. At the urging of her priest, she redoubled her commitment to church activities and daily prayer. Her increased commitment in the form of more committee work and more diligent prayer did not seem to help. Even her priest's admonition to be patient and listen for God's word made no apparent difference. She reported feeling more lost as the weeks passed.

Teresita had no significant disturbances in sleep and eating patterns, or any other common symptoms of clinical depression. She did report feeling discouraged and worried. Further exploration indicated that she was able to function at her job reasonably well, though she reported preoccupation with her loss of spiritual relationship. From her presentation, her counselor was able to rule out clinical depression with its related consideration of medication. Her counselor's interest in and familiarity with Western spiritual traditions made possible discussions about *cataphatic* and *apophatic* spiritual experiences (Cronk, 1991). The former tradition recognizes that individuals enter relationship with God through all aspects of creation, including the beauty of nature, music, art, relationships, and images of God's love in scripture. However, there are times in the life of some individuals in which their traditional religious beliefs and practices no longer meet their spiritual needs. Such experiences need to be considered in light of the apophatic phenomenon. This tradition emphasizes that no images, ideologies, or cultural expressions can adequately convey all that God is, and revelation brings one into mystery characterized by emptiness, dryness, and the absence of the sense of God's presence. Teresita's counselor suggested that she explore the possibility that God was still present, but no longer on Teresita's terms, and that she could consider her experience as an invitation for a new and deeper relationship with the Divine. Including apophatic readings in Western spirituality (Dombrowski, 1992; Progoff, 1983) and spiritual autobiography (Leigh, 2000) helped Teresita begin to experience her journey as a dark night that had been endured by many other devout Christians. Instead of a sign of spiritual death, she began to experience her condition as a sign of *life*, of growth and development of a different kind of relationship with God. She began to sense movement through darkness to the light of acceptance that her relationship with God was maturing from the certainty of earlier times to a letting go of having to "know." Her own process was, in Christian terms, a *paschal death*—a spiritual death of her former self with its ego-based ways of living. Paradoxically, the *absence* she now felt was a *presence*. She gradually took comfort in realizing a sense of solidarity with others whose spiritual journeys shared characteristics of hers. Over a period of months she reported a growing acceptance of her evolving relationship with God, and sensed a dawning of consolation.

A Ritual of Letting Go and Moving On

David is a middle-aged man who sought counseling assistance to help him recover from an unwanted divorce. His wife had left him for another man, making it clear to him that she had not loved him for years and was leaving in part to attain a higher level of material status with her new partner. David was finding it difficult several months after the divorce to begin the process of grieving and letting go. He was a gentle, thoughtful artist who enjoyed nature, hiking into the wilderness, and reflective writing. Much of his spirituality was expressed in his closeness to the land and to the creative symbolism that he enjoyed. With this in mind, the counselor helped David to create a liberating ritual that would help him grieve, bring closure to the broken relationship, and move forward with his life.

One day David hiked into a wilderness setting to a high mountain meadow with a stream ambling through it. There he placed several large stones leading out from the near bank of the stream, careful not to block the flow or to redirect its course. When he was able to stand on a rock midway across the stream, he had a heartfelt conversation with his ex-wife, whom he imagined standing on the opposite bank of the stream. In this cathartic expression, he was able to say without restraint all that he thought and felt about her, their marriage, and the loss of their life together. When he had finished, David left the rocks in the stream to symbolize his belief that he had worked to build a relational bridge to her over the years, and that its incompleteness was inevitable because she had not faithfully built her half of the bridge. Standing on that rock halfway across the stream, he determined that he would no longer stand alone on a half-finished bridge, longing for her.

In the second part of the ritual, David got out a small wooden box into which he had placed photographs, letters, and other mementos of their marriage. He buried this box in the ground, planting a small evergreen sapling on top. He knew that the box and its paper contents would decay and be drawn up into the young tree as nourishment, strengthening it over the years. This was his way of choosing to grow, to become strong and free, turning the sorrow and loss of his experience into character and courage. After returning from the mountains, he talked further with his counselor about the power and personal meaning of the liberating ritual. David felt that he had turned a corner in his struggle and would be moving into healing from that point on.

Rethinking a Marital Mandate

A young married couple requested counseling assistance because of the role conflict they were experiencing. As conservative evangelical Christians, they believed that the Bible was inerrant and that it delineated very specific roles for husbands and wives to follow. While both desired to follow the prescriptions of their faith, the wife was beginning to chafe under her husband's rather authoritarian use of the rights he believed he possessed as undisputed leader of the family. He stated that his wife should obey him, not question his judgment, and trust him to make all the important decisions. While willing to be supportive of his leadership, she complained that he treated her as if she was incompetent, discounted her intelligence, and was quick to quote Bible verses to her if she disagreed with him. An exploration of their families of origin revealed that both had grown up in conservative Christian households in which the unilateral authority of the father could never be questioned.

Instead of questioning the couple's commitment to such self-limiting marital roles, the counselor chose to work within their belief system, challenging them to reconsider their perception of those roles. Knowing that they believed the Bible to be inerrant, he asked them to consider three passages of scripture, specifically Ephesians 5:21–33, Philippians 2:3–11, and Proverbs 31:10–31 (Lockman Foundation, 1973). The first of these passages indicates that wives are to be subject to their husbands *and* that husbands are to love their wives as Christ loved the church. The second describes the self-emptying of Christ, who laid aside the visible manifestations of deity, humbled himself to become a human being, and as a man was a servant to those around him. The sacrificial love emerging from this humble servanthood was unfailing, even if it meant dying to prove that love. The third passage is a classic from the wisdom literature of the Old Testament that describes the characteristics of a good wife. She is not only a skilled domestic engineer but also a strong person, an economically successful entrepeneur who is well known among the community, and a wise teacher who is trusted by her husband.

The purpose for using these scripture passages was to create cognitive dissonance in both clients between their established perception of what it means to be a wife or husband and what their own religious writings said about it. Both were asked to rethink their interpretation of the Bible in light of what the Bible itself said. The husband was challenged to consider whether or not he was actually serving his wife and trusting her judgment in the way he treated her. The idea of leadership from a position of humble servanthood was a new one for him. The wife was empowered to expand her role if she chose to do so, and was able to see that she could be both cooperative with her husband's leadership and free to use her abilities to the full. Both learned that healthy marriages are respectful of the worth and dignity of both partners.

Searching for His Tribe

By the time he reached his mid-40s, Nate no longer believed or practiced the Judeo-Christian religion of his youth. He sought counseling because of a vague sense of being lost, of feeling disconnected, that he did not understand. He described himself as independent, solitary, and friendly but not deeply connected with others. Having read a number of self-help books addressing relationship issues and the concerns of the adult male, he rejected the idea that he was having a midlife crisis. As he said in his first visit to the counselor, "Something else is bothering me, something bigger or more important than just my life."

Over the first few sessions, Nate disclosed a number of facts and feelings that pointed to an unfulfilled longing to be better connected to his Native American roots. He grew up as the middle child in a family with three sons. His father was White and his mother was Cherokee. She left her home abruptly at age 16 to escape the violence of her own alcoholic mother, and soon after married Nate's father. She was proud of her native heritage but never talked about her life among her family or tribe. She reunited with her estranged Cherokee father about the time Nate was born. Nate wistfully described his Native American grandfather as a gentle, strong man who taught him a great deal about life, manhood, and personal honor. He also taught him wilderness skills and the importance of learning from and caring for the natural world. Nate's grandfather died when he was 12 years old, and he was never emotionally close to his own biological father.

During his adolescent and young adult years, Nate had no meaningful contact with any Native Americans except his mother. He attended a large metropolitan high school, completed college and graduate school, and in most ways was successful and happy. During his 40th year, he began to experience the sense of disconnection after a solo backpack trip in the mountains. On that trip he found a perfectly preserved eagle feather lying in the middle of the trail. He described the event as magical, numinous, and soul stirring. Thereafter he became restless, disinterested in former pursuits, and unsure of the direction of his life. The precipitating event that brought him to counseling was talking about the feather to a Native American man he had just met. The new friend said, "Perhaps the grandfathers are talking to you."

With the counselor's assistance, Nate began to explore what he called his "Cherokee side" more fully. He read books about the history of the Cherokee people, including the traumas experienced by those uprooted from their homelands. He also read about native spirituality and the lessons contained in animal folklore. He listened to Native American flute music, attended ceremonial pow-wows, and began to make his own native artifacts. He confided in his mother, who became more open with him about her own troubled childhood. He sought out members of local tribes to continue learning about the culture and spirituality of native peoples. He began to dress in ways that reflected his heritage, rediscovering moccasins and beaded belts.

Despite this understandable searching for his Cherokee self, he was still troubled and lacking in peace. At the suggestion of a Native American friend, he decided to go on a vision quest into the wilderness. Because he was not qualified to mentor Nate on this important spiritual journey, the counselor helped him connect with a Native American elder who agreed to be a spiritual guide for the journey. Nate described their relationship as very much like being with his grandfather. Over a number of visits with the tribal elder, Nate prepared himself for the vision quest.

Nate spent 4 days alone fasting in the high mountain wilderness of his state. He took minimal equipment and supplies, carrying only the essentials for survival. He hiked off-trail and away from people, camping near water in places where he could have the best view of his surroundings. He spent hours just staring out over the wilderness, open to what the mountains, and the sky, and the animals wanted to teach him. At one point he watched a hawk soar above him and asked the hawk what he might understand if he could see his own life from that perspective. He wept openly and bitterly everyday, wondering why there was such sadness in him. By the third day he sometimes felt joyous and free for reasons he could not fully explain.

He later told the counselor about two of the many things he learned on his vision quest. First was the deep sorrow he felt at not being able to grow up among the Cherokee people. He discovered that much of his recent cultural exploration was an attempt to heal this wound. Second was the realization that he did not have a "White side" and a "Cherokee side" but that, like nature, he needed to be whole and only one person. He could not make peace with that person until he also accepted and integrated the truth that the holocaust experienced by his mother's people was created by his father's people. He had been trying to resolve the darkness of that split by choosing one over the other at various times in his life. He learned that, to be at peace with himself, he must live as *one*, aware of the goodness and failings of both sides of his heritage.

When Nate terminated counseling, he described himself as being more aware of himself and the world around him. He stayed in touch with the tribal elder who had helped him, and eventually contacted Cherokee leaders to investigate being registered as a tribal member. He was more focused on community and less on work for its own sake. He continued hiking into the high country, but began more and more to take a number of friends with him, teaching them what he knew of nature and its wisdom. This circle of close friends he fondly referred to as his Tribe.

Recommended Reading

General Reading: Integrating Spirituality and Psychotherapy

Becvar, D. A. (1997). *Soul healing: A spiritual orientation in counseling and therapy.* New York: Basic Books.

Burke, M. T., & Miranti, J. G. (1995). *Counseling: The spiritual dimension.* Alexandria, VA: American Counseling Association.

Cortright, B. (1997). *Psychotherapy and spirit.* Albany: State University of New York Press.

Favier, C., Ingersoll, R. E., O'Brien, E., & McNally, C. (2001). *Explorations in counseling and spirituality.* Belmont, CA: Wadsworth/Thomson Learning.

Fukuyama, M. A., & Sevig, T. D. (1999). *Integrating spirituality into multicultural counseling.* London: Sage.

Griffith, J. L., & Griffith, M. E. (2002). *Encountering the sacred in psychotherapy: How to talk to people about their spiritual lives.* New York: Guilford Press.

Hinterkopf, E. (1998). *Integrating spirituality in counseling: A manual for using the experiential focusing method*. Alexandria, VA: American Counseling Association.

May, G. (1982). *Care of mind, care of spirit: Psychiatric dimensions of spiritual direction*. San Francisco: Harper & Row.

Miller, W. R. (Ed.). (1999). *Integrating spirituality into treatment: Resources for practitioners*. Washington, DC: American Psychological Association.

Moore, T. (1994). *Care of the soul*. New York: Harper & Row.

Palmer, P. (1990). *The active life: A spirituality of work, creativity and caring*. San Francisco: Harper & Row.

Walsh, R., & Vaughn, F. (Eds.). (1993). *Paths beyond ego: The transpersonal vision*. New York: Jeremy Tarcher/Putnam.

Spiritual Traditions and Counseling

Epstein, M. (1995). *Thoughts without a thinker: Psychotherapy from a Buddhist perspective*. New York: Basic Books. [Buddhism]

Frager, R. (1999). *Heart, self & soul: The Sufi psychology of growth, balance and harmony*. Wheaton, IL: Quest Books. [Sufism]

Hanh, T. N. (1995). *Living Buddha, living Christ*. New York: Riverhead Books. [Buddhist and Christian]

Hanh, T. N. (1998). *The heart of the Buddha's teaching*. Berkeley, CA: Parallax Press.

Hart, T. (1994). *Hidden spring: The spiritual dimension of therapy*. New York: Paulist Press. [Christianity]

Hixon, L. (1995). *Coming home: The experience of enlightenment in sacred traditions*. Burdett, NY: Larson. [various traditions]

Johanson, G., & Kurtz. R. (1991). *Grace unfolding: Psychotherapy in the spirit of the Tao-Te-Ching*. New York: Bell Tower. [Taoism]

Kahn, P. V. I. (1982). *Introducing spirituality into counseling and therapy*. New Lebanon, NY: Omega. [Sufism]

O'Donohue, J. (1997). *Anam cara: A book of Celtic wisdom*. New York: Cliff Street Books/HarperCollins. [Celtic]

O'Donohue, J. (1999). *Eternal echoes*. New York: Cliff Street Books/HarperCollins. [Celtic insights]

Wilber, K. (1985). *No boundary: Eastern and Western approaches to personal growth*. Boston: Shambhala. [transtraditional]

Meditation

Hanh, T. N. (1985). *A guide to walking meditation*. New Haven, CT: Eastern Press.

Hanh, T. N. (1995). *The miracle of mindfulness*. Boston: Beacon Press.

Kornfield, J. (1996). *The inner art of meditation*. Boulder, CO: Sounds True Video.

Ritual

Beck, R., & Metrick, S. B. (1990). *The art of ritual*. Berkeley, CA: Celestial Arts.

Biziou, B. (1999). *The joy of ritual*. New York: Golden Books.

Campbell, J. (1988). *The power of myth*. New York: Doubleday.

Driver, T. F. (1991). *The magic of ritual: Our needs for liberating rites that transform our lives and our communities*. New York: Harper Collins.

Feinstein, D., & Mayo, P. E. (1990). *Rituals for living and dying: From life's wounds to spiritual awakening*. New York: Harper Collins.

Imber-Black, E., & Roberts, J. (1993). *Rituals for our times: Celebrating, healing, and changing our lives and our relationships*. New York: Harper Collins.

May, R. (1991). *The cry for myth*. New York: Norton.

Some, M. P. (1993). *Ritual: Power, healing and community*. Portland, OR: Swan Raven.

Web Sites of Interest

http://www.mercycenter.org
The Mercy Center, Burlingame, California

http://www.shalem.org
The Shalem Institute, Washington, DC

http://www.sdiworld.org
Spiritual Directors International

Summary

In this chapter, we addressed the counselor's use of clients' religious and/or spiritual beliefs in pursuit of their therapeutic goals. We described the different ways clients can believe and the ways in which counselors may respond to those beliefs. We discussed a number of specific techniques counselors can implement to work with the client within his or her belief system. We presented several case studies to illustrate some potential client issues and their resolution. We also stressed that the client's way of perceiving and being in the world is unique to that person and deserving of respect. We hope you will experience these ideas as catalysts for your creative and compassionate work with clients, and we invite you to continue exploring your own spiritual/religious path.

References

Allport, G. W., & Ross, J. M. (1967). Personal religious orientation and prejudice. *Journal of Personality and Social Psychology, 5*, 432–443.

Batson, C. D., & Ventis, W. L. (1982). *The religious experience: A social–psychological experience*. New York: Oxford University Press.

Beck, J. R. (1997). Value tensions between evangelical Christians and Christian counseling. *Counseling and Values, 41*, 107–116.

Bishop, D. R. (1995). Religious values as cross-cultural issues in counseling. In M. T. Burke & J. G. Miranti (Eds.), *Counseling: The spiritual dimension* (pp. 59–71). Alexandria, VA: American Counseling Association.

Bragdon, E. (1990). *The call of spiritual emergency*. San Francisco: Harper & Row.

Bragdon, E. (1993). *A sourcebook for helping people with spiritual problems.* Aptos, CA: Lightening Up Press.

Butler, M. H., Gardner, B. C., & Bird, M. H. (1998). Not just time-out: Change dynamics of prayer for religious couples in conflict situations. *Family Process, 37,* 451–478.

Carmody, J. (n.d.). *Toward a male spirituality.* Mystic, CT: Twenty-Third Publications.

Conn, J. W. (1989). *Spirituality and personal maturity.* Mahwah, NJ: Paulist Press.

Conn, J. W. (1996). *Women's spirituality: Resources for Christian development* (2nd ed.) Mahwah, NJ: Paulist Press.

Cronk, S. (1991). *Dark night journey.* Wallingford, PA: Pendle Hill.

Denzin, N. K. (1974). The methodological implication of symbolic interaction for the study of deviance. *British Journal of Sociology, 25,* 269–282.

Dombrowski, D. A. (1992). *St. John of the Cross: An appreciation.* Albany: State University of New York Press.

Egan, G. (1998). *The skilled helper: A problem-management approach to helping* (6th ed.). Pacific Grove, CA: Brooks/Cole.

Faiver, C. M., O'Brien, E. M., & McNally, C. J. (1998). "The friendly clergy": Characteristics and referral. *Counseling and Values, 42,* 217–221.

Frame, M. W. (2003). *Integrating religion and spirituality into counseling.* Pacific Grove, CA: Brooks/Cole.

Frankl, A. D. (1993). Using a funeral ritual in therapy: Changing rigid interaction patterns. In T. S. Nelson & T. S. Trepper (Eds.), *101 interventions in family therapy* (pp. 46–49). New York: Haworth Press.

Georgia, R. T. (1994). Preparing to counsel clients of different religious backgrounds: A phenomenological approach. *Counseling and Values, 38,* 143–151.

Gladding, S. (2001). *The counseling dictionary: Concise definitions of frequently used terms.* Upper Saddle River, NJ: Prentice-Hall.

Grof, C., & Grof, S. (Eds.). (1989). *Spiritual emergency.* Los Angeles: Tarcher.

Guinee, J. P., & Tracey, T. J. G. (1997). Effects of religiosity and problem type on counselor description ratings. *Journal of Counseling & Development, 76,* 65–73.

Helminiak, D. A. (2001). Treating spiritual issues in secular psychotherapy. *Counseling and Values, 45,* 163–189.

Imber-Black, E., Roberts, J., & Whiting, R. A. (Eds.). (1988). *Rituals in families and family therapy.* New York: Norton.

Jankowski, P. J. (2002). Postmodern spirituality: Implications for promoting change. *Counseling and Values, 47,* 69–79.

Jung, C. G. (1933). *Modern man in search of a soul.* New York: Harcourt Brace.

Jung, C. G. (1968). *The archetypes and the collective unconscious.* Princeton, NJ: Princeton University Press.

Kaslow, F. (1993). The divorce ceremony: A healing strategy. In T. S. Nelson & T. S. Trepper (Eds.), *101 interventions in family therapy* (pp. 341–345). New York: Haworth Press.

Kavanaugh, K., & Rodriguez, O. (1973). *The collected works of St. John of the Cross.* Washington, DC: Institute of Carmelite Studies.

Keating, T. (1986). *Open mind, open heart: The contemplative dimension of the gospel.* Warwick, NY: Amity House.

Keen, S. K. (1991). *Fire in the belly: On being a man.* New York, NY: Bantam.

Kelly, E. W. (1990). Counselor responsiveness to client religiousness. *Counseling and Values, 35,* 69–72.

Kelly, E. W. (1995). *Spirituality and religion in counseling and psychotherapy: Diversity in theory and practice.* Alexandria, VA: American Counseling Association.

King, T. (Ed.). (1992). *The spiral path: Explorations in women's spirituality.* Saint Paul, MN: Yes International.

Leigh, D. J. (2000). *Circuitous journeys.* New York: Fordham University Press.

Linder, S., Miller, G., & Johnson, P. (2000). Counseling and spirituality: The use of emptiness and the importance of timing. *Resources in Education,* CG029855.

Lockman Foundation. (Ed.). (1973). *New American standard bible: Reference edition.* La Habra, CA: Foundation Press.

McAuliffe, G. J., & Eriksen, K. P. (1999). Toward a constructivist and developmental identity for the counseling profession: The context-phase-stage-style model. *Journal of Counseling & Development, 77,* 267–280.

McCullough, M. E., & Larson, D. B. (1999). Prayer. In W. R. Miller (Ed.), *Integrating spirituality into treatment* (pp. 85–110). Washington, DC: American Psychological Association.

McCullough, M. E., & Worthington, E. L. (1995). College students' perceptions of a psychotherapist's treatment of a religious issue: Partial replication and extension. *Journal of Counseling & Development, 73,* 626–634.

Miller, G. (2003). *Incorporating spirituality in counseling and psychotherapy: Theory and technique.* Hoboken, NJ: Wiley.

Miller, G. A. (1992). Integrating religion and psychology in therapy: Issues and recommendations. *Counseling and Values, 36,* 112–122.

Miller, S. D., Duncan, B. L., & Hubble, M. A. (1997). *Escape from Babel: Toward a unifying language for psychotherapy practice.* New York: Norton.

Miller, W. R., & Rollnick, S. (1991). *Motivational interviewing: Preparing people to change addictive behavior.* New York: Guilford Press.

Monk, G., Winslade, J., Crocket, K., & Epston, D. (1997). *Narrative therapy in practice: The archaeology of hope.* San Francisco: Jossey-Bass.

Neighbors, H. W., Jackson, J. S., Bowman, P. J., & Gurin, G. (1983). Stress, coping, and Black mental health: Preliminary findings from a national survey. *Prevention in Human Services, 2,* 5–29.

O'Connor, M. (2002). Spiritual dark night and psychological depression: Some comparisons and contrasts. *Counseling and Values, 46,* 137–149.

Pargament, K. I. (1997). *The psychology of religion and coping.* New York: Guilford Press.

Parker, H., & Horton, H. S. (1996). A typology of ritual: Paradigms of healing and empowerment. *Counseling and Values, 40,* 83–97.

Pennington, M. B. (1986). *Centered living: The way of centering prayer.* New York: Doubleday.

Poloma, M. M., & Pendleton, B. F. (1991). The effects of prayer and prayer experiences on measures of general well-being. *Journal of Psychology and Theology, 19,* 71–83.

Progoff, I. (1983). *The cloud of unknowing.* New York: Dell.

Richards, P. S., & Bergin, A. E. (1997). *A spiritual strategy for counseling and psychotherapy.* Washington, DC: American Psychological Association.

Schopen, A., & Freeman, B. (1992). Meditation: The forgotten Western tradition. *Counseling and Values, 36,* 123–134.

Scotton, B. W., Chinen, A. B., & Battista, J. R. (Eds.). (1996). *Textbook of transpersonal psychiatry and psychology.* New York: Basic Books.

Shapiro, V., & Ross, V. (2002). Applications of narrative theory and therapy to the practice of family medicine. *Family Medicine, 34,* 96–100.

Snow, K. (1994). *Keys to the open gate: A women's spirituality sourcebook.* Berkeley, CA: Conari Press.

Sue, D. E., & Sue, D. (2003). *Counseling the culturally diverse* (4th ed.). New York: Wiley.

Suyemoto, K. L., & MacDonald, M. L. (1996). The content and function of religious beliefs. *Counseling and Values, 40,* 143–153.

Tart, C. (Ed.). (1983). *Transpersonal psychologies.* El Cerrito, CA: Psychological Processes.

Watts, R. E. (2001). Addressing spiritual issues in secular counseling and psychotherapy: Response to Helminiak's (2001) views. *Counseling and Values, 45,* 207–217.

White, M. (2000). *Conversation hour* [Audiotape]. In "The Evolution of Psychotherapy: A Conference" (May 25–29, 2000), Anaheim, CA.

Wilber, K. (1996). *A brief history of everything.* Boston: Shambhala.

Wilber, K. (1997, Fall/Winter). A spirituality that transforms. *What Is Enlightenment?, 12,* 22–32.

Wilber, K. (1998). *The essential Ken Wilber: An introductory reader.* Boston: Shambhala.

Wolf, C. T., & Stevens, P. (2001). Integrating religion and spirituality in marriage and family counseling. *Counseling and Values, 46,* 66–75.

Worthington, E. L., Kurusu, T. A., Sandage, S. J., & McCullough, M. E. (1996). Empirical research on religion and psychotherapeutic processes and outcomes: A 10-year review and research prospectus. *Psychological Bulletin, 119,* 448–487.

Wynstrock, N. (1995). The ritual as a psychotherapeutic intervention. *Psychotherapy, 32,* 397–404.

Zinnbauer, B. J., & Pargament, K. I. (2000). Working with the sacred: Four approaches to religious and spiritual issues in counseling. *Journal of Counseling & Development, 78,* 162–171.

Chapter 9

Knowing One's Limits

Christopher Faiver and R. Elliott Ingersoll

Competency: *The professional counselor can identify limits of her or his understanding of a client's religious or spiritual expression and demonstrate appropriate referral skills and generate possible referral sources.*

$\mathcal{N}$ovice counselors idealistically, but naively, often think they can do everything for every client they see. With clinical experience comes the realization of clinical limitations. This is not to say that we must not strive to do our best; of course, we should! An important component of the therapeutic training process, however, involves that of realizing limitations and the consequent setting of therapeutic boundaries. Seeking to constantly upgrade our theoretical knowledge, knowing how and with whom to consult, and knowing when to refer are basic boundary-setting techniques of counseling in general and useful when dealing with clients' spiritual domains in particular. Moreover, implicit in this aspect of competence is the counselor's willingness to self-examine beliefs, needs, and what Jung (1902/1980) called one's "shadow side."

Competence and Definitions of Spirituality

To consider what competence means when referring to the integration of counseling and spirituality, we must operationalize the term *spirituality*. If spirituality simply means the exoteric practicing of a religion or cognitively adhering to a set of beliefs, this will call for one type of competence. This can be dealt with quite nicely with a cognitive understanding of the client's beliefs and empathic understanding of how those beliefs affect the client. If spirituality is a potentially ego-transcending force that may in fact threaten the status quo of an entire society, this will call for quite another type of competence. Here the counselor could be faced with facilitating the client's growth at the risk of tremendous change and the repercussions of that change. Operationalizing spirituality, as most scholars in the area have conceded, is difficult. Exhibit 9.1 summarizes five common understandings of spirituality.

Exhibit 9.1
Five Common Understandings of Spirituality

- Spirituality is its own line of development (Wilber, 1999b).
- Spirituality is the upper reaches of any line of development (Wilber, 1999b).
- Spirituality is a way of being and experiencing that comes about through awareness of a transcendent dimension related to what one considers to be ultimate (Elkins, Hedstrom, Hughes, Leaf, & Saunders, 1988) or as an approach to life or an attitude that you can have at any stage (Wilber, 1999b).
- Spirituality is more about peak experiences rather than stages (Wilber, 1999b).
- Spirituality and religion have public (exoteric) and secret (esoteric) aspects (Bache, 1990). The public side serves the function of translation, and the secret side serves the purpose of transformation. Clients may be involved in one or both of these.

To begin, spirituality can be viewed as its own line of development as well as the upper levels of other lines of development (Wilber, 1999b). As its own line of development, spirituality may be thought of as an amalgam of various developmental lines that progress through the stages of awareness available to human beings resulting in correlative changes in one's experience of the world, behavior, and emotions. As the upper reaches of other lines of development, spirituality is the transpersonal or "trans-ego" stages of the different developmental lines. It is commonly accepted in transpersonal psychology that human beings generally progress through pre-ego (prepersonal), ego (personal), and trans-ego (transpersonal) stages of development. While a person may have a spiritual experience (e.g., peak experience) at any age, they will make sense of it with whatever developmental tools they can access. If the highest level of cognition they possess at the time is concrete operational cognition, that is the cognition through which they will make sense of the experience (Wilber, 2001).

Generally, these understandings of spirituality imply much more for competent practice than is typically covered in the literature. They call on therapists to have a rich background in human development. This background must include a theoretical understanding that human development continues beyond healthy ego development. Currently, most master's programs approved by the Council for Accreditation of Counseling and Related Educational Programs (CACREP) only require one course in human development, and many professors do not teach trans-ego development. Given this state of affairs, counselors are responsible for furthering their own knowledge of human development.

Spirituality as a way of being or experiencing may imply developmental stages, but spirituality as an attitude one brings to situations does not. Both aspects of these descriptions of spirituality are more common in the literature on integrating spirituality and counseling. Many choose more global descriptions of spirituality, because, as Fukuyama and Sevig (1999) noted, "it is impossible to agree upon only one definition" (p. 4). The drawback to such definitions is that they lend themselves to a sort of relativism that is not at all reflected in the literature on spiritual development. Thinking of spirituality in terms of only peak experiences also is problematic as it refutes the almost universal notion that altered states are of little use unless they lead to altered traits (Smith, 2000). This notion is embedded in what Huxley (1945) called the perennial philosophy and cannot be ignored by anyone seeking to develop spiritually. In our current postmodern era, because spirituality is challenging to define, many (counselors included) are tempted to impose their own "pet" definitions without consulting both Eastern and Western wisdom traditions. This can include the error of thinking of spirituality primarily as peak experiences.

While scholars outside of counseling and psychotherapy have discussed how religion and spirituality have both public (exoteric) and secret (esoteric) sides (Bache, 1990), this reality is ignored by many counselors and other psychotherapists who tend to focus only on the exoteric aspects of religion. These include the general beliefs, creeds, and dogmas of the different religions. These public or exoteric aspects of religious or spiritual paths serve the primary function of translation for the individual. *Translation* means that these aspects of a person's spiritual path help the person think in a new way about a difficult world but do not necessarily induce lasting change (Wilber, 1997, 1999a).

While an important part of spirituality (and religion), exoteric aspects and their cultural variations do not address the transformative spiritual experiences clients may have through their spiritual paths. Wilber (1997, 1999a) described *transformation* as a powerful transcendence of the individual's ego and movement to the next developmental level. Wilber discussed how translation and transformation work together developmentally. Translation is more familiar to mental health professionals and is how beliefs, creeds, and practices help a person keep sane in a difficult world and continue growing. Transformation is when the current translation no longer serves its purpose, and the individual either stagnates or moves to the next level, often with a breakthrough insight.

The case of Frank illustrates these different understandings of spirituality and how they relate to therapist competence. Frank began psychotherapy for posttraumatic stress disorder (PTSD), which was the result of his experience as a soldier in the Vietnam war. Frank had witnessed the torture by American forces of two alleged Viet Cong adolescents who were eventually killed. Frank had been charged to guard the two prisoners as they went through their ordeal. Racked with guilt and horror, Frank's ego was barely intact by the time he started therapy in 1976. He suffered the classic symptoms of PTSD and was a polysubstance abuser. With the help of both individual and group therapists, he made fair progress. In 1979 he attended a church service with a girlfriend and had what he called a "born again" conversion. Upon going with others to the front of the church and praying for Jesus to come into his life, he felt an overwhelming sense of love and awe. This was certainly a peak experience for Frank (an altered state), but it also led to altered traits. After this conversion Frank began to reframe his war experience as his "cross to bear" and dedicated himself to various causes to assist oppressed people. In this respect,

Frank's religious involvement helped him (at the ego level) translate a very painful world. He became involved in Veterans Affairs as an advocate and took a job as a caseworker for inner-city drug users on probation. It is important to note we are not "psychologizing" Frank's spiritual experience but rather are setting the context from which he continued to grow.

Although Frank's psychological recovery continued, he had numerous "spiritual crises" over the next 6 years questioning how a personal God could let so many people suffer. These were symptomatic that his translative understanding of Christianity was beginning to fail him. In 1985 he left the church he was in and entered spiritual direction with an Anglican priest who was also well versed in Zen meditation. This priest worked with Frank for another 3 years guiding him in direction and contemplative prayer. Frank reported a "breakthrough" experience in 1988. This experience was similar to his conversion experience but emphasized a sense of connection with a force he called God as well as all of humanity. One of the most powerful aspects of the experience was Frank's sense of identification with the Vietnamese adolescents he saw tortured and their tormentors. With the help of his spiritual director and a different psychotherapist he had been seeing since 1985, Frank came to understand that at some level, the spiritual life force that animates all lives also connects those lives. After this Frank continued practicing contemplative prayer, found a new church to attend, and continued his work in social justice. After his breakthrough in spiritual direction, Frank concluded that his "cross to bear" was not only his but all of humanity's and God's because he came to the understanding that humanity was united by the being of God. While Frank still considered himself a Christian, he noted that his breakthrough experience also gave him a sense that it did not matter what religion a person was, as long as their path led them to the realization of unity in God.

Frank's case illustrates both the impact of peak experiences on a relatively healthy ego and the undulation of translation and transformation. Frank's initial conversion transformed him to a more theological understanding of his war experiences. This theological understanding became his way of translating those experiences. As he continued maturing and developing in his spiritual path, this was followed by the sense that the theology as he understood it at the time was not sufficient to meet the questions he had developed. At the time of his second transformation, he came to a new translation that was more mystically inclined than the first.

Counselors and psychotherapists seeking to integrate spirituality into their practice must be prepared to integrate the breadth and depth of what spirituality means and be able to deal with both translative spirituality and transformative spirituality. Any decent ethics statement on competence needs to include this. Clearly, in Frank's case, he had a distinct sense of the transcendent and came to develop the sense that this transcendent being resided in him as well as outside of him. Granted, had Frank not been engaged in years of therapy to develop a healthy ego structure, his breakthrough experience may not have occurred or he may not have been able to integrate it. This points out another crucial aspect to competence in understanding human development. Counselors need to understand that development proceeds as current developmental levels are transcended and included in the next levels. Thus, one needs a relatively healthy ego to transcend that ego. Otherwise, potential breakthroughs may become breakdowns (Vaughan, 1990). Most publications addressing ethical competence are restricted to translative religion or spirituality. While this is a start, the field will have to consider what ethical competence is in transformative spirituality. We address this later in this chapter.

Ethical Competence and Translative Spirituality

Counseling and spirituality (which includes "psychotherapy" and spirituality) is a relatively new area in the field with most of the literature on the topic written in the last 15 years. A great deal has been written on the general topic of counseling and spirituality (a PsycINFO search from 1994 to the present resulted in well over 1,000 citations), but there has been little written specifically on the ethical aspects of integrating spirituality and counseling/psychotherapy. While current books on counseling and spirituality addressing ethics (Fukuyama & Sevig, 1999; Kelly, 1995; Miller, 2003; Richards & Bergin, 1997, 2000; Sperry, 2001; Wiggins-Frame, 2003) span the therapeutic disciplines, the most recent journal articles on ethical integration come primarily from psychology or psychiatry (Chappelle, 2000; Eck, 2002; Lomax, Jarff, & McKenny, 2002; Tan, 2003).

Most writers address competence by either offering models of integration (Eck, 2002; Richards & Bergin, 1997; Tan, 2003) or more generally suggesting that counselors make every reasonable effort to understand both the client's religious tradition and the cultural context of that tradition (Miller, 2003; Richards & Bergin, 2000; Wiggins-Frame, 2003). It is important to note that this intellectual understanding is most frequently translative in the sense that it is just gaining a basic psychological understanding of how a client practicing a particular spiritual path may explain the world. In addition, counselors want to know how the clients' understanding of their spiritual path affects their life. As Eck (2002) noted, every practicing therapist should "obtain the training necessary to demonstrate competence in understanding the role of spirituality and religion in their clients' lives" (p. 267). This is agreed on by virtually all of the scholars cited up to this point.

As far as translative spirituality goes, reconsider the case of Frank. Assume that a counselor met with Frank shortly after his first conversion experience. That counselor would want to know the general exoteric aspects of Frank's church as well as the impact that Frank's experience had on him. By virtue of most ethics statements, this would be a good start and may serve to support work with Frank over several years. As Frank grew into his more mystical experience, however, the counselor would have to accommodate this even if she or he had views that limited spirituality to Frank's earlier conversion experience.

Ethical Competence and Transformative Spirituality

What is less frequently addressed is ethical competence and transformative spirituality. Part of this is because Western theories of the mind have not adequately mapped spiritual development. Another possible reason is that only a small number of people are estimated to be involved in transformative spiritual practices, and we may assume this includes mental health professionals. Understanding transformative spirituality implies that the counselor has her or his own spiritual practice and has progressed through at least a few cycles of translation and transformation. Having a grasp of transformative spirituality also assumes that the counselor, in addition to understanding the exoteric aspects of her or his client's religion, also has some sense of the esoteric aspects of the religion and how transformative change is developmentally thought to occur for practitioners of that religion.

Consider the case of a young Christian counselor (Pat) we worked with in one of our training programs. This young man was bright, articulate, and passionate about his faith. He had, however, a fairly rigid belief that Christianity was the only true path to God and that he had an obligation to steer people to that path. Pat's spiritual practice was primarily focused on petitionary prayer, and while he stated he felt Jesus' love, he had not had a transformative encounter per se. Pat's approach to counseling was acceptable in the Christian counseling setting where he worked but would not have been in secular settings. We bring Pat into the discussion because it is very likely Pat would have had difficulty counseling Frank after his "breakthrough" experience. This would be a failure to honor Frank's transformation and constitute countertransference. This is where counselor self-assessment becomes an important part of competence.

Counselor Self-Assessment

Fukuyama and Sevig (1999) developed three guidelines that can be applied to counselor self-assessment. First, they noted that it is imperative that counselors examine their own spiritual/religious beliefs. This examination can serve to delineate how one's cultural background is related to one's spiritual/religious worldview. We recommend that this examination include both translative and transformative spiritual experiences. Understanding one's spiritual history and one's chosen tradition may be approached in the form of a spiritual autobiography. Faiver, Ingersoll, O'Brien, and McNally (2001) suggested a format (revised below) that incorporates a series of questions for discussion and reflection. Exhibit 9.2 is a revised version of this format.

Counselors may also use a more traditional spiritual autobiography of the type emphasized by figures like St. Augustine in the Western tradition (Sisemore, 2001). Such an autobiography begins as a developmental exploration of one's spiritual journey and then expands to examine one's values and whether those values are reflected in one's thinking and behavior. For training purposes, spiritual autobiography work can be done in small groups as well. Exploration of the life journey in this manner has been outlined by Birren and Cochran (2002).

As the second guideline to counselor self-assessment, Fukuyama and Sevig (1999) suggested that counselors must assess their understanding of the client's spiritual/religious beliefs and worldview. No spiritual intervention can be in the best interest of the client without first obtaining such knowledge. In psycho-

Exhibit 9.2
The Counselor Self-Assessment Format

- *Introductory statement.* In this statement, use a sense of free association when responding: Any responses may be appropriate, including purpose and objectives for carrying out such an assessment, personal or professional narratives, thoughts, emotions, anything at all that bubbles to the surface. How would you introduce your spiritual journey? How do you describe yourself with regard to spirituality and/or religion?
- *Spiritual themes.* What spiritual themes, topics, subjects, and so on permeate my life? What Jungian archetypes emerge, if any? Are there spiritual themes that set the tone of my life, either positively or negatively?
- *Spiritual influences.* As I complete a look back at my spiritual development, who has influenced me? Are there major religious figures, prominent psychotherapists, and other major figures? Do I note mentors who have affirmed me? Are there certain friends and family on whom I can count for nurturance, caring, and comforting?
- *Life's lessons.* As I complete the life review, influences, and themes, what lessons emerge? What personal and professional discoveries can I glean? What life lessons do I want to pass along to others? How do I intend to pass these lessons along?
- *Personal conclusions.* Finally, are there any conclusions regarding this exercise in self-assessment in this process of personal and professional discernment? Note any and all thoughts and feelings.

therapy, this information emerges as the mutual therapeutic alliance develops with the patience, understanding, and clinical skills of the counselor. In addition, counselors can reflect on the perspective they take of spiritual or religious traditions different from their own. As Miller (2003) noted, "there is a fine line between exploring the views of a client and being judgmental toward him or her" (p. 164). Self-assessment is helpful in situations in which clients practice or adhere to religions around which the counselor has unresolved emotional issues. Neusner (1994, in Wiggins-Frame, 2003) suggested that there are four perspectives one may take of other religions. These are exclusivist, inclusivist, pluralist, and one of empathic interest. The *exclusivist* view is when one believes that his or her religion has a monopoly on truth and is the one true path. The *inclusivist* perspective is when one views different religions relatively with respect to the individual. The *pluralist* perspective is when one feels all religions hold some truth, and the *empathic interest* perspective is when the person views other religions as a way to learn about people. Counselors should assess which perspective most honestly represents them. For the purposes of competent practice, we recommend that counselors, at the very least, be able to transcend exclusivist perspectives.

Third, Fukuyama and Sevig suggested that counselors considering using spiritual interventions take part in supervision or study groups in which the interface of spiritual and clinical concerns may be discussed. This guideline aids the probability of ethical practice. As Welfel (2002) emphasized, formal training and supervision are the foundation of competence.

To the guidelines posited by Fukuyama and Sevig, we include a fourth that derives from Wilber (1999a). Counselors should be keenly involved in their own spiritual journey—a journey that includes practices fitting their chosen spiritual paths. There is no surrogate for personal experience when assisting clients in their spiritual journeys. Naturally, we think that individuals must choose their own paths. Counselors should always reflect on how far they are willing to go with their spiritual practice and whether their level of spiritual involvement and development may limit the types of clients with whom they can work on spiritual issues.

Client Assessment

Integrating counseling and spirituality also can involve systematic assessment of the client. Types of assessment vary according to counseling specialty. For instance, mental health counselors focus on clinical methodology resulting in a diagnosis and treatment recommendations, whereas school counselors and other student development professionals generally home in on developmental and growth issues with consequent plans for students. In all cases of professional counseling, however, the initial assessment may be viewed as an important part of the counseling process, establishing the tone for subsequent contacts. Certainly, too, good listening skills are a requisite for any accurate assessment, which includes planning and referral as necessary. Finally, all assessments include several components: (a) client or student description, (b) description of the presenting concern, (c) relevant background information, (d) current functioning, (e) overall impression, (f) recommendations, and (g) a plan of action. We refer the reader to chapter 3 of this book for a full discussion of the assessment process. Our purpose in talking about assessment in this chapter is to provide a framework for dealing with treatment planning and referral.

We encourage all counselors to gather relevant information about a client's spirituality during the initial assessment, which is in the context of the therapeutic alliance. We propose that counselors examine the client's spiritual culture, background, current circumstances, and worldview. We suggest an assessment format that begins with the global and culminates with the specific. Of course, this examination includes a client's religious/spiritual beliefs, if any. This model offers guidelines for appropriate referral for religious/spiritual issues.

The client assessment affords both client and counselor an opportunity to ask questions and get to know each other, to share therapeutic goals and expectations, and to present an opportunity to raise the topic of religion/spirituality. Conducting a comprehensive interview as the foundation for successful counseling may call for several interview sessions. A sound assessment interview should ultimately provide an opportunity for initial or provisional impressions and treatment recommendations for the client (Faiver, 2001). Ideally, the counselor who actually performs this assessment should provide the counseling as well.

In performing the initial assessment, we have found a number of specific questions, when put to the client, to be of great benefit within the assessment process. Alfred Adler's "The Question" (Adler, 1964) is especially useful for tracing the origin of client conflict. It asks, "What would be different in your life if you didn't have this problem?" Ellis (1989) described anxious types who tend to "catastrophize," exaggerating the gravity of their troubles. To put client problems into proper perspective, Ellis asked, "What is the worst thing that can happen?" Also, the question "Is there anything that I haven't asked that you think I should know?" is commonly used in an effective summary. This last question often brings to light additional information relevant to the assessment process. All of these questions may facilitate client insight, permitting a flow of information leading to improved focus on relevant issues. In many cases, we have witnessed issues of spirituality unfolding within responses to these questions. It is our belief that if the counselor avoids cues or comments in these responses, some of which may be related to spiritual or religious beliefs, many client issues may be misinterpreted or missed.

As counselors examine a client's background and current functioning, we encourage openness to religious/spiritual factors, which may relate to client concerns and issues, including their resolution (Faiver & O'Brien, 1993). Religious and/or spiritual issues may be directly discussed when gleaning general information and presenting problems. We suggest noting both current and past belief system, as well as religious affiliation, if any. Any alterations or incongruencies between current and past beliefs or practices could denote areas of further exploration. Our clinical experience indicates that some clients who refer to themselves as spiritual or religious may actually live in quite a different manner day by day. Thus, we ask, how much does the client really have invested in the religious or spiritual domain? The counselor might ask Adler's question in a slightly different way: "How would your life be different if you didn't have this religion or spirituality?"

In the clinical setting, the assessment of a client's cognitive (thinking), affective (feeling), and behavioral (doing) functioning, which is integral to the general examination of mental status, also applies to assessment of a client's spiritual values and/or religious beliefs. Thus, in the cognitive domain, it behooves the counselor to explore the client's belief system, including concepts, values, mores, and directives or guidelines. Some clients may experience cognitive dissonance, including the complex issue of guilt. What is the source of any guilt? How long, how much, and how pervasive? Does it serve any purpose? Concerning affect, the counselor should note any and all related sources of depression, anxiety, or lability. Certainly, feelings resulting from the belief system may be positive or negative in their effect. It may be helpful to then make use of interventions that incorporate these emotions in therapy. In terms of the examination of behaviors, we recommend an examination of habits or rituals in the client's daily life. Note apparently excessive religiosity or bizarre gestures and behaviors. One should be aware that some rituals and behaviors are developmentally appropriate and encourage growth and positive relations (Worthington, 1989).

Treatment Planning and Referral

Issues exist that may be beyond the scope of the counselor. In all assessments, recommendations such as referral to a psychiatrist, psychological testing, hospitalization, or other modality may be indicated. Moreover, school counselors may want to refer to clinical counselors if psychotherapy is indicated. Only techniques consonant with the client's belief system should be used. For example, clinical hypnosis is not indicated if this modality potentially violates a client's fundamentalist Christian beliefs. Referral to one of the spiritually based 12-step programs also may be considered as one potential referral source.

If the counselor determines as a result of the intake assessment that there are issues involving a client's personal spiritual base or religious tradition, referral to specific clergy may be indicated (Faiver, O'Brien, & McNally, 1998). We recommend that counselors acquaint themselves with nonjudgmental, respected, and caring clergy of various faiths who are open to the psychotherapeutic process and consequent referral for clients with religious or spiritual concerns beyond the counselor's scope of practice. Ideally, these clergy have some graduate-level training in pastoral counseling. We call these people the *friendly clergy*. We do not necessarily presume that knowledge of spirituality or specific religious traditions and beliefs is afforded only for clergy. However, we are cognizant that clergy maintain unique positions of leadership, teaching authority, and influence in churches, mosques, and temples. In these circumstances, clergy assume the role of advisor or faith system interpreter.

Counselors, Gurus: Competence and Boundaries

Many writers have said that mental health therapists serve in many ways the function of priest (London, 1986; Vaughan, 1990) or guru (Kopp, 1976) in our society. The word *guru* means one who leads another from darkness into light. In a sense, counselors do act as gurus or guides for clients. Counselors who are integrating spirituality into their work are potentially working with clients in one of the most powerful areas known to the human experience. This brings tremendous opportunities and tremendous risks. The risks are best detailed by the many abuses of power in guru–disciple relationships (Kramer & Alstad, 1993; Wren-Lewis, 1994) that mirror the types of ethical boundary violations by mental health professionals (Somer & Saadon, 1999; Strom-Gottfried, 1999). While many have documented the healing power of guru–devotee relationships (Bennett, 2002; Braun, 1996; Martignette, 1998) as well as their psychological dimensions, it is important for counselors and other mental health professionals to remember that they are practicing as mental health professionals who recognize spirituality as an important component of the human condition and, thus, the therapeutic relationship.

Boundaries in therapeutic relationships defined as counseling or psychotherapy relationships should be set in accordance with the ethical guidelines of one's professional association. This is complicated as the tools the therapist uses may in fact transcend what is available in the professional literature of the field, particularly if the therapist has integrated transformative spiritual experiences. The supervision scenario that follows illustrates this.

Meenakshi is a professional clinical counselor who is in a supervision group of counselors who are integrating spirituality into their counseling practice. Meenakshi has been practicing meditation for 20 years and had several experiences of transformation. Her "map" of the human mind includes a level that transcends ego as the sense of self most emphasized in Western psychological theories. She was working with a client who appeared to be experiencing what Grof and Grof (1989) called *spiritual emergency*. This is the emergence of transpersonal phenomena that are correlated with the individual making progress in shifting one's sense of identity from the purely personal (ego) to also embrace transpersonal aspects of self. One of the other members of the group, Ed, whose spiritual experiences had been exclusively exoteric and translative, became visibly disturbed when Meenakshi discussed psychological interventions designed to help the client maintain his spiritual practices. Because Ed's map of the psyche did not include transpersonal levels, he saw Meenakshi's intervention as increasing the probability of ego dissolution. As is noted in the transpersonal literature, however, Meenakshi's support of the client's spiritual practice under a recognized teacher was an appropriate intervention. In this example, it becomes clear that the counselor's level of spiritual development is crucial to the therapeutic relationship and the types of interventions that the counselor will be able to draw from. In addition, this example points out that the counselor's spiritual experiences will affect the map of the psyche that they use in their therapeutic work.

Case Studies

What Characterizes Unhealthy Versus Healthy Spirituality?

Joe is racked with guilt. He has AIDS. He is certain that God is punishing him for his lifestyle. Further, he confirms his stance with vitreous speeches and writings of various political and religious figures that maintain this viewpoint. He judges himself unworthy and condemns himself to Hell.

Maria has cancer. She sees a compassionate counselor who encourages her to use symbols of her faith in imagery to sustain and comfort her. At her chemotherapy sessions she is most troubled not by her illness, but by the presence of children with the disease.

What Is the Importance of Counselor Self-Assessment Regarding Beliefs?

Rachel, a counselor, becomes anxious when she sees clients from a certain belief system. Rachel has never examined her beliefs nor has she had counseling herself. These clients, she notes, tend to come less frequently than others.

David leads an examined life. A child of abuse, he has been treated for depression with psychotherapy and medication. During his therapy, David has looked at the recurring theme of depression and its consequent effect on his life. He has noted mentors who have assisted him in his progress, his counselor included. Now on the "other side" of his issues, he desires to start a counseling master's program to assist others.

How Do You Define a "Spiritually Competent Counselor"?

Jackie has a client of another faith. The client says to Jackie that religion is vital to her and is part of her cultural identity, too. Jackie invites her client to teach her about her faith and consults with a member of the clergy from the client's faith to understand how the client is affected by her beliefs.

John always knows what is best for his clients. Thus, when his new client discusses an obviously spiritual concern, John decides to perform pastoral counseling. John has no training or experience in this area.

What Items With Regard to Spiritual and/or Religious Issues Would You Add to the American Counseling Association Code of Ethics?

Mohammed, a Muslim, has been referred to you for counseling. During the third session, he tells you that you, a Christian, do not understand him, his religion, or his culture. He feels angry and not helped.

Patricia, a group member, verbally attacks another client for her stance on abortion. Patricia tells the client that she is wrong and should not return to the group.

How Would You Determine the Necessity of Referral? To Whom? Why? Give Examples

Mildred enters the counseling session looking rather disheveled. During the session she begins to make crosslike gestures on her forehead. She talks of being possessed by the Devil, who tells her she is an evil person.

Dominic is struggling with his drinking. He indicates that he needs help to "stay off the stuff." He points out past abuse, perhaps dependence, on alcohol.

Elena, age 60, has been a client for several months. During a recent session, she notes that she, a Catholic, is troubled at having married a Protestant man decades ago. She now feels that she is unworthy of receiving communion.

Recommended Reading

Cameron, J. (1992). *The artist's way: A spiritual path to higher creativity*. New York: Putnam.

Emery, M. (1994). *Intuition workbook*. Englewood Cliffs, NJ: Prentice Hall.

Frankl, V. (1992). *Man's search for meaning: An introduction to logotherapy*. Boston: Beacon Press. (Original work published 1963).

Fulghum, R. (1993). *All I really need to know I learned in kindergarten: Uncommon thoughts on uncommon things*. Westminster, MD: Faucet.

Fulghum, R. (1996). *From beginning to end: The rituals of our lives*. Westminster, MD: Faucet.

Moore, T. (1994). *Care of the soul: A guide to cultivating depth and sacredness in everyday life*. New York: Harperperennial.

Moore, T. (1994). *Soul mates: Honoring the mysteries of love and relationship.* New York: Harperperennial.

Moore, T. (1995). *Meditations: On the monk who dwells in daily life.* New York: Harperperennial.

Peck, M. (1978). *The road less traveled.* New York: Simon & Schuster.

Peck, M. (1997). *The road less traveled and beyond: Spiritual growth in an age of anxiety.* Old Tappan, NJ: Thorndike.

Wicks, R. (2003). *Riding the dragon: 10 lessons for inner strength in challenging times.* Notre Dame, IN: Sorin.

Web Sites of Interest

http://www.americapress.org
America Magazine

http://www.igc.apc.org/atp/
Association for Transpersonal Psychology

http://www.infoasis.com/people/grof/HBinternet.html
Grof Transpersonal Training Program

http://www.concentric.net/~Lemckay/wilber/
The PL Ken Wilber Web Site

http://www.mindspirit.org/
Psychotherapy and Spirituality Institute

http://www.spiritualityhealth.com
Spirituality and Health

http://www.spiritslaughing.com
Spirituality and Humor

http://www.geocities.com/RodeoDrive/1415/index1.html
Spirituality, Yoga, Hinduism

http://www.spiritweb.org/Spirit/workplace-1.html
Spirituality in the Workplace

Summary

In sum, all competent counselors seek out relevant training and maintain clear boundaries to best serve their clients in an ethical manner. These precepts extend to the integration of the spiritual domain in therapy as well. We have presented a variety of understandings of spirituality with consequent implications for competence, including referral of clients to others when their spiritual issues are not within the expertise of the counselor. We have endeavored to clarify a rather contentious and murky area of the profession while recognizing that wherever spirituality is concerned, there is bound to be ambiguity.

References

Adler, A. (1964). *Problems of neurosis.* New York: Harper & Row.

Bache, C. M. (1990). *Lifecycles: Reincarnation and the web of life.* New York: Paragon House.

Bennett, H. M. (2002). Four dimensions of experiencing Sat-Guru Adi Da's spiritual heart-transmission (Hrdaya-Saktipata): Phenomenological, lasting effects, setting (internal and external), and personality set (Da Free John). *Dissertation Abstracts International: The Humanities and Social Sciences, 62,* 8-A.

Birren, J. E., & Cochran, K. N. (2002). *Telling the stories of life through guided autobiography groups.* Washington, DC: American Psychological Association.

Braun, A. S. (1996). Beyond the limitations of ego: The guru-path as a vehicle for transformation and transcendence. *Dissertation Abstracts International: The Physical Sciences and Engineering, 56,* 9-B.

Chappelle, W. (2000). A series of legal and ethical decision-making steps for using Christian spiritual interventions in psychotherapy. *Journal of Psychology and Theology, 28,* 45–53.

Eck, B. E. (2002). An exploration of the therapeutic use of spiritual disciplines in clinical practice. *Journal of Psychology and Christianity, 21,* 266–280.

Elkins, D. N., Hedstrom, L. J., Hughes, L. L., Leaf, J. A., & Saunders, C. (1988). Toward a humanistic-phenomenological spirituality. *Journal of Humanistic Psychology, 28,* 5–18.

Ellis, A. (1989). Rational emotive therapy. In R. Corsini & D. Wedding (Eds.), *Current psychotherapies* (4th ed., pp. 197–240). Itasca, IL: Peacock.

Faiver, C. (2001). Components of effective treatment planning. In E. Welfel & E. Ingersoll (Eds.), *The mental health desk reference* (pp. 83–88). New York: Wiley.

Faiver, C., Ingersoll, R., O'Brien, E., & McNally, C. (2001). *Explorations of counseling and spirituality: Philosophical, practical, and personal reflections.* Pacific Grove, CA: Brooks/Cole.

Faiver, C. M., & O'Brien, E. M. (1993). Assessment of religious beliefs form. *Counseling and Values, 37,* 176–178.

Faiver, C., O'Brien, E., & McNally, C. (1998). Characteristics of the friendly clergy. *Counseling and Values, 42,* 217–221.

Fukuyama, M. A., & Sevig, T. D. (1999). *Integrating spirituality into multicultural counseling.* London: Sage.

Grof, S., & Grof, C. (Eds.). (1989). *Spiritual emergency: When personal transformation becomes a crisis.* Los Angeles: Jeremy Tarcher.

Huxley, A. (1945). *The perennial philosophy.* London: Harper & Brothers.

Jung, C. (1980). *The archetypes and the collective unconscious* (R. Hull, Trans.). Princeton, NJ: Princeton University Press. (Original work published 1902)

Kelly, E. W. (1995). *Spirituality and religion in counseling and psychotherapy: Diversity in theory and practice.* Alexandria, VA: American Counseling Association.

Kopp, S. (1976). *If you meet Buddha on the road kill him.* New York: Bantam.

Kramer, J., & Alstad, D. (1993). *The guru papers: Masks of authoritarian power.* Berkeley, CA: Frog Ltd.

Lomax, J. W., Jarff, S., & McKenny, G. P. (2002). Ethical considerations in the integration of religion and psychotherapy: Three perspectives. *Psychiatric Clinics of North America, 25,* 547–559.

London, P. (1986). *The modes and morals of psychotherapy* (2nd ed.). New York: Holt, Rinehart & Winston.

Martignette, C. A. (1998). Gurus and devotees: Guides or gods? Pathology or faith? *Pastoral Psychology, 47,* 127–144.

Miller, G. (2003). *Incorporating spirituality in counseling and psychotherapy: Theory and technique.* New York: Wiley.

Richards, P. S., & Bergin, A. E. (1997). *A spiritual strategy for counseling and psychotherapy.* Washington, DC: American Psychological Association.

Richards, P. S., & Bergin, A. E. (Eds.). (2000). *Handbook of psychotherapy and religious diversity.* Washington, DC: American Psychological Association.

Sisemore, T. A. (2001). Saint Augustine's confessions and the use of introspection in counseling. *Journal of Psychology and Christianity, 20,* 324–331.

Smith, H. (2000). *Cleansing the doors of perception: The religious significance of entheogenic plants and chemicals.* New York: Jeremy Tarcher.

Somer, E., & Saadon, M. (1999). Therapist–client sex: Clients' retrospective reports. *Professional Psychology: Research and Practice, 30,* 504–509.

Sperry, L. (2001). *Spirituality in clinical practice: Incorporating the spiritual dimension in psychotherapy and counseling.* Philadelphia: Brunner Routledge.

Strom-Gottfried, K. (1999). Professional boundaries: An analysis of violations by social workers. *Families in Society, 80,* 439–449.

Tan, S. Y. (2003). Integrating spiritual direction into psychotherapy: Ethical issues and guidelines. *Journal of Psychology and Theology, 31,* 14–23.

Vaughan, F. (1990). *Thinking allowed with Dr. Jeffrey Mishlove.* Monterey, CA: Thinking Allowed.

Welfel, E. R. (2002). *Ethics in counseling and psychotherapy: Standards, research, and emerging issues.* Pacific Grove, CA: Brooks Cole.

Wiggins-Frame, M. (2003). *Integrating religion and spirituality into counseling: A comprehensive approach.* Pacific Grove, CA: Wadsworth Publishing.

Wilber, K. (1997, Fall/Winter). A spirituality that transforms. *What Is Enlightenment?, 12,* 22–32.

Wilber, K. (1999a). *The collected works of Ken Wilber: Vol. 3.* Boston: Shambhala.

Wilber, K. (1999b). *The collected works of Ken Wilber: Vol. 4.* Boston: Shambhala.

Wilber, K. (2001). *Ken Wilber: Speaking of everything.* Boulder, CO: Enlightenment.com

Worthington, E. L., Jr. (1989). Religious faith across the life span: Implications for counseling and research. *The Counseling Psychologist, 17,* 555–612.

Wren-Lewis, J. (1994). Death knell of the guru system? Perfectionism versus enlightenment. *Journal of Humanistic Psychology, 34,* 46–61.

Chapter 10

Epilogue:
Where Do You Go From Here?

J. Scott Young and Craig S. Cashwell

*W*here do you go from here? The competencies discussed in this book are broad and general. How the competencies will apply to a particular client will depend on you as a counselor and the individual client before you. Therefore, the competencies are but a starting point, and they are by no means an ending point. In other words, the competencies are aspirational in nature. As counselors, just as in life, we spend our professional lives *becoming*, but do not arrive. Subsequently, the competencies are not intended to communicate that you do not "know" enough to do this work. Rather, the competencies are intended to provide a template for your own development as a counselor who integrates spirituality and religion into your practice.

We are sure you remember your first client, and the feeling that you did not know enough to help the client. Yet neither you nor the client was hopelessly damaged because of your inexperience. The same is true of spirituality in counseling. Your work will be sufficient if you are sincere in your seeking and open in the process and obtain supervision when you need it. As with all healing work, *intention* is vital. You do not need to know everything about religion and spirituality to connect with a client along those lines. What you do need is clarity about your purpose for doing this work as well as an awareness of when you are outside of your own zone of competence. We don't "fix" our clients. Rather, through the counseling process, a healing space is created that exceeds either person's abilities alone. When Spirit is invited into the process, the work becomes even more powerful. Larry Dossey (1989), in his book *Recovering the Soul*, recounts research in which batches of germinating seeds were prayed for while others were not. Repeatedly, the prayed-for seeds grew more shoots. Even more interesting, when experimenters stressed the seeds by adding salt water to their containers, through multiple repetitions of the study and when more salt water was added, prayer was even more beneficial when the seeds were under stress. Needless to say, the extrapolations from these experiments to the clients with whom counselors work are easy to make. Further, the power of intentionally including the spiritual healing energy in the process cannot be discounted.

While some clients will clearly identify a spiritual or religious problem as their presenting issue, much more common is the *process* of integrating spirituality into counseling when the problem presented has potential spiritual relavance (e.g., loss of a relationship, substance abuse, death of a child). In other words, while the *content* may not always be spiritual, the *process* can be. Counselors can pray for their clients. Our responsibility to the clients with whom we work is to first and foremost do our own work, the work of both developing spirituality and staying grounded in this work. Working our own path and entering into each counseling relationship with the intention of being a healer is enough.

We eat food to have the energy to go out and "do something." Reading this book is the fuel to go out and "do something" about spirituality in counseling. What you do with this fuel is up to you. If you do not already have a daily spiritual practice, be it prayer, meditation, yoga, tai chi, breathwork, or a religious tradition, you need a starting place. Most people will benefit from a *sangha*, or community of practitioners, to begin their spiritual practice. Both the emotional support and the instrumental support of others who are practicing the same discipline are helpful. In our society, we are often told, "Don't just sit there, do something!" We believe that counselors can benefit greatly from some form of contemplative practice to center and quieten the mind. Thus, our adage might be, "Don't just do something, sit there!"

Many academic pursuits are also personal pursuits. The process for you now is one of reformulating the content of this book, making it unique and personal. Academic explanations will sustain you to a point, and then the process is a personal one. Thus, this book is merely a starting point for your work as a counselor who integrates spirituality and religion into counseling, and it provides a map. Clearly, the map is not the territory.

Spirituality cannot be fully understood, at least not in the traditional ways of knowing. Integrating spirituality into the counseling process, then, is by design a movement into the unknown and mysterious. An anonymous mystic of the 14th century referred to spiritual development as necessarily moving beyond the constraints of rigidly held beliefs and dogma and passing through a *cloud of unknowing*. Such, too, is the mystery of developing as a counselor who intends to integrate spirituality into the counseling process. As Huston Smith (1996) wrote,

> Problems have solutions, but mysteries don't, because the more we understand a mystery the more we realize how much more there is to it than we had realized at the start. The larger the island of knowledge, the longer the shoreline of wonder. (p. 4)

Developmentally, the counseling profession is in an interesting stage regarding the integration of spirituality and religion into the counseling process. There is a clear recognition of the importance of spirituality and religion in the counseling process, yet there remains a substantial need for writing and training on skills and methods for doing this effectively. In this sense, we recognize the need for shelter, but we are still learning how to build the house. This text may be a tool that assists in adding a few bricks to the foundation. However, more empirical support is needed to continue the work. We must find some balance between scientific inquiry and acceptance in faith that the cloud of unknowing will never be fully known and understood. It is this balance of science and faith that will enable us as counseling professionals to more competently and ethically promote spirituality and religion as an integral part of the counseling process.

Namaste (the light within me honors the light within you).

Recommended Reading

The following is a list of recommended readings on spirituality. Special thanks to Jan Holden at the University of North Texas and Mike O'Connor of Seattle University for their work in compiling this annotated list of readings.

Counseling

Burke, M. R., & Miranti, J. (2001). The spiritual and religious dimensions of counseling. In D. C. Locke, J. E. Myers, & E. Herr (Eds.), *The handbook of counseling* (pp. 601–612). Thousand Oaks, CA: Sage.

> An excellent, concise overview of the issues of, and strategies for, including spirituality and religion in counseling, including counselor competencies.

Frame, M. W. (2002). *Spiritual issues in counseling and psychotherapy.* New York: Wadsworth.

> A concise yet comprehensive and user-friendly summary of "what you need to know" to work with clients' spiritual and religious issues. Makes links with traditional therapeutic approaches and adds religious and spiritual interventions; also addresses special populations. Rich with suggested activities and multicultural case examples.

Griffith, J. L., & Griffith, M. E. (2002). *Encountering the sacred in psychotherapy: How to talk with people about their spiritual lives.* New York: Guilford Press.

> A thoughtful, culturally sensitive presentation of therapy as sacred encounter involving several genres of symbolic expression, including idiom, metaphor, story ritual, and community. Cultural anthropology and narrative theory inform this work, which is textured with case studies and excerpts from session transcripts.

Kelly, E. W. (1995). *Spirituality and religion in counseling and psychotherapy: Diversity in theory and practice.* Alexandria, VA: American Counseling Association.

> Perhaps the first text to offer an integrated overview of theory, research, and practice related to spirituality and religion in counseling.

Richards, P. S., & Bergin, A. E. (1997). *A spiritual strategy for counseling and psychotherapy.* Washington, DC: American Psychological Association.

> An outstanding text that addresses counselor stance as well as assessment and intervention with clients.

Religion

Smith, H. (1991). *The world's religions: Our great wisdom traditions* (Rev. ed.). New York: HarperCollins.

> This classic text addresses Buddhism, Christianity, Confucianism, Hinduism, Islam, Judaism, Taoism, and primal religions.

Smith, H. (1995). *The illustrated world's religions: A guide to our wisdom traditions.* New York: HarperCollins.

> An abbreviated but still extremely rich version of the classic text that satisfies the reader's left brain, with visual material related to each religious tradition that satisfies the reader's right brain.

Spiritual Experiences

Bragdon, E. (1993). *A sourcebook for helping persons with spiritual problems.* Aptos, CA: Lightening Up Press.

> A valuable survey of spiritual emergence, spiritual problems, and spiritual emergency detailing diagnosis and developmental interventions during the counseling process. Concludes with a useful list of texts, sources for video and audiotapes, and relevant motion pictures.

Cardeña, E., Lynn, S. J., & Krippner, S. (Eds.). (2000). *Varieties of anomalous experience: Examining the scientific evidence.* Washington, DC: American Psychological Association.

> The American Psychological Association's first text on various spiritual/religious experiences. Excellent chapters on topics such as mystical experiences, psi experiences, out-of-body experiences, near-death experiences, past life experiences, and lucid dreaming.

Kason, Y. (2000). *Farther shores: Exploring how near-death, kundalini and mystical experiences can transform ordinary lives.* New York: HarperCollins.

> Comprehensive description of the varieties of potentially spiritually transformative experiences, their aftereffects, and suggestions for coping. The author, a near-death experiencer who describes her experience in the book, is also an MD and a researcher.

Transpersonal Perspective

Boorstein, S. (Ed.). (1996). *Transpersonal psychotherapy* (2nd ed.). Albany: State University of New York Press.

> Chapters on a variety of topics related to the transpersonal perspective in psychotherapy by most of the major figures in the field of transpersonal psychology.

Scotton, B. W., Chinen, A. B., & Battista, J. R. (Eds.). (1996). *Textbook of transpersonal psychiatry and psychology.* New York: HarperCollins.

> Unparalleled in scope and depth, this essential text addresses theory, research, and practice, including the contributions of the major religious traditions to transpersonal psychiatry.

Wilber, K. (2000). *Integral psychology: Consciousness, spirit, psychology, therapy.* Boston: Shambhala.

> Overview of Ken Wilber's theory that integrates science and spirituality, past and present, East and West. Places various psychotherapies in a sequence corresponding to the three phases of human development: prepersonal, personal, and transpersonal.

General

Lesser, E. (1999). *The new American spirituality: A seeker's guide.* New York: Random House.

> An engaging spiritual autobiography by the co-founder of the Omega Institute chronicling her explorations of various traditions and insightful "pearls" from conversations with various world famous spiritual teachers. Lesser includes dozens of spiritual exercises she has developed or been taught by various mentors. A very enjoyable narrative companion to the more "text-bookish" resources that compose most of this list.

Walsh, R. (1999). *Essential spirituality: The 7 central practices to awaken heart and mind.* New York: Wiley.

> A distillation of the practices found in common between the mystical traditions of the world's religions and designed originally to facilitate spiritual development. Written by a psychiatrist well known in the field of transpersonal psychology, the book offers, as the cover states, "exercises . . . to cultivate kindness, love, joy, peace, vision, wisdom, and generosity."

References

Dossey, L. (1989). *Recovering the soul: A scientific and spiritual approach.* New York: Bantam Books.

Smith, H. (1996). Foreword. In W. Johnston (Ed.), *The cloud of unknowing* (pp. 3–5). New York: Image Books.

Index

Date Due

JUN 0 1 2009		
6/1/20/0		
JUN 0 9 2010		
JUN 01 2011		
JAN 0 3 2011		
APR 1 3 2012		
JUL 0 3 2013		
SEP 2 6 2013		
SEP 1 7 2013		
MAY 0 7 2014		

BRODART, CO.   Cat. No. 23-233-003   Printed in U.S.A.